GERHARD ON MUSIC

for Nigel Fortune

Gerhard on Music

Selected writings

edited by Meirion Bowen

Routledge
Taylor & Francis Group
LONDON AND NEW YORK

First published 2000 by Ashgate Publishing

Reissued 2019 by Routledge
2 Park Square, Milton Park, Abingdon, Oxon, OX14 4RN
52 Vanderbilt Avenue, New York, NY 10017

Routledge is an imprint of the Taylor & Francis Group, an informa business

Gerhard's writings copyright © Roberto Gerhard.
Commentary copyright © Meirion Bowen, 2000.

The editor has asserted his right under the Copyright, Designs and Patents Act, 1988.

All rights reserved. No part of this book may be reprinted or reproduced or utilised in any form or by any electronic, mechanical, or other means, now known or hereafter invented, including photocopying and recording, or in any information storage or retrieval system, without permission in writing from the publishers.

Notice:
Product or corporate names may be trademarks or registered trademarks, and are used only for identification and explanation without intent to infringe.

Publisher's Note
The publisher has gone to great lengths to ensure the quality of this reprint but points out that some imperfections in the original copies may be apparent.

Disclaimer
The publisher has made every effort to trace copyright holders and welcomes correspondence from those they have been unable to contact.

A Library of Congress record exists under LC control number:

Typeset in Sabon by Express Typesetters, Farnham, Surrey

ISBN 13: 978-1-138-71052-8 (hbk)
ISBN 13: 978-1-138-70840-2 (pbk)
ISBN 13: 978-1-315-20058-3 (ebk)

Contents

Acknowledgements

I should first like to thank Ashgate for agreeing to publish this book and the music books publisher Rachel Lynch for her sympathetic help in bringing the project to fruition.

Gerhard's writings are published by permission of the Gerhard Estate: I should like to thank Dr Rosemary Summers for not only giving such permission, but also encouraging all my efforts to make the work of Roberto Gerhard more widely appreciated, and meeting some of my editorial expenses out of the Estate's funds.

In the difficult task of preparing English versions of texts originally published in Catalan or Spanish, I have received a considerable amount of help from Agustín Prunell-Friend and Francesc-Xavier Canals. Their patience and good humour in guiding my efforts towards translations that were true, not just to the letter but to Gerhard's spirit and intentions, are much appreciated.

The research for this volume took me often to the University of Cambridge Library, where the Head of Music, Richard Andrewes, patiently brought forth all the manuscripts, documents, books, photographs that I needed from the Gerhard archive there. I enjoyed some happy sessions, also, at the Institut d'Estudis Catalans in Valls, where Francesc Domingo gave me free rein to explore their important archive focused specifically on the early part of Gerhard's career.

I should mention the work of Joanna Crespi and Margarida Estanyol in documenting Gerhard's manuscripts, writings and effects and their advice and personal co-operation lightened my task considerably. Sharing my enthusiasm for Gerhard's early works, Josep Dolcet and Llorenç Caballero at Tríto Edicions, Barcelona, helped fill the large gaps in my knowledge of the Catalan musical scene of the 1920s and 1930s and smoothed the way for my researches in Barcelona and Valls.

I should like to thank Julian White for reading through the manuscript and helping me to correct glaring errors and omissions. Any flaws that may remain are naturally all my responsibility.

Quotations from Gerhard's *Don Quixote*, Stravinsky's *Symphony of Psalms* and *Canticum Sacrum* are included by kind permission of Boosey & Hawkes Ltd; quotations from Schoenberg's *Von Heute auf Morgen* are reproduced by permission of Schott & Co. Ltd, London and Belmont Music Publishers, USA; and from Schoenberg's Suite Op.25 by permission of Alfred A. Kalmus Ltd, London (Universal Edition A. Wien); and a quotation from Schoenberg's Piano Concerto is by kind permission of G. Schirmer & Co.

With one exception, the photographs reproduced here have been provided by the Cambridge University Library and Boosey & Hawkes Ltd. I am grateful to David Allenby and Richard Andrewes for their specific assistance in this respect, as well as to the Gerhard Estate for permission to include them. The one exception is the picture of Gerhard with Aaron Copland and their pupils at Tanglewood (Plate 9), which I first discovered on the Internet. Dr Jan Bach – one of the Gerhard pupils portrayed therein – provided me with his own personal copy, along with some personal reminiscences of his teacher: for all of which I am exceedingly grateful.

Lastly, I should like to thank Stephen Kristian for helping me avert many a nervous breakdown when progress on my work was disrupted by a wily, temperamental word-processor. In parallel with this book, he collaborated in the creation of an official Roberto Gerhard internet website – which from now on should be a central source of information on everything relating to this important composer. The address is: http://www.roberto-gerhard.com

Meirion Bowen

List of plates

(between pages 156 and 157)

Chronology of Gerhard's life and work

1896	Born in Valls, Catalonia, 25 September; his father was of Swiss origin, his mother French-Alsatian
1908	Begins studying commerce in Zofingen
1911	Continues his studies in Neuchatel
1913	Moves to Lausanne and undertakes commercial studies there for six months; undertakes musical studies with a local German musician, Hugo Strauss. Moves to Lucerne, fails his commercial exams and decides to devote himself exclusively to music.
1914	Moves to Munich and enrols (April) at Royal Academy of Music. Studies piano with Karl Roesger and has private lessons in counterpoint with Walter Courvoisier. At the outbreak of First World War (July), Gerhard returns to Barcelona
1915–16	Studies piano in Barcelona with Granados and Frank Marshall
1915–22	Studies composition in Barcelona with Felipe Pedrell (his last pupil)
1917	Song-cycle: *L'infantament meravellós de Schahrazada* (first published work)
1922	*Seven Haiku*, for voice, wind instruments and piano
1923–38	After writing a long letter to Schoenberg, he is accepted as a pupil, studying composition with him, first in Vienna, then at the Prussian Academy of Arts, Berlin
1928	Wind Quintet (in homage to Schoenberg); *14 Catalan Folksongs*
1929	Returns to Barcelona; first concert of his music presented at the Palau de la Música, in December, by Associació de Música da Camera
1930	Marries Leopoldina (Poldi) Feichtegger, whom he had met in Vienna
1931–36	Writes articles for *Mirador*, etc; translates music books into Catalan Founding member of CIC (Independent Composers of Catalunya); Professor of Music at the Escola Normal de la Generalitat in Barcelona
1932	Co-founds *Amics de l'Art Nou* (ADLAN – Friends of New Art) with Salvador Dali, Lluís Montanya and Sebastiá Gasch). Cantata, *L'Alta Naixenca del Rei en Jaume*, for soloists, chorus and orchestra

	Orchestrated versions of six of Gerhard's Catalan Folksongs premiered at the ISCM Festival in Vienna, with Anton Webern conducting
1933–38	Administrative and editorial work in the music department of the Biblioteca di Catalunya Edition of Six Quintets by Antoní Soler (published by Biblioteca di Catalunya)
1934	Composes ballet, *Ariel* (surrealist ballet on *The Tempest*, in collaboration with Joan Miró and J. V. Foix)
1936–38	Ballet, *Soirées de Barcelone*
1936	*Ariel* premiered at the ISCM Festival in Barcelona with Hermann Scherchen conducting
1937–38	After the outbreak of the Spanish Civil War appointed Adviser to Ministry of Fine Arts in the Catalan Government and to the Central Musical Council of the Republican Government
1939	Invited to Warsaw as a member of the jury of the International Society of Contemporary Music. With the defeat of the Republicans in the Second World War, decides not to return to Spain and takes temporary refuge in Paris with his friends Joan Miró and Josep Lluís Sert; then moves to a suburban artist's colony at Meudon, where his friends include Hans Arp and Theo von Doesburg In June, he is recommended by Professor Edward J. Dent for a minor research fellowship at King's College, Cambridge. He and his wife settle permanently in Cambridge
1940–41	*The Adventures of Don Quixote:* ballet conceived in the context of incidental music a BBC for radio production
1941	Symphony: *Homenaje a Pedrell; Cancionero de Pedrell* Begins series of arrangements of Spanish Zarzuela music
1943	Ballet, *Alegrías,* presented by Ballet Rambert in Birmingham
1934–35	Completes Violin Concerto
1943–66	Incidental music for many BBC radio drama productions
1944–45	Ballet: *Pandora*
1945–47	Works on *The Duenna,* opera after Sheridan's play
1947–49	*Don Quixote:* second version as fully-fledged ballet presented successfully at Sadler's Wells with choreography by Ninette de Valois
1948	Gerhard and his wife return to Spain for the first time since before the war. This was the first of a series of visits for vacation spent with Gerhard's Catalan pupil Joaquin Homs and his family
1949	BBC presents *The Duenna* for the first time in a radio production conducted by Stanford Robinson
1949–62	Incidental music for stage-productions of plays, mainly by Shakespeare

1951	Visits Germany for the first time in 20 years to attend a concert performance of *The Duenna* at ISCM Festival in Frankfurt Concerto for piano and strings (Gerhard's first fully-fledged twelve-tone composition) first performed at Aldeburgh Festival
1952	Music for five BBC TV documentaries, *War in the Air* Collaborates with Lionel Salter on a lengthy series of BBC radio programmes offering a conspectus of the art music and popular music of Spain, from the earliest origins to the present Commissioned by British film director, Thorold Dickinson, to compose the score for his political thriller film, *Secret People*
1953	Onset of heart condition from which he suffered the rest of his life. While recovering, he composes his Symphony No.1
1955	String Quartet No.1 Incidental music for BBC TV production of J. B. Priestley's *You know what people are* First performance of Symphony No.1 at ISCM Festival in Baden-Baden, conducted by Hans Rosbaud
1956	Invited by William Glock to teach at Dartington Summer School of Music Special edition of *The Score* magazine, edited by Glock, in celebration of Gerhard's 50th birthday Keith Prowe brings out the first scores of Gerhard's works to be published since 1933 Composes Harpsichord Concerto and Sonata for cello and piano
1957–60	All Gerhard's works from the 1950s published by Mills Music Ltd Composes Nonet
1959	Composes *Lament for the Death of a Bullfighter* (Lorca) Completes Symphony No.2, commissioned by BBC
1960	Visiting Professor of Composition, University of Michigan, Ann Arbor Symphony No.3 (*Collages*) for orchestra and tape Signs exclusive publishing contract with Oxford University Press
1961	Teaches composition at Berkshire Music Centre, Tanglewood
1962	String Quartet No.2; *Concert for Eight*
1963	US premiere of Symphony No.1, with New York Philharmonic Orchestra conducted by Leonard Bernstein *Hymnody; DNA in reflection* (electronic music for film)
1964	Cantata, *The Plague* (Albert Camus), premiered by BBC Symphony Orchestra conducted by Antal Dorati Incidental music for BBC TV productions of *The Count of Monte Cristo* and *Macbeth* Music soundtrack for *This Sporting Life* (film, directed by Lindsay Anderson)

1965	Concerto for Orchestra, commissioned for US tour by BBC Symphony Orchestra is premiered in Boston under Antal Dorati First commercial recording devoted to Gerhard's music issued by EMI (Symphony No.1; *Don Quixote* Dances)
1966	*Epithalamium* (a re-working of music originally composed for *This Sporting Life*) first performed in Italy, conducted by Ettore Gracis
1967	Symphony No.4, commissioned for 125th anniversary of the New York Philharmonic Orchestra, premiered with William Steinberg conducting Last visit to Spain as guest of Joaquim Homs, who has led the campaign there against official indifference to Gerhard's work Awarded CBE
1968	Onset of serious illness Interrupts work on *Metamorphosis* (reconstruction of Symphony No.2) to compose *Libra*, and begins work on Symphony No.5 (commissioned by Fromm Music Foundation for Stockholm Philharmonic Orchestra) Awarded Honorary Doctorate of Music, University of Cambridge and Fellowship of University College
1969	*Leo* (last completed work)
1970	Dies at his Cambridge home on January 5
[1994	Poldi Gerhard dies on 24 February]

Introduction

When Roberto Gerhard died 30 years ago, his star was in the ascendant. His music was being published and recorded. At the BBC, William Glock, foremost amongst his British advocates, continued to champion his works, featuring them not only on the recently created all-day Music Programme, but in the summer season of Promenade Concerts that brought them to the widest possible audience. Near the end of Gerhard's life, Barrie Gavin at BBC Television was able to direct a 50-minute documentary about him – a serious arts programme of the sort now considered an almost extinct species. The brilliance and originality of the works Gerhard composed in the last decade of his life was winning him new admirers. An up-and-coming generation of performers and conductors had come to regard his work as essential to the modern repertoire – always a good sign, if the music itself is to survive. Domiciled in Cambridge since just before the Second World War, Gerhard had lately come to be known in the USA: he gave lectures and seminars at the University of Michigan, Ann Arbor and the Berkshire Music Centre, Tanglewood; he also received some major American commissions. In England, he had been honoured with a CBE; even Cambridge *academia* woke up to his existence and bestowed upon him an Honorary Doctorate. Spain – which he had left when Franco came to power – still largely ignored his achievements: only very recently has there been an increased awareness of Gerhard in his native land.

Since Gerhard's death, there has been no backlash, no dismissive revaluation, so much as a stalemate situation. Admirers still abound, but ignorance is also widespread. It would have helped if there had been more recordings of his music, but these only began to appear after his death; and many were quickly deleted from the catalogues. Happily, that is changing now: the celebrations for the centenary of his birth in 1996 have already prompted many new recordings, including one devoted to his opera *The Duenna*.

It would have helped if so many publishers had not been involved in bringing out his scores: these ranged from the Spanish and French ones who produced his early works to the British and American ones who, a decade or so after he settled in this country, began issuing editions of his later music. This dispersion of effort made it difficult for performers and other enthusiasts to track down copies of specific works. Forming an overall picture of his output has only lately become possible.

If recordings cease to be available, if scores are difficult to obtain, if his writings are unpublished, if the only book about him is a small volume by his one-time pupil Joaquim Homs, available until now only in Spanish and Catalan, small wonder that Gerhard has of late been ignored. Moreover, Gerhard was never the sort of flavour-of-the month composer suddenly attracting a great welter of superficial publicity from the press and media, only to be discarded just as quickly in favour of the next cult figure. His challenging, pioneering, creative temperament, unswerving integrity and seriousness made him an inconvenient entity in purely commercial terms.

In 1973, the conductor David Atherton and the London Sinfonietta mounted a memorable series of concerts in London, featuring the chamber music of Gerhard and of his teacher Schoenberg. After that, there was never any major presentation of Gerhard's work, except for a sprinkling of major performances here and there, amongst them, the eventual staging of *The Duenna*, in 1992. The programme book for the Sinfonietta series remains one of the best sources of information on Gerhard: but, like other attempts to focus attention on the composer and provide up-to-date reference materials (such as the special issues of the magazines *The Score*, September 1956 and *Tempo*, December 1981) it is incomplete and provisional. That was unavoidable. Exiled composers have never been the tidiest subjects for precise documentation. Important scores of Gerhard's are still coming to light, are still about to obtain first performances in their original or completed format. The composer's wife, Poldi, outliving him by 24 years, was often capricious and difficult in dealing with her husband's legacy of manuscripts, books and papers. She subverted an early attempt by Ates Orga to collect together Gerhard's writings for publication. But whether aware of it or not, she acted wisely in bequeathing the Gerhard Estate to Dr Alice Roughton – who early on had provided financial support and accommodation for the Gerhards when they arrived, almost penniless, in Cambridge.

Subsequently, Dr Roughton's daughter, Dr Rosemary Summers, gave to the University of Cambridge Library those of Gerhard's manuscripts, books and other materials that survived at his home; she also provided funds to enable Margarida Estanyol to make a *catalogue raisonné* of the entire collection. Even the most cursory examination reveals this to be a treasure trove of previously unpublished musical and literary effects. Much the same could be said of the somewhat smaller collection, given by Gerhard's family to the Institut d'Estudis Vallencs at the composer's birthplace, Valls, in Catalonia: this too has been efficiently catalogued by Joanna Crespi. Sa. Estanyol's list of writings by and about Gerhard, together with her up-to-date catalogue of his music, comprise the most useful feature of a booklet issued (in 1996) by the Department de Cultura at the Generalitat de Catalunya. Now, at last, real Gerhard scholarship can begin.

The structure and purpose of this book

The present book – the first in English to be devoted to Gerhard – will inevitably be regarded as yet another interim stage along the way to a full appreciation of Gerhard's artistic character and achievement. For that we shall have to wait a year or two, until publication of the forthcoming study by Julian White. Nevertheless, this volume, which collects together the bulk of Gerhard's writings, should be found useful, coming, as it does, a few years after celebrations of the centenary of the composer's birth, which prompted a number of concerts and many new recordings.

Looking at the outline chronology of Gerhard's life and work, which precedes the selection of his writings, one can see that it is virtually split in two – in essence, before and after exile. Not surprisingly, therefore, most people's awareness of the composer to date has centred simply on a particular phase or on an aspect of a career spanning nearly half a century. This book attempts to demonstrate something of the composer's full breadth and the continuity of his artistic and creative thinking: his evolution from a composer whose early attachment to Spanish and Catalonian traditions broadened into a fascination with folk music in its widest manifestations; who gravitated decisively towards Schoenberg, in the mid-1920s, as the one composer capable of helping him to discover his own creative individuality and direction; who thereafter remained capable of taking on board – albeit on his own terms – innovatory ideas of all kinds; who made significant incursions into the realms of electronic and concrete music; and at the end of his days seemed still capable of breaking fresh ground.

Gerhard never liked programme notes and regarded discussion of compositional technique as primarily a matter for the composer, not the listener. Looking at the complete list of his writings (Appendix I), the reader will observe that there are precious few descriptions of specific works of his own. On the other hand, Gerhard's articles, reviews, lectures and broadcasts reveal great speculative skill, are full of fascinating insights into creativity amongst both artists and scientists, and are always tempered by humility and lightened by humour. For some readers – particularly those who are new to Gerhard and his work – they may unlock the door to a proper understanding of his intentions and accomplishments. My aim has certainly been to preserve and communicate something of the integrity of Gerhard's vision.

This means, firstly, that the selection of his writings here is not blandly chronological; secondly, I have omitted quite a lot that would have simply overloaded what is meant to be a purposeful anthology. Gerhard once described his own music as "a braiding of many strands": this, perhaps more than anything, provided me with a guiding editorial principle, in that various fascinations – musical and non-musical – stayed with him throughout his life, and others were woven into the fabric of his creative and intellectual thought as his career unfolded.

From early on, Gerhard was impelled occasionally to step back from the task of composing and consider his relationship with performers and with audiences: hence the first of the six sections of this book. Gerhard's tastes in music were eclectic in a deep sense: he was forever quick to seize upon any experiences of sound, timbre, gestures and techniques of musical presentation – anything that could be absorbed into his own music. The context for this was his profound awareness of musical traditions and the primal springs of music-making: thus pre-classical music was not just some kind of historical curiosity; and Catalonian folk-music – indeed, all the ethnic musics – stimulated not just sentimental affection, but provided a wealth of ideas relevant to Gerhard's compositional aims and strategies.

The second section of this book demonstrates the importance to him of certain key figures in his early life – his teacher, Felipe Pedrell (whom he probably valued more for his folk-music research than as a composer) and the musicologist Higini Anglès, with whom he collaborated from 1916 until the early 1930s. Although he made arrangements of the folksongs collected by Pedrell, Gerhard never narrowed his creative aims to become the Vaughan Williams of Catalonia: rather he became perhaps its Bartok, absorbing the raw, physical ferocity of rural folksong and its moods of stillness and contemplation – essential facets of his style which are evident right the way through to his late works, such as *Gemini.* Gerhard himself reveals also that the insights provided by research on medieval and Renaissance music introduced him to new techniques that he already put to good use in works such as his *Concertino for strings* (1929).

Gerhard began writing extensively on music, just after he had settled in Barcelona in 1929 and married Leopoldina (Poldi) Feichtegger, whom he had met during the period of his studies in Vienna. Writing was both a way of earning some money to supplement his meagre income as a composer and also a propaganda vehicle for innovation. For Gerhard had by this time become something of a local figurehead for new artistic ideas, alongside other *avant-gardistes* such as Salvador Dalí. A 1929 concert of his music at that Mecca of conservatism, the Palau de la Música Catalana, precipitated a public debate between an affronted Lluís Millet – the locally revered guardian of traditional musical values – and the young upstart Gerhard, with his new-fangled Schoenbergian atonalism and whatever. This is the backcloth to the second sequence of articles in the second section of this book.

Stylistic developments in Gerhard's writings

The task of preserving some kind of continuity of style and tone between Gerhard's early journalistic writing in Catalan and his later writings in English was not at all easy, even acknowledging that the later writings are more obviously "mature". Gerhard was multi-lingual – speaking and writing fluently in Catalan, Spanish, German, French and English – and alert to etymological nuances of all kinds. (Small wonder that he became an active member of the International Society for Contemporary Music and got on so well with its President, Edward J. Dent – another noted linguist – who was to negotiate a Fellowship for him at King's College, Cambridge, when he fled from the Franco regime.) Even so, when Gerhard wrote in Catalan, he was naturally inclined to be more florid and repetitious, using superlatives to excess, which is how they might seem to an English reader.

Taming these tendencies, tightening Gerhard's prose to conform to English succinctness, has been difficult and dangerous. I particularly wanted to avoid losing both the natural flow and what, to my mind, seemed like a mock-obsequiousness of tone in Gerhard's response to *Mestre* Millet. Likewise, in subsequent reviews of music by some of Gerhard's contemporaries, the contrast between his plaudits and his criticisms seemed to me at least in part a deliberate strategy – condemnation laced with fulsome praise. While scrupulously courteous and positive when writing about Spanish contemporaries, Gerhard remained the enemy of a parochial artistic vision.

Gerhard's music

The traditional orientation in Gerhard's make-up enabled him to contribute notably to the repertoire of ballet and, in the 1940s, to compose an opera whose lightness of touch (he himself acknowledged) ran counter to any supposed *zeitgeist*; small wonder he was out of sympathy with Adorno's advocacy of *angst* and "anxiety" as prime ingredients in post-Holocaust artworks. Part IV of this book introduces Gerhard's early notions on opera and film music and sketches in the background to the creation of his two major stage-works, *Don Quixote* and *The Duenna.*

From the mid-1940s onwards, Gerhard earned an income of sorts from composing incidental music for radio plays, the live theatre and (belatedly) film. Much of this music is still in manuscript and he wrote relatively little about what, compositionally, it entailed for him. Indeed, from the point of view of this volume, it is a pity that the Gerhard of the late 1950s and 60s, making eager forays into electronic music and *musique concrète* provided no counterpart to his cautious, sceptical early article on music and film (1930).

In Gerhard's own development, the five years he spent first in Vienna, then in Berlin, studying with Schoenberg (1923–28) proved absolutely crucial – manifestly the turning-point in his career. As the fifth section of this book should demonstrate, he acquired from Schoenberg not a set of rules or a fixed method, so much as a mixture of rigorous discipline and openness – an anti-dogmatic approach to composition that prevailed throughout his career. It should be evident from his reminiscences, here, that Gerhard revered Schoenberg – though such reverence stopped short of idolatry. He felt free to be critical of Schoenberg's music or of his ideas and he took quite a time, in fact, to incorporate twelve-note technique into the forefront of his own compositional procedures.

But he was always loyal to his teacher. Soon after he returned to Spain Gerhard arranged for Schoenberg to come to Barcelona for concerts of his music: he also championed the works of Berg and Webern there in the early 1930s. Later on, in the 1950s, after Schoenberg's death, he was very disturbed at the way he had been toppled from his pedestal by the post-war avant garde, who allotted much greater significance to Webern. Gerhard too admired Webern but thought of him as a brilliant miniaturist, rather than the consummate master which he considered Schoenberg to be. In his later writings and talks, Gerhard engaged intensely and profoundly with post-war developments in serial music – its theory and practice – and his arguments took him sometimes into an esoteric technical domain. Still, however, he kept his head, invariably displaying a mixture of discernment, objectivity and wry humour that would put everything neatly in perspective.

Gerhard as artist and thinker

The overall trajectory of this book has been planned to take the reader from the general matters considered in Part I, through a sequence of specific topics: composers and compositions past and present – including some of Gerhard's own works; styles and techniques; finally, some mature reflections on broader aesthetic issues.

Writing, lecturing and broadcasting so frequently, Gerhard naturally drew upon a personal store of anecdotes and quotations that recur in more than one context. In the versions published here, I have pruned his texts as judiciously as possible, trying at the same time not to lose the flavour or the slant of the original. Immensely well-read, Gerhard quoted from or paraphrased an array of literary sources which, where possible, I have tried to identify. Consciously or otherwise, Gerhard often altered the words he quoted, or conflated different passages: here again, where appropriate, I have noted such modifications, always bearing in mind that Gerhard was a creative, speculative artist, not a fastidious scholar.

The ultimate objective of this book is that through access to his writings on music, readers might come closer to Gerhard the composer and realize that in his chosen field he was someone of enduring international stature and quality.

Meirion Bowen
London, 1999

I Composer and Public

1 Listening to music (1930)[1]

Phèdre: "Je confesse qu'il m'arrivait de me détacher sans le savoir de la musique ... Je me distrais a partir d'elle-même qui m'y invite. Puis je rentre dans son sein." (Valéry, *Eupalinos ou l'Architecte)*

[I confess that sometimes it happens that I have detached myself from the music to which I am listening ... Distracted, I used it as the starting-point for my own thoughts. Then once more I re-discover its essence.]

Have you ever wondered about how you listen to music? It's a question I like to ask my amateur musician friends, people from diverse professions. The replies are very interesting to a musician. They teach him, at least, how to consider the musical work from a "secular" point of view, one he would never have discovered on his own. It's an important viewpoint which has to be taken into account, as it is that of a huge majority of his possible audience.

The musician has a big surprise when he finds that, in most cases, the amateur seems to listen mainly to himself rather than to the music. It is as if music gave wings to his own interior monologue, or as if it poured highly flammable fuel on the embers of his fantasy, sparking off exuberant fireworks that bewitch him. Once this show has been initiated, the music itself is shifted discreetly into the background.

It is difficult to know how much of the delicate play of shapes the music keeps instigating and how much of its immaterial substance actually reaches the mind of the listener. His imaginative flights autonomously follow the events of the performance. One could say that music is merely a "pretext" by means of which the absorbed listener embroiders a new "text": and this can be about the most unexpected subjects – just ask any listener.

I obviously exaggerate somewhat. Perhaps I am marking out the extreme position of distraction in itself to which music seems to invite us. Without defining the degrees of distraction, it is undeniable that the listener has this tendency – which music seems to favour remarkably – to "digress", to *rêver*, to let himself slide down *par la plus douce pente de sa durée*, to use Valéry's words. It is a remarkable fact. I don't think any of the other arts achieves such high emotional output with such little attention directed to the real object proposed for our contemplation.

Hence the superior charm of music, then? Is that what has made it the most accessible art to the masses? Is that why music would be the most musical of the muses?

Here we are faced with a sensitive issue which we should handle with care.

One should also attempt to approach it from the musician's standpoint. Do you think Phèdre listened to music correctly? Most musicians would reply in the negative. Then, how should your ideal listener listen?

There is an extraordinary story about Mozart transcribing Allegri's *Miserere* totally from memory after a single hearing. Even if we regard the story as apocryphal, it gives us an idea – albeit, indeed taken to an extreme of an absolute degree – of the essential nature of listening to music.

Listening to music is perceiving organic relationships between sounds and rhythms. To the extent that the listener is able mentally to create a synthesis of the series of sounds heard and perceive the "shape" in time, he is a musician. Perceiving the "shape" means, first, to discern the autonomous musical figures; that extends to making a rhythmical synthesis of relationships of intervals. The first intuitive action is a perception of the musical sense of the interval, that is of the relationship between two sounds. Secondly, perceiving the "shape" means to add up the collection of autonomous musical figures within the superior collection of a musical phrase; in other words, perceiving its articulation, punctuation and flexible rhythm. Thirdly, it means synthesizing the phrases within the symphonic cycle: that is to say, perceiving articulation, punctuation, the architectonic rhythm of the cycle. And finally, it also means synthesizing the cycles within the whole symphonic shape.

These operations – thus excessively summarised – are done by the spirit. Melody is a purely spiritual action which only exists in the listener's spirit. The listener listens to music to the extent that he can mentally re-create the *melos* (melody, rhythm and character). That is why he needs to have recreative fantasy, a capacity for musical imagination, of audition *in mente*. Perhaps there is no essential difference between this listener and the composer other than a simple gradual difference. Musical men are gifted with this natural disposition of combining sonorous shapes and an intuition of their untranslatable musical meaning. The aesthetic pleasure of listening comes, perhaps, from the activation and concrete form that composition gives to a latent disposition, innate to the listener, to create sound architectures.

It is so elementary, that I nearly forgot to mention the initial condition of the true music listener: *he mustn't be deaf*! There are physically deaf people who listened to unheard-of music (Beethoven). There are people with a very awake sense of hearing who still haven't managed to hear music. Our concert halls are teeming with spiritually-deaf people. And finally, we all know there is no worse deafness than ... well, need I say more?

2 The composer and his audience (1960)[2]

In a questionnaire, I was once invited to respond to the following: "If, prior to the performance of a work of yours, you were given the opportunity of addressing the audience, what would you like to say?" My answer was: "Not a word." This may have had the merit of brevity but it is not entirely unambiguous; indeed, it lends itself to misinterpretation. Above all, it needs to be made clear that not every enquiry would deserve such a negative reply. It was a matter of addressing, specifically, a concert audience. My answer applied to such a case.

It is an obvious fact that the gap between the composer and his contemporary audience has sometimes been wider, sometimes narrower. That gap is wider, perhaps, now than at most comparable periods in the past. The idea of asking the composer to address his audience is inspired by the wish to help narrow down that gap, offering the audience some guidance, some listening-aid. And who better?

Considered from this point of view, my reply seems distinctly unhelpful, stand-offish and aloof – as if to say: as a composer I am concerned with the making of a piece of music; audience reaction is none of my concern. For all its apparent abruptness, this take-it-or-leave-it attitude is, I feel, basically right. It stresses the importance to the composer of the detachment which he knows he must maintain *vis-à-vis* his audience. Only it tends to obscure one fact which, I think, is of almost equal importance: namely, that a piece of music is made for a listener. It is meant to be listened to by other people besides the composer. Unless the composer is willing to shut himself up in an ivory tower and play there a kind of solipsistic game, he is clearly bound to have in mind some sort of rapport with his potential audience. This relationship is, I think, worth exploring.

The human factor is met with at the very first stages of even the most abstract composition. The composer has certainly got to reckon with this at the outset in the person of the performer or performers of his work, since he is not simply writing for an instrument or group of instruments. His instruments will be played by human beings capable of such and such a length of breath or bow, and with similar limitations in the speed of their reflexes, on which the successful handling of the instrumental mechanics depend.

Admittedly, these considerations drop out when it comes to electronic music, since it dispenses with the human performer altogether. Even in this extreme domain, the necessity of a rapport between the composer and his potential audience remains in full force. Indeed, it is significant that no noted composer of electronic music is (as yet) willing completely to renounce traditional instruments or, least of all, the vocal medium, in favour of purely synthetic sound. Most significant is the fact that, in the compositions which electronic composers are writing for traditional media, the major enterprise afoot now could properly be labelled: *récuperation de l'interprète* – win back the performer!

One may certainly argue as to the proposed ways and means for allowing the performer a degree of "free choice" which is supposed to amount to an almost "creative" cooperation on his part not only in the rendering but in the actual shaping of the work. Winning back the interpreter is a good thing in any case – however wrongly one might go about it – if it succeeds. But there cannot be the slightest doubt that the rapport with one's audience remains the crucial issue.

To my way of thinking music is, in its essence, dramatic. I am using the word in the largest sense in which any phenomenon that is bound to the *péripêtie* of a given temporal cycle or lifespan – and has, therefore, a beginning, a period of growth and an end – can be said to be dramatic in essence: the life-cycle of a blade of grass, the course of an avalanche, the impact of a drop of rain on a sheet of water, no less than the lifespan of a tune or of a symphony. The drama is, of course, in the mind of man, the beholder. This is the level at which the listener's mind must be engaged. I believe in plunging my listener straight away *in media res* and keeping him there. In other words, the vital affair for me is to hold his attention. This is my work's life-line. The moment it snaps, my work dies.

From a painting hanging on the wall you may take your eyes away, and come back to it as often as you like: it is always there in its wholeness. Not so with music. A work of music takes shape only in the mind of the listener. It does not exist, apart from this, as a thing in itself. Or rather, it does exist, but as something entirely different. It exists as a catalogue of specifications or directions for use (known as a score) which stands in a far more distantly mediatory relation with regard to the actual sounding work, than that in which the pigments can be said to stand to the image which the roving eye reads on the canvas. Until, and not until, the work of music comes alive in the mind of the listener, my score is but the possibility, the promise of a work. In order to arise in the mind of the listener, it must *become*, eventuate, actualize in time. It is never there all of a piece, since it only comes into being as a temporal succession. In order to achieve its particular kind of existence and wholeness, the work has therefore got to be lived through in its total lifespan.

As long as the listener's attention is held, the composer may do anything he likes: the one thing he cannot afford to do is to bore his listener and lose him on the way. Because the moment his attention lapses, be it only for a few bars, there is no knowing what might follow, how many bars may be irrevocably blotted out in the listener's consciousness, as a result of that momentary eclipse of attention.

Whereas in the experience of a work of music "communication" must remain, probably forever, an unknown quantity, attention can be directly "observed"; if it were necessary, it would perhaps even be measured. It is therefore a much more objective *datum* on which to base and to gauge one's rapport with the listener. But it is far more than that.

Attention – deep, sustained, undeviating – is in itself an experience of a very high order. There seems to be a direct relation between the quality of a work of art and the quality of attention it elicits in the perceiver. We know that it is the works which have held our attention most strongly, that we can bear to experience most often. The work to which I can listen time and again with ever-renewed freshness of approach and a seemingly inexhaustible sense of discovery, is also the work which seems to prove my capacity for inexhaustible attention.

This is a happy match and when it does occur, it is as if the listener in his turn had been able to achieve a degree of detachment in the act of perception matching that of the composer in the act of origination. The listener's mind is emptied of all the petty preoccupations of the day; on exceptional occasions it may even succeed in temporarily suspending that feeling of separateness which we call our individuality. Detachment in the composer, matched by detachment in the listener, thus results paradoxically in the strongest possible bond between the two.

The social side of man has been defined as that part of the person which is entirely "made up of other people", in other words, of borrowed patterns of behaviour, mostly unconsciously imitative. The feeling of being *different* – an oppressive feeling at most times – is perhaps what drove some people to become artists. Yet in that stage of perfect detachment which a great work of art can induce, both originator and perceiver seem, on the contrary, to find access to that part of ourselves where we are all essentially the same, but where the common ground lies far beyond the place of superficial social conformity. I believe that this is one of the major aims of every true work of art.

To return to my questionnaire, it might be asked: is not the artist sometimes effectively hindering, if not frustrating, this very aim, as, for instance, when he becomes boldly experimental and upsets accepted conventions by too many or too radical innovations? Temporarily this may indeed be the effect of innovations. Could not the artist then make it easier for his audience to grasp his intentions by explaining what they are? The answer is still: no.

If the composer could *say* something that might effectively help to make his intentions clearer to the listener then, surely, something must be missing in the work. Intelligent listeners and critics know very well that full justice cannot be done to every new, unfamiliar, work at the first hearing. Repeated hearings will almost certainly modify, for better or for worse, their first impressions. Only growing familiarity through repeated hearings can test the work to the full. And I am convinced that no verbal explanations the composer could provide can possibly affect the way in which the listener will finally come to terms with the work, as a result of the immediate and spontaneous experience of his own.

This statement may surprise listeners who have grown accustomed to the now fashionable technical exordia handed out at the performance of new works – a practice needing a word of caution. One has to distinguish between the sham and the genuine declarations. They are not difficult to tell apart. The sham ones are unmistakeable: they are aimed at the listener. The genuine ones, especially when they come from the composer himself, and are to be found in learned journals, are intended mainly for other composers who may happen to be working on similar lines, and whose criticism is implicity solicited because it may prove useful. The ordinary listener ought to disregard both.

The sham declarations set out deliberately to foster the fallacy that the more the listener knows about matters of technique, the better his understanding of the music. The truth is that a little knowledge can go a long way to confuse the layman, *a fortiori* when the information is false. Among young serialist composers today, a certain amount of deliberate humbugging is practised on the innocent listener, in the claim as to how many aspects of a composition, how many "parameters" are being serialized. For some dark reason this is supposed to impress the listener or, more likely perhaps, a certain type of critic. I would have said that what this amounts to is an implicit admission that it matters little if everything is lost, bar some sort of "intellectual" prestige, even though this is based on false pretences. The composer who is advancing such spurious claims can feel quite safe against detection, since none of them can possibly be checked aurally. Also, very few people will go to the length of checking by analysis of the score, which, while immensely arduous, is the only possible means of establishing the truth.

Of far greater concern, however, are the serious misunderstandings that arise out of the genuine claims put forward by composers that are are given careful consideration by the student. Once again we are up against the fallacy that music can be *explained*; that more knowledge about how the piece is made will lead to a better understanding of the music. But it is evident that knowledge – here as in many other fields – does not necessarily lead to understanding. The danger is, on the contrary, that more and more knowledge may lead to less and less understanding, particularly where the layman is concerned. Paradoxically, understanding must come first. One must have grasped intuitively the heart of the matter before the factual bits of knowledge can even begin to make sense. And this holds good for all of us, listener, critic and composer alike. It is a case of strict one-way traffic. The direction is from the centre of an intuitive understanding outwards to the factual data, never the other way round. Technique is only illumined from within, from the core of the creative experience, with the composer, or from the core of the perceptual experience, with the listener or the critic.

Approached from the outside, the facts that can be known – rules, technical devices, points of method – are barren. They are bound to be read from the outside in a spirit of literal-mindedness. Taken at their text-bookish face value, these data have a knack of often turning into the very opposite of what they are really meant to signify. They become then rigid static formulae. Their inner dynamic and shifting relatedness, apparent to the artist in the act of compositional engagement, is entirely lost on the armchair analyst.

Technique will never explain the work, but experience of the work could give valuable – indeed invaluable – clues towards explanation of the technique. So, even if that is all one really cares about, one obviously would be better advised to start, as an unprejudiced listener, with the experience of the work pure and simple.

"Pure and simple" is, of course, a manner of speaking, considering all that is involved even in the most elementary act of sensorial perception. What I mean to say is that immediate perceptual experience is the analyst's only chance even from the point of view of his own particular pursuit. Thus it turns out that my argument against answering questionnaires for the benefit of a concert audience goes further than I foresaw; indeed, it applies quite as much to the person who looks for technical information, be it professionally or simply for the new dimension which the acquired knowledge may give to his enjoyment of the work. There is no doubt in my mind that to those who have intuitively grasped the heart of the matter, more and more will be revealed, not through the conscious straining after knowledge, but out of their own genuine experience of the work. Whereas in those who lack this intuitive understanding, even the correct factual information they may gather will, in the end, only serve to increase prejudice and confusion.

Contemporary art undeniably shows a powerful accession of increase of intellect. It is not a freak, but a fruit of our time and has got to be accepted as such. But when the extremes are about to meet, it sometimes becomes difficult to tell the cybernetic robot apart from the mystic. The artist without faith *must* believe in calculation, that beauty might possibly be achieved by *perfect* calculation. It is the logical creed of the *sceptique créateur*. He has no alternative. There is no going back from the intellectual rigour which has become our second nature. It would be foolish to expect the contemporary artist to trust to the "reasons of the heart" with the same naïveté with which it is (probably mistakenly) thought that artists did in other ages. Intellectual rigour has come to stay, at least for our time. It is not in the least surprising, therefore, that given the alternative of being an inspired imbecile or one of the exponents of Darmstadt-style calculation, the budding composer today should unhesitatingly plump for the latter. His only mistake is to think that he has a choice. The truth is that the only way of working out his salvation is to harness both inspired imbecile and calculating prodigy to the common task.

The paraphernalia of rational, systematically organized thought that goes nowadays into the composing of music, is but one very partial aspect of the creative effort. Serial technique, for example, is in the end nothing but a kind of cradle of scaffolding which allows the composer to work at certain aspects or levels of the sound-fabric, which were inaccessible. But what matters is the work. Once this is finished we want the scaffolding removed. It is not meant to attract attention. If the work has been successful, the props must have become invisible in the end. Correct as I believe the simile to be, it is yet only half the truth. Seen from a different angle, there is another, more important aspect of the intellectual approach and of the constraints to which the artist bends his gift of imaginative invention. By these constraints, he endeavours to achieve yet another kind of detachment – undoubtedly the hardest – namely, detachment *from his own work*. In the measure in which the artist can make the work obey immanent laws, conform to a "programmed" order (randomness taking care of itself), he correspondingly reduces the range of his "will", of his power of "causation". It seems to me that the artist who directs attention to the disciplines which enable him to approach such an aim is like a man sawing off the very branch on which he sits.

Communication is, no doubt, a function of language. But music is improperly called a "language". For all the obvious similarities in their respective structural organizations, it has become an increasingly misleading analogy to call music a "language". The sign, or rather the signal, in music never points to a "signified" beyond and other than itself. On the contrary, it is intransitive, as it were; it arrests and focuses attention upon itself, and yet not so much upon itself as upon the mobilization of a vast constellation of signals in their courses. The ear, said to be the musician's intelligence, is so very difficult to assess, that I keep on giving it the benefit of the doubt. One of the hardest discoveries for a musician to make, it seems, is that music, contrary to a generally held belief, is not made with notes. The eye leads the ear astray; it easily persuades it that the notes are really there – and nothing but the notes. As far as one can see, the ear, therefore, misguidedly concentrates on locating notes, on disentangling their clusters, on tracing the patterns they form. Yet the basic stuff of music is sonic motion, not notes or sounds. Manoeuvre is the *raison d'être* of the formations. The notes, the actual discrete sounds, are like the bits of straw on the waves in Leonardo's description of the phenomenon of "tremor": "the bits of straw are not carried along by the waves in the direction of the spread, but only bob up and down." The true business of the composer is to release the flow and shape, and steer the stream of sonic events in time.

Time is the drama; drama is time.

Hans Arp once said that the man who invented the excruciating phrase "time is money" deserved to be horse-whipped. A society that has adopted this saying has nothing more to learn about devaluation.

3 Sound and symbol (1957)[3]

Victor Zuckerkandl's book, *Sound and Symbol*[4] is described on the dust-jacket as "a philosophy *through* music", rather than a philosophy of music. As such, it is unlikely to find much favour, I imagine, either with the professional philosopher or with the practical musician; indeed, it seems a very good way of making the worst of both worlds. But my concern here will be to examine the merits of the book on musical rather than philosophical terrain: this, after all, is the ground on which Zuckerkandl's premises are based and where practically the whole of his argument is conducted.

He begins by exploring the concepts of "tone", "motion", "time" and "space". He then proceeds to contrast his findings with the notions generally held on these topics in the field of natural sciences, physics in particular. From the comparison, certain conclusions are drawn. In Zuckerkandl's own words: "In so far as disparities between experience and concept are brought to light in this way, our investigation will become a critique of these fundamental concepts...: music makes us revise these concepts to bring them into agreement with our experience."[5]

In other words, Zuckerkandl's book attempts not so much to prove to us musicians that, for all the beautiful music we've been writing for centuries, our theoretical notions of sound, motion, time and space were wrong: more than that, it is these very concepts, as held by modern science, that are being challenged. To be sure, science itself has been engaged for over half a century in re-defining these concepts, and it continues to do so. But this is the first time that music wants to testify and demands that its voice should be heard in such matters.

One thing which, I dare say, will surprise every musical reader, is the astonishingly narrow range of Zuckerkandl's musical interests. It made me rather suspicious to realize that the whole inquiry was going to be based on a meagre collection of a dozen-and-a-half or so musical examples – mostly stripped to the bone, so that they were playable on the piano literally with one finger! They are taken from Bach, Beethoven, Chopin, Mendelssohn, Weber, Johann Strauss, Wagner, Bruckner and a couple of bars from – the *Marseillaise*! All non-European music is quietly dropped; not a word about Chinese or Indian music; much less about music of the so-called primitive cultures or the non-learned traditional music of the people in the world at large. And even within the area of western art-music, such important domains as plainsong, the music of the Middle Ages and the Renaissance, let alone contemporary music since, say, Debussy, are not so much as mentioned.

What is left conjures up, of course, a familiar picture: a picture of the Warden of the so-called Grand Tradition, for whom music is at its zenith in the span of time comprised within the famous four German B's: Bach, Beethoven, Brahms and Bruckner. It is tacitly implied that the rest, both before and after, are negligible.

To this Zuckerkandl might retort, firstly, that the examples he has chosen suit his purpose well enough; secondly, that he is not talking about *music as art* but rather about *music as a phenomenon of nature*! In other words, that actual music, quotable in music-type, had only to come into the picture in so far as it would help him draw the outline of what he calls "a musical concept of the external world"[6]. For the purpose of the book is none other than to find an answer to the following question: "How is music possible?" or, to put it differently, "What must the world be like, what must I believe, if between the world and me such a thing as music can occur? How must I consider the world, how must I consider myself, if I am to understand the *reality* of music?"

But this would not dispose of my criticism. It simply isn't possible to study music as a "natural phenomenon" alone; in addition to whatever aspect offers *qua* "natural phenomenon", it is also and always an historical reality. As such it occupies its niche in historical time and is rooted in ideas and conventions which, for the most part, have no universal validity, but only an historically circumscribed validity.

To this, it might be observed, Zuckerkandl does, in fact, conform, since he has chosen the historical period of the so-called Grand Tradition for his musical illustrations. But *with* the historical period goes also the contingent view of what *that* period understood by "musical reality"; the two are inseparable. This Zuckerkandl overlooks. He takes it for granted, for instance, that he's looking at the material of music in a pristine state when he starts making his observations on the material of music as it is known in the West during the eighteenth and nineteenth centuries. This is, of course, a complete fallacy. He is by no means isolating in that music pure natural phenomena that could be found anywhere else as well say, in Chinese music or in plainsong. He is, in fact, dealing with an historically determined state of the musical material exhibiting characteristics which belong to this particular historical period and none other – such as, for instance, the dynamics of harmony, based on the diatonic scale and on diatonic tonality. But diatonic tonality is not valid for the music of all times; it is no longer valid, for instance, for all our own music today. Therefore, when Zuckerkandl generalizes on the historical basis of tonality he's really rather like someone who, in post-Copernican times, would be arguing on the basis of a Ptolemaic view of the universe. In this, he is paying the penalty for the narrowness of his musical interests.

There are other biased notions of his that spring from the same cause. For instance, he propounds a cogent theory of the "dynamic field"[7], which makes *relatedness* the cornerstone of all musical experience.

But it then comes as a surprise that Zuckerkandl should revert to a primitive sort of materialistic animism that refers to note – or rather "tones", as his American translator makes him say – as if they were things or bodies, and locates not only forces and trends in the "tones" but even intentions and wishes. A tone, we are told, "wants to pass beyond itself", another "wants itself", yet another "wants *nothing*"[8], that is, wants to eliminate itself, says NO to itself and so on and so forth.

Obviously, the preconception underlying this way of thinking is that music is made *with* notes or "tones". This is a time-honoured and widely held belief which will be very difficult to uproot. Yet Zuckerkandl himself takes a step towards doing so. In fact, the tantalizing thing about his book is that so often it makes one feel that he's on the brink of a new insight. "There are 'tones'", he says, "because there is music, not the other way round"[9], which is very well put. Eventually, in the book, there does emerge a more definite image of music as *pure eventuation*, in the sense of a lived-through experience. Pitches are then no longer required as bodies or carriers, but rather as something more like high-water marks that are touched by the continuous stream of dynamic events.

The philosophical problem of motion – a notorious one that has puzzled mankind for the last two thousand years – is first approached by Zuckerkandl with the same animistic preconceptions which are bound up with his settled views of classical tonality, understood as a kind of closed system of gravity. His book contains much talk of "unfulfilment", a feeling attributed to notes or "tones"; of their "desire for completion"; of "tones pointing beyond themselves" and "reaching hands to the next tone" – and so forth. However, a more up-to-date conception emerges eventually in this field too.

Taking his cue from Bergson's definition of real motion as "rather the transfer of a state than of a thing"[10] – in which the choice of the word *state* is not very fortunate – Zuckerkandl arrives at a formulation which now perhaps overshoots the mark, as when he writes: "Not unjustifiably may we say that musical motion is at the core of every motion; that the very experience of motion is, finally, a musical experience."[11] Surely that is going too far.

If "music *is* motion" – as this implies and as, elsewhere, he literally asserts – then a journey in a lift would be a musical experience. Yet here again, a much more cogent phrasing is arrived at later on:

> "Since ... there is nothing in music that moves, and no places in which things are, we now say that it is precisely *because* there are no things and places in music that the 'passing over', the 'between', the core of motion can be manifested in absolute purity and immediacy. It is precisely *because* hearing music is a perception of purely dynamic phenomena that the core of the process of motion can be elementally experienced in music, and *above all*, in music ...".[12]

Philosophers and aestheticians are wrong when they talk of "ideal" motion, or of "abstract" motion in music. There is nothing ideal or abstract in it. The elimination of thing and place takes away nothing of the reality of motion, of the concreteness of its experience: on the contrary, it reveals its innermost core.

Tonal motion is the most real motion. With *this* Zuckerkandl is not in opposition but agreement with modern science. He can, for instance, quote an atomic physicist, who asserts that: "motion in its pure state seems to refuse to enter our space-time framework"[13] – and that's a view with which a musician can sympathize. Now when music is defined as a temporal art, what do we mean? What is time?

The ambiguity of the notion was once amusingly illustrated by Sir Arthur Eddington, when he imagined a discussion between the Astronomer Royal and Monsieur Bergson. He dated it 20 years or so before Einstein and was letting Bergson have the best of the argument. But at the end of it, Bergson had to look at his watch and rush off to catch a train, which was starting by the Astronomer Royal's time. So we seem to have at least two different sorts of time, just to begin with. Zuckerkandl quotes the following definition by Lobachewsky: "The motion of one body taken as the measure of the motion of another body is called time."[14] That is obviously the Astronomer Royal's time. It is divided into hours, minutes and seconds. Yet hours, minutes and seconds are not really measures of time itself but, by the previous definition, measures of spaces, of extents of spaces traversed by moving bodies. Time seems to slip through our fingers. To be sure there is another sort of time, the time familiar to our consciousness, of which we have an intimate experience. Yet generations of philosophers and psychologists have taught that although an awareness of time goes along with all our sensations, perceptions and feelings – as the order or form of their appearance (namely, succession) – in itself, time can never been the object of any sensation, perception or any kind of experience. "Time", says Leibnitz, "is idea, not reality." To which Zuckerkandl tersely replies: "To whatever else this doctrine may appeal for support, it is *not* compatible with the facts of music."[15]

We come now to the part of the book which contains the author's most challenging views. The *musical* concept of time is contrasted with the *physical* concept of time in four separate propositions.[16]

"Time is *order* [or] *form* of experience", he confronts with, "time is *content* of experience." What is meant is that, whereas there can only be effects *of* time, but not effects *of* time, according to natural laws, in music, according to Zuckerkandl, we encounter "processes that cannot be comprehended except as effects *of* time, in the literal sense." In other words, whereas for Eddington, time is "a mere formality", for Zuckerkandl time is "an active force".

The second proposition – more a corollary of the first, really – breaks no new ground. Against "time measures events", in music, according to Zuckerkandl, "time produces events". The third proposition states: Against "time is divisible into equal parts", in music "time knows no equality of parts." Lastly, "time is perpetual transcience" Zuckerkandl confronts with "time knows nothing of transcience."

One can't help wondering what a natural scientist would have to say to this collection of propositions. Will he be persuaded to discard his own concept of time in favour of the one which, according to Zuckerkandl, is alone compatible with the facts of musical experience? Another question which the natural scientist might like to put to me, as a musician, would be: "Is it true that the facts of musical experience make it imperative for you, as a musician, to accept Zuckerkandl's new concept of time?". The answer would be: no. It remains for me to try and justify my rejection of the Zuckerkandl doctrine.

The question is: do the facts of music warrant Zuckerkandl's new concept of time, or not? First of all, we must ask ourselves what are the "facts of music"? What do we mean by the "facts of music"? Is music something that we encounter in the world because it is simply "out there somewhere", in the same way that we encounter natural phenomena? A scientist from Mars who could read Zuckerkandl's book, but had no experience of music might very well come to some such conclusion. Music seems to yield for Zuckerkandl three different classes of "facts", dependent on whether we take music as a natural phenomenon, located in the outer world, or as an experience of a listener, or as an experience of a player, of someone who *makes* music, who presents us with the *object* of our actual musical experience.

The real maker of music, namely the composer, is here conspicuous by his absence. Now it would be unfair to accuse Zuckerkandl of not wanting to talk of what he doesn't know, namely – since he doesn't seem to be a composer himself – of the experience of *making* music, in the sense of originating it, of "producing it *ab ovo*". But surely the "facts of music" as experienced by the composer, *in* composing music, and in particular his experience of time, should be considered too.

Now, what is *time* in the composer's experience? To be sure, it's not Astronomer Royal's time. It doesn't elapse in intervals of absolutely equal length as measured by the clock. But it is no less certain that the composer's experience of time does *not* resolve, in the last analysis, into the dynamics of the "metrical wave" as Zuckerkandl would have us believe. That the metrical to and fro, the dynamics of a descent *from* the crest of a wave and ascent *towards* the next crest must be something of a basic experience to the performer of music is, for obvious reasons, pretty certain.

Less understandably, it seems to be something of a basic experience, too, for the more naive listener who can't help beating time with the music, wagging a finger, stamping a foot or nodding his head. Yet for all that, the experience of the dynamics of the metrical wave is no longer demonstrably present in the performance of many types of non-European music, it is also conspicuously absent in some types of folk-song – the *cantilenae* sung by Spanish peasants on the threshing floors, for instance, as anyone can testify who has tried to transcribe their freely swaying lines in metrical notation. As for the composer, there is no question at all that the dynamics of the metrical wave are of entirely subordinate importance.

Conclusive proof of this can be seen in the fact that it is possible for a composer like Stravinsky to re-bar entire passages, in revisions of some of his works, that is, to give them alternative metrical readings without thereby affecting the music in the smallest degree. To be sure, no musician could agree with Eddington that time is a mere formality in music: but metre, certainly, is nothing else; it's purely and simply a matter of convenience. Polyphonic and concerted music would be unthinkable without it; except of course, for the rigidly fixed and fairly rigidly maintained traditional repertoires that lack a system of notation anyhow, like the art-music of the Arabs. In western art-music, however, metre is a formality and not, as Zuckerkandl would have it, a sort of ultimate substratum, let alone something like the "grain" of time, which would combine with sound in producing music, in the same way that the coating of a film in combination with light brings about the pictures I can take with my camera. The notion is rather extravagant but nothing as fantastic as that of a "dynamic field of metre", which Zuckerkandl propounds; in my opinion there is nothing in the composer's experience of time that could remotely be said to correspond to this hypothetical "dynamic field of metre".[17]

The composer's experience of time is, in reality, essentially rhythmical. Rhythm *can* but *need not*, by any means, be associated with metre: granted that the experience of musical rhythm comes very near to, or might perhaps be analysed as wave dynamics. The push and pull, the trajectorial thrust of the rhythmical wave, has nothing metrical about it: nothing (necessarily) regular, that is to say, that becomes a measure by the fact of its being regular. What *is* present and immediately apprehended in the rhythmical time-flow is a play of time-proportions, steady or changing to every imaginable degree. Now proportions spell form. Rhythm is the form of a flux, the shape of a stream, even more accurately: the shaping of the streaming. This also explains why there cannot be in musical experience – the composer's, the listener's or the performer's – anything like equality of parts of time, as there is for the Astronomer Royal: precisely because rhythmical experience of time is *not* an operation of measuring. What equality of parts is to metre, equivalence of parts is to rhythm. Equivalence is not a matter of pointer-readings, it is more in the nature of a judgment passed; it is a feeling of balance, of compensation; it is, in the temporal dimension, the exact counterpart of balancing bodies of ponderable weight on one's hands.

Even linguistically, *compensation* seems to signify a thinking with or in weights. Only the notion of weight must be taken purely figuratively in the realm of experienced time. This figurative weight has, in addition, another really crucial dimension, namely the living, the experiential intrinsic weight of the given event in time. It would be inexplicable, otherwise, that one can so often have a convincing feeling of balance, equivalence or compensation in spite of the greatest disparity of the parts of time, as compared chronometrically.

Who has not experienced, for instance, that sometimes one moment of "sublime uneventfulness" – to use the beautiful Melville-ian phrase – can truly counterbalance and compensate for the commotion in the rest of a whole symphonic movement? Zuckerkandl's book, eminently worth reading, is chock-full of provocative ideas.

4 The contemporary musical situation (1956)[18]

What is it that makes a composer tick? And how is it that in great compositions, music can give us such an impression of consistency: how is it that it can and does hold our attention for an improbably long time and, occasionally, even succeeds in moving us deeply? I suppose it is all largely your own doing. It happens when you lend the musician a willing ear – the accent being on "willing".

A symphony has perhaps no objective existence in reality. But the recreative process by which your mind apprehends it is an undoubted reality to you. And what is more: this immediate experience of yours is also an absolute reality. These are not my own words. I am quoting a mathematician-philosopher – Hermann Weyl. In his opinion, the objective world is of necessity relative: "it can be signified by definite things, numbers of symbols, only after a system of coordinates has been arbitrarily carried into its sphere."[19] Whoever desires the absolute, Weyl concludes, "must take subjectivity and egocentricity into the bargain: whoever feels drawn towards the objective faces the problem of relativity."

Simone Weil would probably have put it differently: "Our thoughts", she says, "are in a state of constant flux, subject to passions, fancies, fatigue. Yet the mind's activity must be continuous, every day, many hours a day. "Therefore", she adds, "a motivation, a driving power is required that is capable of freeing itself from our changing thoughts: we need an absolute, we need idols. Idolatry is a vital necessity in the cave" (she is referring, of course, to Plato's cave and the play of shadows on the wall) ... "let us, therefore, choose the less evil idolatries. *Chercher les idoles moins mauvaises.*"[20] It seems to me that with these words Weil is also justifying the musician. He too sits in the cave with his back to the light. So to the question as to what makes the musician tick, my short answer would be: idolatry. Or even shorter: IT.

If we look, then, at music-making from the listener's side, we could perhaps say that it is a matter of re-creation – and I hope it is often true in both senses of the word. From the composer's standpoint, the major problem is one of presentation; objective presentation requiring, as Hermann Weyl says, numbers or symbols and a system of coordinates arbitrarily set up. And *arbitrarily* is the key word. There are no systems based on immutable natural laws, as some musicians too readily assume. A system of coordinates is to the musician something like a pair of pincers for joining time and sound and making them work in harness, in what he means by form.

I hesitate to go into this more explicitly. It seems to me that in theory, as distinct from practice, as observable in the works of the masters, the matter is as yet not too well understood. What do we mean by form? Is it not one of those concepts which seem to be best understood when least defined? But perhaps we might agree if we go no further than to say that it is an order, an order of some sort. Let us take a rudimentary example. You have a pile of ordered letters on your desk. With a flick of the hand, you can make them tumble onto the floor in complete disorder. It won't take you a second. But if you wanted the pile to assume a specified and definite disorder, it might take you very long indeed. And supposing you had finally achieved this end, I don't see why you shouldn't just call it a new order; you probably would. That, in a word, is the contemporary musical situation.

You have the pile on the desk, in the old order, long taken for granted; you have the mess on the floor; and you have also the third pile, or rather several, sometimes widely differing, attempts at achieving a specified, definite disorder which – if your specification were meaningful – can of course be taken as equivalent to a new order under a different system of arbitrarily set-up coordinates.

Unfortunately it is very rare that a metaphor will fit an example with perfect accuracy, agreeing with it in every respect, as two congruent geometrical figures do. There is nearly always something that turns out to be either too short or too long, too tight or too loose. Let me therefore hasten to say that it is by no means by a simple flick of the hand that, in matters of art, an old established order can be superseded. Nor is the finding of a new order just a question of shuffling your cards. It is all rather more involved than that. But if you retain the metaphor so far as it holds, we shall make progress. I shall not touch the pile on the desk: for I am mainly concerned with the third pile.

Yet the mess on the floor must claim our attention for a moment. Confusion, I would say, is the hall-mark of the contemporary musical situation. One has to go a long, long way back to find anything comparable in the history of Western music. Some of the more eminent music critics of our time have repeatedly and unequivocally made it plain that the confusion is a little too much for them. They frankly admit to a complete lack of critical standards that could be said to possess any proven general validity in the contemporary field. This is an attitude one can respect. And a blank mind is occasionally the best receptacle for an unfamiliar truth. Unfortunately, the daily routine of a professional music critic does not allow him to conform in practice to such an idealistic attitude. Works put before the public must be assessed, judgments must be passed.

Consider for a moment the parties: the composer, the musical public and the mediating critic. On the other hand, the map of contemporary music: a criss-cross of rival creeds and schools of thought. On the receiving end: a bewildered audience; and in between, acting as an umpire, the critic who, in moments of sincerity, admits to no longer knowing the rules of the game. It would obviously be unreasonable in these circumstances to blame the listeners for not knowing what's what and getting it all mixed up. Not that it matters who is to blame and for what. It is much more interesting, I think, to try to sort out the difficulties and to see where they lie. In my opinion they are fairly evenly distributed among all the parties concerned; I mean: composer, critic and society.

To begin with us: obviously the reticent or downright inarticulate composer is precious little help to the critic who seriously tries to understand and clarify. If you blame us for it, we shall answer: it was never our mission to enlighten the critic – even supposing we could enlighten him. Besides, the code is to have no dealings with the critic, whether friend or foe. Furthermore, we do not start – as in physics or natural sciences – from theoretical assumptions or from theory *and* experiment carefully combined.

The concept of verification is alien to us unless you choose to call by that name the general opinion that the proof of the pudding is in the eating. But surely, that is not quite the same. It isn't a matter of checking results against intentions clearly defined and stated beforehand. The emergence of theoretical concepts and the gradual building up of a consistent, rationalized picture is an after-event. First come the works and then the theory. It couldn't be otherwise, since a consistent picture can only be arrived at by way of analysis of already existing works, many works, sometimes covering long periods of production. The newspaper critic has of course little to do with that. The analysis – an arduous task – is the labour of a few isolated studious minds especially equipped for it; they appear to me the creative critical minds.

The underlying assumption here is that the changes we observe in the way music is composed in different epochs do not constitute a random process, but a logical evolution. Many factors are involved. The composer himself is only one of them. I admit, he is very often just feeling out in the dark, though not exactly like the Spanish philosopher Unamuno's blind man in a dark room, at midnight, groping for a black cat which is not there. The cat is certainly very much there. Only, all the composer is concerned with is catching it, not telling you how it is done.

It is the studious man, the creative critical mind who will finally be able to tell you. He could already tell you quite a few things by now – among other things, for instance, how the old classical order started disintegrating some time in the 1880s, what a painful struggle new musicians had with the old ideas, the impact of changing social conditions on this evolution; the influence of other contemporary developments, especially in the scientific field; the slow blending of the startlingly new with surviving elements of the old, and the gradual shedding off of the older elements, just like (if I may be forgiven the everyday comparison) an onion growing from the inside and peeling off as it grows, and showing in its new layers, as they appear, new colours, new textures, new shape: in short, appearing in every way such a new onion as scarcely to remind you of the old one.

We have travelled a long way indeed from the classical music ideal. Of course no sane person has ever dreamed of regarding it as synonymous with progress. There is no such thing as progress in art. But there is continuous change; change is the fundamental fact; even stagnation, when it occurs, *is* change, because it means decay, that is, change for the worse. But surely the changes in music have been no greater than those, say, in physics.

It must be remembered that the rise of classical physics after the seventeenth century and the rise of the classical system of musical composition were in fact contemporaneous. The quantum theory of atomic processes was proposed by Niels Bohr in 1913, which about coincides with the time when the break with the classical concept of tonality in Schoenberg's work can be regarded as definitive. It really looks as if, in every age, men were compelled to tackle their particular problems in terms of the topic of which they dispose: and that includes, of course, ideas, in so far as they can be regarded as tools. Pioneer work consists in finding new and unexpected paths of development. It constantly requires the discarding of concepts or techniques that prove inadequate.

I submit, therefore, that no-one should be surprised if you find that a whole series of fundamental classical concepts such as tonality, dissonance, theme and many others are abolished and that new structural principles are at work; that in important works of contemporary music a new morphological conception is present, to a more or less radical extent – and to varying degrees free from vestigial elements of the old order. And what is more important: the whole process is in full swing, has to continue and cannot possibly be reversed, as some people – and even many contemporary composers – seem to be hoping for in the secrecy of their hearts.

This, I think, may already give you a kind of picture of the contemporary situation. *Contemporary* is a loose description; we are all contemporaries who happen to be breathing today. You might try to distinguish, as in politics, between left-wing, right-wing and centre, or, in other words, between those of us who are in favour of going ahead, those who wish to cling to the glorious past or try to revive historical styles in a new garb, and the clever ones who are able to make the best of both worlds. I am perhaps over-simplifying, but roughly speaking that is the picture. And it seems to make sense, even like this.

God forbid that there should only be radicals in this world. I am told that geneticists assume the existence of some agency, whose mission it is to act as a brake on the rate of mutation, and without which mutation might go on at such a rate as to imperil or indeed make illusory the very identity of a species in time. In a similar way, it may be that the conservative composer is very necessary for an overall, general balance and correct rate of development. What we do want is probably a kind of controlled instability. In other words, it takes all sorts to make a world of contemporary music. To say that only this or that school of thought is justified nowadays, and all the rest are waste and rubbish, is in my opinion thoughtless, arrogant foolishness.

As regards the social aspect of the contemporary situation, there are at least two sides: the conditions of the society in which we live and the composer as a member of that society. Let me take the composer first. We might ask ourselves: what kind of person chooses composition nowadays as a profession? Here, too, we shall find a great change. The professional type today is no longer what it was.

At one time, the musical profession seemed to be, like so many others, a matter of family inheritance and tradition. One thinks of the families of the Bachs, Scarlattis, Mozarts and many others of lesser eminence. During the eighteenth century there was also a time when a great number of composers were recruited, seemingly lost by accident, from amongst waifs, strays and orphans. In Italy, then the leading musical nation, conservatoires were called *ospedales* (hospitals or hostels), in fact they were both things in one. They had such beautiful names as *dei Mendicanti* (hostel for beggars), *della Pietà* (hostel of mercy), *di Poveri di Gesù Cristo* (hostel for the poor people of Jesus Christ), or, most remarkable of all, *degli'Incurabili*, the hostel for incurables! The children were trained there in singing, playing instruments, harmony, counterpoint and all the rest, just as we train our blind in making baskets. That is where many eighteenth century composers came from. Of course, if we cared to look further back, we might find that our direct ancestors are probably mediaeval goliards, a tribe of roaming students or clerics. I'm afraid the Troubadours have had no descendants. They remain a brief aristocratic episode in our musical history. The type that came perhaps nearest to them was the nineteenth century romantic composer, especially in the glamorized version that lingers in the imagination of Hollywood.

All these variations that the profession has attracted at one time or another are largely due to the ways in which society has treated us in different epochs. For centuries the composer worked for the Church, the theatre or the enlightened wealthy patron. In a large measure he did commissioned work. Naturally, there are always strings attached to commissioned work, even when they don't show, even if it is simply a question of the *rapport* the artist's mind establishes with an assumed audience, whether consciously or not. Not knowing for whom he writes, not being able even to pretend to please anybody in particular, he has decided, rightly or wrongly, to please himself. One can see only too clearly how this gradual loosening of his social attachments favours the composer's emancipation from every kind of traditional convention. In extreme cases it leads to experiment for experiment's sake and the public be damned!

The ear is incomparably less intelligent and quick on the uptake than the eye. Visual images play a vastly more important part in thought than aural images. When we understand, we say: I see, not: I hear. The very word *theory*, as you know, is the Greek for "a sight", something visualized, a "point of view", as you would say. The eye is intellectual. The ear is really rather stupid, I'm afraid. It is like a shy horse refusing to take hurdles. When something frightens it, it will stop abruptly and throw you. To the ear, depending apparently so largely on memory, on a memorized code of signals, anything unfamiliar is at first rather irritating. New, unfamiliar music mostly strikes us as downright ugly at a first hearing. It does so because it is so confusing. But confusion is not necessarily always in the object. It is probably just as often in the frightened, rearing horse, who needs to be taken repeatedly to the obstacle, made familiar with it and calmed down; then he will perhaps change his mind and, in the end, take it quite easily, in perfect style. As I said before, it is largely a question of the willing ear.

The reason why this is so often misunderstood is easy to see. When you read a poem and to some extent also when you look at a painting or a sculpture – the work seems to borrow its life almost entirely from you; it doesn't come fully to life without a very active *reading* or animating on your part. It seems to yield comparatively little of its own accord.

But musical sound possesses a kind of physical life of its own: we can sit back in a state of almost complete passivity and let it work its spell upon us. As long as nothing disturbing (because unfamiliar) occurs, we are quite happy. If the experience happens to be very intense we are simply spellbound. Our feelings and imaginative powers seem to be splendidly enhanced and, before long, we may discover that we have escaped along a tangent, that we are no longer there, that we are floating in the void and dreaming our favourite daydream; that, in fact, we are no longer listening to the music, we are taking it like hashish. Many people who fancy themselves serious lovers of music are like this. Of course it's not the way! The pleasures of genuine listening are quite different.

The very effort of pure, undeviating, sustained attention is, in itself, an experience of a very high order. It is also a thrill to discover that the world of sound, which to most people is just a blurred mass of glowing or shimmering impressions, with some tuneful thing riding on top or sometimes darkly in the deep region of the orchestra, can be perceived, with a little training, as an articulated multiplicity which you grasp more and more clearly as your listening becomes more discriminating. Again, it is in itself a pleasure of a rare quality to be able to hear several things at once, to grasp the way they are related and fall into meaningful patterns the moment you get them into focus. When the orchestra starts that entrancing process of weaving an immaterial fabric of sound, the genuine act of re-creative listening is a complex business; it must be attended to, literally, body and soul, because not only the higher centres are involved, but even the body itself is a receiver.

There are certain wave-lengths of a more somatic nature which require the whole bodily frame to be attuned to the process. There can be no doubt that kinaesthetic sensations are of paramount importance. The naive listener who keeps on wagging his head or beating time with his foot is only registering the lower mechanics of the process. The perfect abandon to the rhythmic stream is a much more subtle and harmonious working together of mind and body.

Again, stresses and tensions have always a corporeal echo. Even the specific individual qualities of sound which, with the placing and the spacing of the notes, create what we call the musical texture, seem to have some analogy to what the painter understands by "tactile qualities". Think of the smoothness, the velvety quality of a perfect *legato* phrase on the clarinet; of the silky touch the high strings can lend it; of the hardness of a strong *staccato* attack on the violins, when the notes come down and bounce off like ice-pebbles in a hail-storm; of the sharp edge of violent stabs of sound in the brass and so forth. If you miss these sensuous qualities, then your listening must be fearfully dull. I would certainly recommend you to fasten on to this life which is in the material body of sound and to grasp the living behaviour of the structures thrown up in the aural stream, rather than concentrate intellectually on the formal or rhetorical aspect of music, as some pedagogues advise.

For one thing, we are not all agreed as to what we mean by musical form. To me form in music means knowing at every moment exactly where we are. Consciousness of form is really a sense of orientation. If at every moment you know in what quarter you are, at what point of a curve, and in what direction you are going, then you can be said to be aware of the essentials of the form of the piece in its time-dimension, which is the crucial one. It matters little that you should be able to discover whether you are listening to sonata-form or rondo or what. These are nothing but schemes of presentation. As with life, the experience of musical form consists in living it, in living it through, such as it is.

In this sense, the concept is more akin to the idea of conduct, of pattern of behaviour, than the old-fashioned and misleading comparison with so static an art as architecture. My favourite simile is the experience of flying. Imagine yourselves sitting next to the pilot of a glider aircraft. Your first problem is that of getting airborne. So it is, metaphorically speaking, with musical form. Your second problem is to keep airborne; how to take advantage of every condition that may confront you in the air, currents, counter-currents, air-pockets and so forth; how to navigate your craft and set a course. Your third problem, when in sight of your destination, is, naturally, how to come down.

The hazards of the take-off and the landing are no less conspicuous in musical form too. If you have been watching your pilot all the time, you will have realized how his stillness, his reflexes, his compass-readings, his judgment of hazards and chance happenings combine, instant by instant, and result in choice, in doing this rather than that. In short, you will have been witnessing an activity which consists of a chain of decisions taken in full course of the operation. That, I submit, applies exactly to musical form. A chain of decisions, sub-serving an overall design and steering a course in action. Naturally, they ought to be the right decisions every time, or things may go wrong. If you have to bale out or crash-land the thing is not considered to be quite so successful. Fortunately, the musical pilot or passenger can go wrong without loss of life or limb.

One final point which I think my simile can make clear is that the conscious perception of trajectory is essential to the experience of musical form. The mind is exhilarated when feeling itself in gear, as it were, with the very impetus that gives rise to musical form and when it discovers that pure abstract motion can be understood as a language, with a world of images which are specifically its own. It is strange to think that as vital a theme as this has attracted little or no attention so far, from a theoretical point of view. It is not mentioned in any text-book I know of. Contemporary music and contemporary theory are still completely out of step in this field. The key concepts used are mostly static concepts, borrowed from the world of things solid and at rest.

A composition is studied as one takes a machine to pieces. Naturally, to do that the machine has got to stand still. When the component parts are reassembled, the analyst seems to think that he then knows everything there is to know about it. No motorist, I am sure, would dream of judging a machine before taking it onto the road. He knows that the real points are those that are only revealed in performance. They are matters of behaviour. Yet the music pedagogue is apparently quite happy with the result of his armchair scrutiny. The whole field of motion and its rhythmical organization, in other words, the morphological characteristics which belong specifically to it, are so entirely lost sight of that we can't even properly talk about them: we haven't got an adequate vocabulary.

It was always felt that the crucial problem of musical form is the question of unity. Yet the static musical analysis has profoundly vitiated the whole approach to it. A musical work that can only be presented and become intelligible in "time", is thought to need something which will make for coherence or consistency. By definition, music is flow; flow is change; what is wanted is something which will suggest a kind of permanence within this unceasing change. Analogies with the devices of rhetoric and syntax have provided the answer for many centuries. Repetition, similarities, the putting of two and two together, effects of symmetry, recurrence of conspicuous aural landmarks that can be missed etc: these are the methods we have long been used to. Too long, indeed. Contemporary musicians have grown weary of repetition. Symmetry has been terribly overworked, it has become a boring device. Besides, all the devices in the world cannot make unity a less elusive thing.

It is something very much like the problem of identity in time, with regard to the human personality. The child is father to the man; at different ages you are the same and yet not the same. What is it that assures the identity of the personality in time, through so much change, physical and mental? Here I've reached a point bordering on ethics or psychology and I must not trespass.

By way of conclusion let me take you back to the contemporary arena I mentioned earlier, in which several attempts are at present being made to organize sound on an entirely new basis. If I may remind you of my simile of the piles of letters, I should like to single out two rather different ways of making a third pile, ordered to certain specifications. I'll take radical one first: it is also the most recent development.

Recently, a beginning has been made in what is called pure "electronic music". It has nothing to do with so-called *musique concrète*, neither has it anything to do with electronic instruments, with *performing* on instruments, such as Ondes Martenot, Trautonium, Novachord, electric guitars and such like. Indeed it dispenses with every kind of performing instrument, traditional or modern, and what is more, it dispenses even with the performers. Electronic music needs only frequency-oscillators, plus an array of mixing and filtering devices, plus a tape-recording machine. Every sound is produced electro-acoustically and fixed on tape for further treatment. The required manipulations are complex. Even the first compositions in which only pure – or sinusoidal – tones were used, progressed at a rate of weeks or months of intricate operations for each second of composed music. The advances made in a comparatively short time are quite astonishing and the results are sometimes fascinating.

This latest development means, of course, a radical and complete break with the past. Whether or not the traditional instruments, the orchestra itself, are doomed to extinction in the foreseeable future it would be rash to anticipate. For the moment it is interesting to realize that certain social and economic conditions plus modern technology have made possible a development which is entirely unprecedented in the history of music. The suppression of the performer as an intermediary between composer and audience may seem at first sight a positive gain; it means that the composer's work will reach his audience exactly as the composer has made it, as the painter's, or the sculptor's does. But this turning one's back on the human interpreter has some disquieting implications.

The composer might soon find it possible to dispense with an audience as well. For with the advent of electronic music the composer himself retreats into a strange de-personalized neutrality. Only the musical object counts; you must take it or leave it. Now emotional detachment is certainly a good thing in itself, as long as it doesn't mean throwing out the baby with the bath-water. But when objectivity turns into something like a temperamental deep-freeze, it becomes a little alarming.

Above all, when the attitude becomes a dogmatic pose, based on loose talk about our age of anxiety and this foundering world of ours, it is difficult not to become impatient with ponderous philosophers like Adorno, who proclaims, in as many words, the "illegitimacy of expression" for the artist of these out-of-joint times. According to him, the only honest thing the contemporary artist can do is to let the "material speak for itself", taking good care that the treatment he gives it conforms to the strictest rules of asepsis; in short, the artist should beware of leaving fingerprints on anything he touches. What this really amounts to is a new peculiar form of *angst*. This headlong flight from expressiveness, carried to its logical end, would lead to perfect silence, or as a penultimate stage, to the fiddler in Grillparzer's tale, playing his solitary note forever, rapt in timelessness;[21] except, of course, that to him the note was charged with "infinite" expression.

However, we may be fairly sure that only the more naive composer is likely to be taken in by the fashionable catch-phrases. The few really gifted composers who are doing pioneer work in the new medium seem to have seen the red light already. It is a very short step that leads from: "I am measurable, therefore I exist" to "only in so far as I am measurable, I exist" – which, obviously, leaves out the imponderables. Yet, as these begin to take their rightful place again in the total scheme, there is little reason to doubt that we can expect significant and artistically valid works from electronic composers. In addition, the very nature of the new medium is bound to lead to new structural ideas which may well have considerable repercussions on the ways of using and organizing sound in the traditional media.

As far as these are concerned – and this is worth stressing – it is perhaps a little premature to conclude that they have run their course, as some of the spokesmen of the electronic school seem to be taking for granted. Twelve-note composition – to whose methods "serialists" and *pointillistes* are most particularly indebted – is, perhaps not unnaturally, especially selected for kicks under the table; but it lies in the nature of the operation that they cannot always be well-aimed. This much, at least, ought to be clear: what twelve-note technique has been up to since Schoenberg and Webern is for the twelve-note composers to say.

II Tradition and Innovation

5 Music at the court of Alfonso V the Magnanimous (1936)[22]

The special kind of musicology practised by the priest Monsignor Higini Anglès inhabits a rigorous scientific domain. As a result, only a handful of Catalans sympathetic to these areas have some idea of the real importance of his work and know that in the international world Mgr Anglès is amongst three or four names of central importance. His publications, issued by the Music Department of the Library of Catalonia, are invaluable contributions on account of their knowledge of Hispanic musical culture. In many ways so far unknown to historiographers, Mgr Anglès has even somewhat revolutionized the traditional historical perspectives. The role of our country in the Middle Ages – considered to be virtually non-existent until recently – has gradually been revealed by Mgr Anglès' erudite research to be a leading one in the musical culture of the period.

Thanks to the scholarly publications of this distinguished musicologist, the court of Alfonso the Magnanimous can be understood in relation to the famous courts of France and Burgundy. Mgr Anglès speaks of this area of almost arcane research in an informal manner. He knows a wealth of anecdotes that can delight all audiences. Furthermore, he is so passionately involved in his subject, improvising his discourse with ease and assurance and coming across as truly enamoured of the old masters he is portraying, so that it all becomes quite contagious. His audience is likely to take musicology as one of the most captivating and entertaining sciences available.

The music at the court of Alfonso the Magnanimous has become an exceptionally interesting subject both for its content and because all accounts by Mgr Anglès are a result of personal direct research, much of it still unpublished. The archives of the Cancilleria de Barcelona (Chancellery) are immensely rich in historic documentation on the music and the musicians encountered at the royal court of Catalonia-Aragó during the late fourteenth and first half of the fifteenth century. As it happens, it is precisely in this period that other countries lack data. Music from the this time in France and Italy is preserved and documented, but some of the composers that appeared here remained unknown until now. Thanks to our archives it is demonstrated that many of these composers travelled to our royal courts.

The court of Alfonso V the Magnanimous coincides with the blossoming of accompanied love songs in the Flemish school of Dufay and Binchois. Alfonso got to know and love this music, which was encouraged at the court of Burgundy as well as at his palace. He loved and personally practised music from an early age and, when he became King of Catalonia, surrounded himself with fine groups of musicians, one for his residence and another for his chapel.

The precedents for love music at the court of Castile of the end of the fifteenth century can already in fact be found at Alfonso's court. Johannes Cornago,[23] for example, wrote compositions with Castilian text, at first discreetly following the Dutch style and later introducing typical Hispanic idioms, 40 or 50 years before the repertoire of Castile was widely heard in the period of the Catholic Monarchs. This was the kind of music that Magnanimous delighted to hear at his court in Catalonia and Naples – songs with beautiful lyrics and undeniable musical charm, sometimes elusive in character, shrouded with a primal virginal grace.

6 A note on Felipe Pedrell (c. 1940)[24]

The importance of Felipe Pedrell's work as a pioneer of modern Spanish music and, at the same time, as a restorer of a great part of Spain's musical heritage, is too complex a subject to be covered adequately here. I shall simply concentrate on a single aspect of his life's work – the most fundamental one, in my view.

Towards the end of the eighteenth century, a Spanish theorist, the Jesuit Padre Antonio Eximeno (1729–1808), in his book on the laws of music, expressed the idea that "every country ought to base its art-music on its own folk-song."[25] This was a remarkable opinion for an author to adopt at that time. It amounts to a clear forecast of musical nationalism. It is now curious to think how much nineteenth-century music was in exact accordance with the Jesuit's view. One can imagine how delighted Pedrell must have been with this, which confirmed the course he had already set himself. For he had begun collecting and sorting out materials for his monumental survey of the traditional sources of Spanish music. The outcome of this was his *Cancionero Musical Popular Español* in four volumes,[26] which is now one of his best-known works. It was my good fortune, I am glad and proud to say, that I happened to find a publisher for it.

The service Pedrell rendered his country with the *Cancionero* is in many ways comparable to that Bartók had done with regard to Hungarian folk-music. In both countries we find a special repertoire of sophisticated popular music which does not belong really to the common people but to a special class of semi-professional musicians who provide entertainment for paying audiences. Both Hungarian gipsy-music and the "Andalusian gipsy" of Flamenco guitar-music and *cante jondo* were highly glamorous stuff that easily caught the fancy of audiences and composers at home and abroad, and which generally is held to represent the very essence of these two countries' national music. In truth it does not. When Pedrell – like Bartók later on – started collecting his songs amongst peasants, fishermen, artisans, children, itinerant pedlars, beggars and so forth, he revealed to us the real vernacular musical idiom of Spain. This is something much less glamorous than Flamenco but it goes much deeper towards showing the musical grain of the nation. It can attain sometimes a quality of pure lyricism, at its most spontaneous and naive.

Besides his studies in folklore, Pedrell had become more and more involved in antiquarian musical research. His final achievement both as a music historian and as the first modern editor of the works of Victoria, Morales,

Cabezón and a host of minor masters of different periods is of such proportions that a proper description is beyond my scope here.

Suffice to say that Pedrell's studies in both these fields of Spanish folk-music and music history led him to the conclusion that when Eximeno had advised that every country ought to base its art-music on its own folk-song, he had just formulated, without knowing it, one of the distinctive characteristics of the Spanish school. This was precisely what Spanish art-music has done throughout its history, as a traditional constant and nearly general practice of composition.

Taken at face value, such a statement may appear to be a rather sweeping one. Yet when looking at the material Pedrell offers in the last two volumes of his *Cancionero* one cannot deny that he has assembled a good deal of striking evidence in support of this claim. Of course this ought not to be understood as evidence of a really conscious aesthetic attitude, such as that of Padre Eximeno.

To my way of thinking it points to a much deeper and general characteristic of the Spanish mind. The divorce between the highbrow and the popular, between the vulgar and the aristocratic has never been accepted in Spanish art to the extent it has been in other nations. The smoothest ivory of Spanish ivory towers will always show streaks and veins of popular idioms that reach down to the earth. Think only of the poet Góngora. A modern poet with a popular streak like Lorca is in the true line of Spanish tradition – something he acquired through the influence on him of Manuel de Falla.What Pedrell considered to be his main purpose in life was the re-awakening of Spanish consciousness as a musical nation: and to this end he would have us regard equally his work as a scholar and as a creative artist.

7 New musical methods (1930)

[On December 22, 1929, a concert organized by the Associacio de Música da Camera and devoted to the music of Gerhard, took place at the Palau de la Musica Catalana in Barcelona. This was a daring venture, an intrusion into the territory of the Orfeó Català, the right-wing conservative, bourgeois choral organization, modelled on Vincent d'Indy's Schola Cantorum in Paris, which had been co-founded in 1891 by Lluis Millet and Amadeu Vives (later to achieve recognition as a composer of zarzuelas). A review of the concert by the 63-year-old Millet – by then an esteemed figure in Catalan culture – led the generally hostile press criticism. Published in the *Revista Musical Catalana*, the official organ of the Orfeó Català, it focused specifically on Gerhard's Wind Quintet and Concertino for Strings. These works in particular seemed to Millet to undermine the traditional values embodied in both his cherished organization and the Palau itself, which had been designed to Millet's specification by Domenech í Montaner, and featured an extravagant proscenium sculpture symbolizing the twin aspects of the Orfeó ideology – Catalan folk music and "universal" music as represented by Beethoven and Wagner.

Millet wrote "... we found no joy in this music, on the contrary, we often felt discomfort rather than aesthetic pleasure"; in his view, artistic creation was "...the diffusion of an indescribable feeling of comfort and harmony, the irradiation of joy within the whole being". Some of his comments are somewhat exaggerated, e.g. "... the first two movements [of the Concertino], totally atonal, with a random thematic presentation and dreadful contrapuntal textures, sounded like those breaks in a rehearsal when each instrumentalist is independently trying out different passages." Describing Gerhard as a "pseudo-musician", Millet was nevertheless more complimentary about his arrangements of Catalan folk-songs and *Sardanas*, which he considered "a branch of salvation for our composer".[27]

Gerhard responded in *Mirador* – a weekly newspaper founded in January 1929 by Amadeu Hurtado which had quickly become an important forum for the literary, artistic and political avant-garde. Gerhard's sequence of four articles triggered a second article in the *RMC* by Millet, in which he re-asserted his aesthetic standpoint even more vividly, in terms such as "a stirring equilibrium, true intuition, a noble enjoyment of supreme pleasure".[28] Although he valued discipline and hard work, regarding them as indispensable, he ends up stating that "the essence of art can be found in spontaneity." Gerhard replied to this in his article, *Coda.*][29]

Prelude[30]

I am honoured to have been invited by *Mirador* to write in its columns. Some of my friends, whose opinion I value greatly, have also pressed me to expound for the benefit of the general public my ideas regarding present-day music –

words which will help those who are sympathetic to become orientated. Both have defeated my attempts at resistance.

Nevertheless, though defeated, my arguments are still valid – especially this one: the composer fights for his ideals with music. The dialectical fight, theory, analysis, must be entrusted to a different person – the "creative critic", the *schöpferischer kritiker* of the Germans.

I must add that the general ideas exposed here are not new. In Berlin, Vienna, Paris, in Leningrad, they are common subjects in any conversation amongst musicians. Let us bring them to Catalonia, for they are truly worthwhile.

Obviously, I should like to do more than this. And as a result you should be on your guard. Nobody should expect me to show a critic's impartiality – if to ask for this virtue in a critic is legitimate. The contemporary music I want to defend is that which needs to win friends in Catalonia, not the kind whose interest is limited to its "present-day-ness". Alongside music that is merely "modern" there is in Europe nowadays a more ambitious variety. Certain intellectuals have already thought out this distinction quite well. Nevertheless, it would be unfair to lower too much the category "present-day". Although it is a neglectable category in the private lives of certain people, it is not so in the life of a community. Having alluded to this, I would like to indulge a personal fantasy.

I like to imagine the "communal conscience" divided into a series of zones of sensitivity, progressively diminishing towards the periphery. In the zone of maximum sensitivity there are some maligned beings who discover that in the world the problems never end – even the systems that are apparently most perfect are not fully fledged yet! Close to the realm of these sad individuals there is the zone of transitory human solutions. Let us leap over them to reach the periphery. There we find the zone of the "person of well-being", who enjoys all comforts and will defend it at all cost.

From this small exercise, let us extract a maxim: We have jumped a few zones, so let me begin again in the opposite direction, to greet in passing the zone of the simple "dilettante", a noble type worthy of revival. To him I address the words of Paul Valéry: "*Les hommes n'inventent rien qu'ils n'y soient contraints par les circonstances. Les damnations ne sont que des expédients qui répondent a des expédients. Elles n'émanent que de juges extérieurs qui ne sentent pas ce que nous sentons. La séverité est nécessairement superficielle.*"[31]

Men invent only that which is restricted by circumstances. Damnation is only the expedient that answers other expedients. They emanate only from exterior judgements which are not those we feel. Severity is necessarily superficial.

Remember, too, that a prelude does not have a strict form; it belongs to the category of so-called improvisatory forms. Its principle is that of anticipation of veiled allusion – sometimes gradually revealed – to the theme or themes of the fugue.

Chorale[32]

One of the most confusing words that have been "thrown" into the small arena of new music during these last few years has undoubtedly been the word "atonal". Who is responsible for this? Useless question! I confess that, in general, all these words, all these "-isms", make no difference to me. These battle-cries are the ideological signs that give the discussions of critics and aesthetes some force. The Germans say *Schlagworte*,[33] which means "slogans". I think it is very good. One cannot ask for a better definition. However, I am not so indifferent to the atonal "ism". Could it possibly be because someone has wanted to appoint me its "representative" in Barcelona? I do not think so. My feeble indifference is more unselfish in this case.

I have talked to people whose information about the tendencies of the poorly-named "atonal" music was so suspect that it only made them think of *acrata* or Bolshevik. It is curious – but, God help me, I would not want to compromise myself with this information – there are a few significant musicians in the atonal school who are, in fact, militant communists.

But – and here is the but – a no less curious fact is the following: the majority of the young Russian composers nowadays write with such old-fashioned aristocracy of procedure and of spirit that one has the sensation of having one's name preceded by a "de". On the other hand, I do not know today anything more authentically revolutionary than the procedures of certain neo-Italian composers who have just discovered the value of the fascist symbol in tonality. Do you still want any more paradoxes? I think that is enough.

Therefore, no: this word "atonal", which makes one frown and has a nihilist past, is today applied, despite the protests of those concerned, to a series of musicians who are the ones that have the deepest respect for a good musical tradition. For my part, modestly, I have confessed to conservative ambitions. It seems to me, though, that this nuance has not been interpreted with sufficient accuracy. One should understand "conservative" in the manner of a doctor who, as long as he could save the life of a patient suffering from a temperature of 41 degrees centigrade, would not hesitate to make him bathe in cold water. This is what Schoenberg has done with tonality. It had a very high temperature – remember *Tristan* – it had a foot in the grave. Everybody realized this. There was a birth-crisis. Once the crisis had passed, it progressed so far in such a short period that its old acquaintances found it unrecognizable, in a word "atonal". I have immense satisfaction in informing you that "tonality" is in splendid health. Schoenberg has just enjoyed a great triumph in Frankfurt with an *opera buffa*, *Von heut auf morgen*,[34] written in strict obedience to a more rigorous system than Old Dutch.

This system is an order deeply rooted in tonal and pre-tonal music. It is neither historic reversion, the fruit of an archaeologist's spirit, nor the accidental personal invention of an unashamed innovator. Tonality was a thought, maybe the central thought in all Western music, a thought that wanted "to keep on being thought upon". Here we have an arduous task that most of us loathe. It is nicer to live on one's income. There is nothing more comfortable than a well-solved thought, complete and rounded-off; a portion of certainty won the hard way through the effort of other generations and offering to our impotence the chance to embroider epigones and make delicate personal variations.

What do you want? All the divergence between the friends of immutable tonality and the friends of "atonality"– we shall keep this name merely to avoid inventing a worse one – could be reduced to very little: for instance, to the difference concept of what they think "tradition" means. For some it means, to be carried; for the others, to carry. Or: some go on horseback and we go by foot. You can see how old a new thing like "atonality" really is. Another day, if you like, we can talk of how tonality is managed by its present exponents. And another day, even more explicitly, about where tonality comes from and where it goes.

Fugue[35]

Noble *mestre*, I consider it not merely a polite duty, but a pleasure to accept your invitation in the pages of the *Revista Musical Catalana*, which I have recently received. I feel honoured by the words you dedicate to my music, coming from such a noble and representative personality like yours in our musical world. They make possible a debate I had not thought about before reading your well-intentioned article. I must say I read it with true emotion. Your words, even when you treat me as a "pseudo-musician", have a tone of sincerity that irritates my sensibility, the sincerity of a genuine artist confronted with an aesthetic fact, without losing critical curiosity or a worthy desire for comprehension. The kind and paternal tone with which you reprimand me has made me feel for a moment like a prodigal son returning from remote countries and hearing from his father's lips what it was in the mood of the period that led him astray.

Truly, you have made me think of my father, who came from Valls to listen to my works. His reaction has been very different from yours. On asking him what effect they had on him, he replied that he had enjoyed them all very much. Mestre Millet, you understand this, don't you? However, you would not believe that my father is not a musician.

If you could hear him when he walks up and down the mountains of that wooded region not realizing that a possible audience might be listening, he goes whistling Swiss or Catalan songs. You would be surprised sometimes by the melodic variations and ornaments he invents. We descend from a race of Swiss peasants. We, the Gerhards of Valls, are the first generation that has entered yeomanry. My father tells me an anecdote of those peasants that you might find interesting. They used to live in an idyllic valley in Switzerland, a valley "with their houses in the deep green ...".[36]

He still remembers when, in earlier times, they used to form an orchestra or band in which all the musicians belonged to the family and carried our surname. One of them, the conductor, was also a composer. My father can still sing some dance- or march-tunes which, I assure you, sound beautiful. I like telling you this anecdote as it might make you believe that in myself, a humble Catalan descendant of those humble musicians, the first impulse of musical invention comes from a region over which I have no control. The second impulse, though, is already controlled. And all the systematization in my works that annoys you, still seems minute compared to the desire I feel always to make the genesis of the work more ordered and conscious, independent of all suggestions of comfortable emotion and the dictates of absolute fantasy.

Your definition of artistic creation as an expansion of an ineffable feeling of consolation and harmony, the irradiation of the joy of a whole being – not only could I not accept it, but, at most, I can't even say I understand it. I cannot see clearly what kind of activity these terms can define. Both artistic creation and the same attitude of propagation of aesthetic contemplation seems to me much more complex, much more spiritually active. If you mean that artistic creation is above all a natural fact, essentially unreflecting or inspired, the product of a spontaneous and inoffensive behaviour, or without the pains of giving birth, it seems to me that you would be defending a thesis with which you could only do youth a poor service. Watch out, *Mestre*, for I feel that young people in our country are already inclined enough to believe that the work of art is born as in a trance, or as leaves grow on the trees in spring. We are not questioning the fact of inspiration, which is private to the composer. What we are questioning is the artistic fact that begins where inspiration ends. Of all the definitions I know, I prefer Baudelaire's dictum: inspiration is to work every day!

I can see that you have been led into error by that disgusting word "atonal" – which we will never be able to get rid of – when you suppose it means "liberation of the whole hierarchy of sounds". That would be literally absurd unless you explicitly mean that you accept as a natural hierarchy, as a unique order, as irrefutable as the laws of the physical world, the historical order of the age of homophony or the harmonic style with its hierarchy of tonal chordal functions. Nevertheless, you cannot ignore the historical process through which this tonal order has been constituted, which in part belongs to convention.

The artistic facts are that in the last 50 years there has been an evolution of this order at least as important as the introduction of the English techniques of *gymel* and *fauxbourdon* were, in the fourteenth century, providing the germ of harmony in Western music, before that solely contrapuntal. But this order, let me stress, is merely the order of the sonorous materials which have an inherent rationality that has made them apt to take on very different orders from the tonal order during history. I do not believe, *Mestre,* that you suppose that the sound with which Orpheus used to tame the wild beasts would respond to our tonal or modal one. I find that this question of the tonal or "atonal" order of the materials, at heart, has no artistic interest; it is an essentially theoretical question, almost of acoustics and not of morphology

Fugue (Ending)[37]

I am much more interested in picking up this assertion of yours: "A melodic line, without a *certain* determined tonal or modal sense becomes incoherent, it has no meaning." I underline the word *certain* which you use implicitly in an exclusive sense, since you refer to a single determining system. And permit me to disagree with you on the following: a melodic line that would respond to your tonal or modal determination, can be musically as incoherent as an inarticulate scream, if its rationality is not guaranteed by a principle of a higher and more subtle organization than the elementary mathematics that could be derived from its reference to a certain scale of seven sounds.

Conversely, a melodic line that would present this rational organization will be coherent and intelligible even though it is not referred to a tonal or modal scale, but to an "atonal" scale, for instance, to one of the innumerable possible permutations of the twelve sounds of our well-tempered scale. You yourself, *Mestre*, prove the accuracy of this fact, when you do not mind saying that you find "more successful" the third movement of my Wind Quintet, and you attribute it to the virtue of the rhythm. Exactly, *Mestre*: the rhythm is one of the essential elements of that rational organization of the melody, of which I talked to you earlier. You know how a basic rhythm reaches the point of ensnaring the musically dullest person. You yourself found that in that context we mentioned – "the incoherences were saved, in part, by the rhythm". I cannot ask for more: it is a concession I take to support my previous affirmation and which you cannot use to support your point of view, since it invalidates your avowed conclusion.

The rhythm, however, is still the most "physical" of all those elements which can give a melodic line or musical "idea" an intelligible organization. Next to the rhythm we have the purely logical elements that directly appeal to the intelligence and which you, *Mestre*, do not tend to ignore. These elements have a value *per se*: therefore they do not depend on any historical convention.

Finally, let me point out the necessary corollary to this: that which is valid in a melodic succession is also valid in the phonic simultaneity: they are two dimensions of a single idea. "Harmony, genuinely, only means perfect concordance, logical congruence between these two dimensions." This is the central thought of the old tonality inherited, also as a central thought, by the new "atonality". In order to understand this, one may look for the true meaning of tonality in the great "classic" works: but not in *fin-de-siècle* works, where the elements of a historical system begin to appear spoilt or disproportionate under the pressure of "expanded" forms which announce a new order and a new creative mentality. In a country like ours, isolated from the process of chromaticization that characterizes the end of the nineteenth century, there will obviously be great difficulties in understanding these present facts. It could be that the musician makes his own nineteenth century. It is he who will investigate the genuine meaning of the pure tonality of the classic masters, the secrets of which very few modern composers still retain.

Schoenberg has taught us to see and admire this rational sense of the old tonality, nowadays hidden and forgotten by the majority. He has taught us to compose "tonally", not "atonally" – the latter is something he does not teach – but with the severity with which he has communicated the compositional secrets of the old masters, severity to which 99 per cent of his disciples have succumbed. Beware all lovers of spontaneity!

I suppose you must be surprised by this. "How come", you will say, "this 'systematic reformer' teaches you the technique of the old masters and not his new system?" Precisely because he is an intelligent teacher who recognises that perfect technique, if you like, has an eternal value; today it can be considered *sub specie aeternitatis*. It is a tightly knit organic whole, whose principles shine radiantly. For all the problems, for all the concrete compositional intentions we can find a paradigm in the classical system one of intelligible order. Today, after 200 years, we know all the morphological laws; the established convention is clear to us even in the smallest ornamental details. Could there be a more general "school", a better founded discipline? One cannot say the same about the laws that govern the evolution of music nowadays.

The musician-creator is not a theoretician: therefore, he has no obligation towards nor any interest in the possibility of establishing a collective, conventional and impersonal "system". But at the time of the creation, or, if you want, of the inspiration, that is the most lucid and intense human faculty, he has, undoubtedly, a more or less profound and broad intuition of these still not formulated laws, to which, however, his spirit is compliant. On the other hand, we already know that the codification is always an *a posteriori* fact. Zarlino and, above all, Rameau, deduced the harmonic laws from the immanent rationality offered by the artistic fact that began with Dunstable, for instance. But, what was there before? It was not our tonal order. How then did those musicians of the thirteenth and fourteenth centuries like Machaut, Dufay or Binchois, compose? I am not very sure myself, but you will understand from the following anecdote that I am enormously interested in this.

Not very long ago, I had the opportunity to see in the Catalan Library the transcriptions of a manuscript, probably of the thirteenth century, discovered by Mgr Higini Anglès, in an archive God knows whereabouts.[38] One of the compositions I could read – I do not remember the text now – surprised me in a way I find difficult to explain. That anonymous, maybe Catalan, thirteenth-century composer used a contrapuntal technique that I have never yet encountered anywhere else and which I have used myself with absolutely identical intention and procedure in the central development section of the first movement of my *Concertino*.

This coincidence through seven centuries is, I think, worth mentioning. That technique, the particular, concrete aspect of my general lineal concept, has been for me a logical consequence of the Schoenbergian definition of "polymorphic canon". The value of this extraordinary intuition of Schoenberg has been greatly corroborated a few years ago by the admirable discoveries (of which I believe you are aware) of one Wilhelm Werker in Bach's musical techniques.[39] The anonymous thirteenth-century musician belonged to that long line of pure pre-tonal contrapuntal composers, whose spirit has survived through the whole harmonic-tonal era until Bach: and Bach took away with him the secret of a hidden contrapuntal technique which was not inherited even by his own sons.

Nowadays, when we hear in Schoenberg's works the renaissance of that immortal contrapuntal spirit, it isn't strange that we refuse to be seduced any more by the fantasy of a particular folkloristic paternalism. Ours is a different time. Let me then answer you, *Mestre*, with that symbolic song with which, through the centuries, Belgian, Dutch, French, German, English, Italian and Spanish musicians were brothers, members of that broad international brotherhood called "the Dutch School", whose figurehead was always J.S. Bach. Can you not tell, Sir, emerging from the foundations of our time, that old *cantus firmus* that makes itself felt once again in the latent society of a new period? Can't you feel it? – "the man, the man, the armed man" – *L'homme armé*?[40]

Coda[41]

In the last number of the *Revista Musical Catalana*, Mestre Millet honours me by answering the articles I dedicated to him from these same columns. It would be courteous to let him have the last word in our dialogue. But I am pleased to note a positive advance in the debate: I refer to the new amplitude you give to the concept of "tonality", inside which the whole "atonality" will fit despite the few new concessions you may allow to the logic that leads you to accept the legitimacy of a "musical system based on quarter-tones".

Here we have, then, a basis for agreement. You admit that the tonal hierarchy can operate in "thousands of ways". This is what I have striven to emphasize. One of these ways is the one that has been named "atonality" (not the first time I've regretted this inaccurate word). You have well seen, Sir, that in this word the negation is addressed against the formula of an exclusive, obsolete system, and not against the essence of the concept. We have already, then, moved a good way along the path towards a possible final understanding.

But you affirm, Sir, that in your view I am lacking in Mediterranean clarity. It would hurt me if this were true. Did you expect me, in my *Mirador* articles, to provide you with the key to the new compositional methods of the Schoenbergian school? No, Sir, that was not possible! How many years does one need to teach one's pupils a very approximate vision of that which one finds so interesting – the laws and hierarchies that guide me personally in bringing new music into being. You realize I suppose, this is asking for an entire course in musical composition. You don't know how gladly I would impart it to the first person I found who was positively interested in these problems.

Ah! if I could have replied to you with a fully formulated recipe, what a joy ... for others! No, we will leave this task to future theoreticians. Like the musicians of the first "tonal era" did, who composed responding *avant la lettre* to the laws of historical tonality.

The first man sang. The second man, who was a theoretician, no doubt, found the scale that underlies that singing. He proved the first one had sung well. But the first already knew it: he had known the scale by intuition.

Does it concern you that the intellectual techniques of the Schoenberg school can provide such ample space for intuition? Does it upset you that not everything can be analysed into theoretical concepts? Does it surprise you that at the beginning of a new stage of musical evolution, a rational system cannot rise *a priori* armed to the teeth, incorporating all the possible modulations? Your surprise would surprise me!

You even say that you have missed in my music "the true artistic purpose", that is, beauty. Ah, *Mestre*, if you become allied with that lady, I will evidently lose! I shall be glad to lose against you in this domain. I would rather have to lose against a critic, who is the only man – history proves it – who possesses the secret of Beauty. It is his professional secret. I am sincerely convinced, Sir, that we, the artists, understand none of these things.

Variations[42]

My heart tells me, good-natured, imaginary reader, that you are ready to tell me to go to hell if, before next Lent, I try to talk to you once again about "tonality" or "atonality". I would not reproach you for that. Everything has its limits and your patience – if you haven't lost it a long time ago – would have been strained already by the frequency with which this topic has been raised here. It would be a serious mistake, on the other hand, to suppose that those terms amount to an artistic issue. No, it's rather a question of almost pure acoustics, referring to the internal regulations – the domestic arrangements, as it were – of sonorous materials. The issue is thus prior to the technique of musical composition itself. And if, strictly speaking, this is hardly a matter for the musical "amateur", then clearly he would be even less interested by the previous one. It would be just as big an error to believe that, without being initiated into the secrets of "atonality", the listener couldn't understand atonal music. I'm thinking of the amateur who understands the language of Mozart without needing to know about the theoretical basis of tonality.

The only true thing is that atonal music is as hard to understand today as chromatic music was in the heroic times of Wagnerism. Why? The answer is so banal that it is a pity to mention it: because we aren't used to it! Because all that is new involves a sudden expensive payment for the pleasure of the surprise, the emotion, the enjoyment, the charm, the beauty it could give us. It makes us renounce familiar associations of ideas – no mean effort for us.

Moreover, it forces us to perceive mentally in a melody or chord, sounds we had never before perceived. The effort this demands is superior to our desire to be surprised, to be charmed, to enjoy, to be moved or consoled by the music. It is a price we aren't ready to pay for this pleasure. We prefer to become bored. We prefer to feel a sonorous cascade fall upon us, just like someone who senses the rain on looking at the storm clouds through the window, and hopes that tomorrow, God willing, the weather will be nice again.

Functional music[43]

If it is already difficult, simply relying on the elements of essence and form, to establish a clear distinction between absolute music and music with a "programme", it is still more difficult to draw a clear dividing line between "pure" and "applied" music – rejecting, naturally, a severely literal sense, according to which all music that sets a text or accompanies dance would be "applied" – a *lied* by Schubert, for instance, the same as "I want to be happy ...".

Within the same sphere of objectively defined concert music – which embraces equally the symphony and the string quartet as examples of "pure" music, not to mention Mozartian Divertimenti and Serenades – there are of course concertos, that typical institution of the past century, whose character is in proportion to the skills of this or that artist. Strictly speaking, we cannot easily find examples of pure music from which the concept of "usefulness" is completely excluded: a concept centred on the application of music to a practical purpose, foreign to the existence of the work itself; likewise, on the other hand, "applied" music can't help but incorporate a good degree of "pure" music.

Nowadays, the distinction is acquiring a precise character. Amongst the younger generation, especially, the desire to take music out of its splendid isolation, to tie its production to practical uses, satisfying the needs of particular groups, is alive and evident every day. Hanns Eisler, for instance, has written political music for his proletarian choirs – typical *Zweckmusik*, music serving a useful purpose, as opposed to pure, self-indulgent music, to be enjoyed disinterestedly. Here we have maybe the most fundamental difference: in the first instance, the composer thinks above all, or exclusively, about the "performer"; in the second, he thinks about the "audience".

In the first case, the composer's concept of a mass of performers determines the plan, the means used and the content of the composition: musical inspiration facilitates the enjoyment of those performing rather than the passive audience.

In the second case, the composer situates himself at a level of practically unlimited freedom. This explains, in part, why the extraordinarily fast and complex recent evolution of "pure" music has simultaneously distanced itself from the mass audience. The other reason for that distance, however, is the evident decay of the public concert as an institution: previously alive and vital, it is now a dead form, mummified, a cult of the Art of Music that is unresponsive to the spirit or practical necessities of our time.

It would be rash to prophesy the disappearance of the concert as a form of musical presentation within the reach of large audiences, however much radio, in countries more fortunate than ours, has advanced in range, quality and vitality. But there is no risk in foreseeing the disappearance of the public concert in its present form, wherein the attitude of the audience and the character of the programmes are both wearisome and soporific.

But to return to our topic: the desire to make the relationship between the producer and the consumer of music – to put it at its most trivial – more alive and efficient is something that increasingly engages the attention of composers today. With reference to the performer, I mean, concretely, the "amateur" performer, be it singer or instrumentalist, who makes music for his own pleasure and who, at the end, constitutes the elite of the musical audience. It is therefore a question of injecting the spirit of new music into this realm of music-making, simplifying the technical means in order to make it within the reach of those executants with the most modest capacities.

Thus, *Zweckmusik* has, very often, an educational, sometimes overtly didactic tendency. Hindemith, Kurt Weill and Bertolt Brecht have created the genre of *Lehrstuck* or school-piece, in which this tendency is explicit. Weill's *Der Jasager* has evolved this genre into a school opera, designed to be performed entirely by state school students. It was premiered last year in a Berlin school and has been presented in a significant number of schools since, by groups of students.[44] The aim of this work obliged the composer, presumably, to favour extreme simplicity in all its aspects. The vocal and instrumental parts – with an orchestra made up of three wind instruments *ad libitum,* two pianos, percussion, strings, without violas – are written in such a way that they can be easily encompassed by students. Nevertheless, the composer has not made the music so easy going as to be childish. His starting-point has been the interest and practical value of the study the work entails, rather than the final performance, less important from a pedagogical point of view.

The idea that the student, through this study, becomes steeped in the underlying ideology of the subject-matter is an apt psychological intuition. Notwithstanding the musical results, this is bound to be a secondary result.

We should regard these attempts as exemplary, because of the transcendant value they contribute to the musical culture of a nation. If we want a normal musical life, it isn't enough to create concert societies all over the country, or to make intelligent use of the medium of radio. The musical culture of a nation begins in school.

It's indeed worth noting these new tendencies in the production of music. As opposed to gala performances, towards which an audience, every day more distant, cold and disillusioned, pays conventional tribute, music aspires to become an object of prime spiritual necessity. *Zweckmusik*: a utilitarian concept, in opposition to a self-indulgent view of music – this is the yardstick. It was logical that this aspiration amongst musicians should be taken into schools, so as to inculcate a feeling for the spiritual necessity of art within the minds and hearts of tomorrow's generation.

8 Music and poetry (1935)[45]

I'm not ashamed to say quite freely that I've never given serious theoretical attention to the relationship between the musician and poetry. I have, however, responded to the affectionate but lively demands of some esteemed poets – accidentally; but how could I resist? – so that I can risk coming out of the shell wherein the musician finds refuge.

The musician must twist his true line of thought if he wants to impose on it a theoretical or speculative slant. Such a purpose obliges him to express something he has no true need to express, at least in that way.

The notion of that arduous exercise which consists of opening and undoing something which, if it was folded once or twice, had probably good reasons for being the way it was, only makes me desolate. I have never asked myself any of the questions which my subject-matter is now directing towards me. I am more interested in the answers given by the artist, than the enquiry itself. Those pre-paid answers, that received message, one doesn't know where from, permits him sometimes to write *ex abundantia*.

The accidents of the imaginative and affective existence of the artist deter him from entering the world of knowledge. Not even artistic reflection itself, more or less intellectual according to the musician's temperament, offers an entrance into that internal world which stubbornly resists analysis. The reason for this seems obvious. The intelligence of the artist is not disinterested enough. But just the opposite, as well: it is too interested an intelligence, so intimately linked with its aim, that any attempt to separate it from the emotive-imaginative complex which it mirrors would leave us a residue of void or insignificant informational value.

On the other hand, the topic that my poet friends propose to me is of a magnitude excessive for my strength – the relation of a musician with poetry: it is the creative act itself. The music act *par excellence*. The agreement with the muse is secret and no artist, probably, would ever betray it.

What can I say, then, about the act of setting a poem to music? Nothing important from the musician's point of view. My considerations might end here, but such an abandonment is unfair. Several questions arise – some irrelevant, others unpleasant. Before the "how", the "why" demands immediate attention.

For instance, how can we explain, given the richness of the forms of pure music, how the musician's imagination leads him to link up with an external, finished fact, an end in itself as poetry is; something that involves the musician in a considerable sacrifice of his freedom of movement, as can easily be foreseen?

It is clear that the union of words and music is as old as poetry and music themselves, maybe even previous to the Muses themselves. A word dense in emotive content, allied to an exalted musical expression, to an interval or an apt and appropriate musical motif, to repetition, implies a whole series of strange roads leading to enchantment and magic.

The idea of vocalization obviously brings up the question of the human voice itself, the very best musical instrument; and immediately afterwards, the idea of "singability", a supreme emblem in an expressive concept of music. However, before all this, there is an even more obscure and difficult point to be expressed. A disconcerting statement relevant to this has been made by a musician, and a modified interpretation of it by a poet – both worthy of consideration. It appears in Berlioz's introduction to his *The Damnation of Faust* and Paul Valéry used it as the subject-matter for his essay, *Introduction to Leonardo da Vinci's methods*. Berlioz says: "Someone asks the composer why he made his character travel to Hungary. 'Because he wanted the audience to hear a piece of Hungarian music', the composer confesses frankly. 'And I would have sent him further, if I had had the smallest reason to do so.' "[46]

If we avoid taking this declaration literally, we shall hear the resonances the quotation stirs up – we can feel something very restrained, hidden from view, hint at a realm of knowledge with the sharpness of a blow with the elbow.

To reproduce musically that limited world of feelings and images, the lyric experience of poetry, to bend and fix our own imagination upon the alien objectives set out in the poem, is probably nothing but a veiled way of satisfying a deeply original intention. It is an affective pre-disposition, a secret, not always conscious plan: a plan which might superficially be thought childish or absurd, like most of the voluntary operations of the artist. Deep inside a work there probably exists, more often than we know, the desire to make an audience hear a piece of Hungarian music. It would be convenient to know up to what point a text is often a pretext.

It makes sense also to ask ourselves what poetry gains and loses in its alliance with music. I do not feel too impelled to examine what it gains; I prefer to consider the list of losses. In the first instance, I observe the sacrifice of the formal and musical values of the poetic text set to music. The sonorous effects of versification, that which the poets call the music of the verse itself – that fine music of coloured vowels and consonants; the internal harmonies and chords of the verse; the resonances of the rhyme; all that sustained melody that the poet knows how to obtain sometimes with the sensitive accidents of language, as superior counterpoint to the other more serious melody which generates the significant, lyric flow of the verse – all this is almost completely invalidated by the musician's music.

When music gets hold of the verse, it penetrates and deforms it; dilates, contracts and multiplies its members, as if it were struggling to impose on them a new body; all that fine and small-proportioned music created by the verse remains quiet and faded, as if muffled by the more powerful voice that is swamping it. Only the pre-eminent effects of the language still emerge from the musical ballad through the potential of simple accidents of vocal articulation.

Here we have a first negative result for poetry: an important loss, from the poet's point of view. The musician is lucky, probably, not to think too much about it while he composes, and to notice it generally *a posteriori*. If he were too obviously conscious of the positive good which he destroys at the expense of another still problematic good, he would lose the ingenuousness necessary for creativity. Fortunately, these are not an artist's reflections, but an aesthete's (or the other way round?).

The artist, when he protects himself, does so without explanation because of a daring ingenuousness: he goes his own way and does what he feels. And it is probably both necessary and inevitable that this is so. In its union with music, poetry loses all the autonomous beauty of its formal organization.

The most subtle results of the periodical return of clearly ordered sensitive effects – internal rhythm of the verses, the formal rhythm with which they interlink all the harmonious elements of the best prosody – are reduced to a weak metrical rule that does not confine the musician, merely offering him clauses for the formal articulation of melody.

The autonomous outline of verse and stanza disappears when faced with the greater freedom and physical dynamism of the musical rhythm imposed upon the body of the poetry. The static harmony of its constituent parts melts into a different, more ample, flexible and dynamic harmony. From the fine architecture of poetry, the new symmetries and synthesis of music respect only the simple quantity of the stanza, when not still multiplying its verses and constituent elements.

What is there left from the poem, after having sacrificed to music all the most important features of its formal anatomy? A text, poetic matter and a lyrical substance, still retained exactly in the text, but deprived of rhythm and identity, of that resistant body which the poet carves in language and which he regards, justly, as the supreme proof of his creative act.

After these considerations, we could almost ask ourselves whether it is possible that a poet could agree with the musical setting of a poem he might admire. This question can only be answered by a poet. It would probably be excessively modest on the part of the musician, however, to leave the question in so disadvantageous terms. Of necessity, though I do not wish it, I must take account of a possible counterweight, capable of compensating for the damages mentioned.

It could probably be formulated in the following way: if music, with the plenitude of life it transmits and imposes on us almost physically, manages to give us the illusion – which it sometimes does – of making us live the same lyrical substance as the poetic expression, beyond its significant symbols, it is possible that in that case we can overstate the list of losses, the sacrifices in the formal craft of the poem, like an unfounded scruple, since the poem remains, in fact, intact, in its independent existence.

And a beautiful poem lasts, and mediocre music passes and does not change.

III Contemporary Composers 1929–1939

9 Hanns Eisler[47]

Amongst so many young composers who have been more attracted to "classic" forms and (alas!) past styles than to those of today, and amongst those who feel the present only in terms of "tomorrow", there is one musician who finds himself in his element in his own time: Hanns Eisler. His music is very much of the *present*, with all that such a word can mean: it's impossible to imagine him in another era other than ours; and if he could have chosen an era to live in you can be sure he would have chosen this one and no other.

I don't think we can expect to find compositions either like the sort of communist oratorio, *Die Massnahme,* he has just premiered in Berlin[48] nor his revolutionary *choruses* in the repertoire of our choirs. Our choirs prefer more "appropriate" works for current performances. But just in case someone wants to take note; just in case there is a pianist who wants to tackle Eisler's Sonata[49] or one of his piano pieces;[50] or a group of people who play music at home want to try out his *Palmström,* a series of *lieder* for flute, clarinet, violin and cello on poems by that strange poet Christian Morgenstern[51] – and so on: let us give this new figure some time and consideration. So far his works have been published by Universal Edition of Vienna.

Beneath a gentle, harmless exterior, with blue eyes that don't betray his Jewishness, gold glasses and the large pink bald patch and polite manners of a shy university lecturer, Hanns Eisler is a formidable demagogue and a man of disconcerting mischievousness. Faced with someone he doesn't know, he reacts like a dog to a cat. You can be sure that, on your first encounter, his infallible instinct will make him find out the subject which most disturbs you and make the rudest comments. Attacking and scratching, he keeps a finger on the pulse of the person he is speaking to. This manner of his can become unpleasant indeed and doesn't work for everyone. Those who persevere, however, find it worthwhile, as they discover the sweet man that Eisler is deep down, the excellent comrade who passes all tests of loyalty and sincerity.

The day I met him, as I was coming out of Schoenberg's class, I remember we fought lividly over ... Proust! Had we been carrying guns we would have had a duel. We parted feeling angry with each other after exchanging some rude words. The day after, we shook hands and became friends at the keyboard of a terrible, rented boarding-house piano, having played though four-hand versions of three or four of the Beethoven symphonies – which, incidentally, managed to disturb the whole establishment. But we had made it up.

This amusing man has three great passions: *kirsch*, music and the

Revolution. Or the other way round. In any case, music occupies a central position. He gets there from one or the other extreme. But once he has reached it, the only outcome, an obligatory one, is propaganda, social action. With his extreme anti-individualism, stuffed with Marxist doctrine, he is the most relentless enemy of art, the art of our "bourgeois" music. Music – explains Eisler – is the most social of all arts. Without a society there is no music and without collective ideals society does not exist. Great musicians have only existed during periods of great social ideals. The Beethoven who was a protégé of the Archduke Rudolf and the great lords of the Austrian aristocracy, was the singer of the Revolution, of universal fraternity, of human rights. Wagner himself, the greatest bourgeois musician, was supported by the wave that lifted up the great German industrial capitalist bourgeoisie, with their imperialist ideals.

But today for whom is music to be made? The dominant social class is on the defensive, has no ideals and it puts its efforts exclusively into conservation. For this reason, the musician who cannot make music for a society without ideals, makes music for himself and only for himself. As a result, the most unbridled individualism was necessarily going to lead to the present hybrid music situation. *Ergo*: music, today, has no choice but to cease to be the refined, though sterile exercise of aesthetes, the luxurious cultivation of private feelings which has reached a dead end. This situation necessitates a new social transcendence, putting music at the service of a future society. As the active force of propaganda, music demands words as a necessary complement: thus we have the reason why Eisler abandoned pure music a few years ago in order to cultivate the choir, the *lied*, oratorio, films and theatre, in which he is currently the main collaborator with Erwin Piscator.[52]

Hanns Eisler plays indeed one of the most singular roles in current musical life. Although he hardly ever appears in "bourgeois" concert programmes, he is one of the young composers whose works receive a high number of performances nowadays in Germany. Coming from the Schoenbergian school and having one of the most subtle techniques and the deepest spiritual quality, he has lately evolved a voice of authoritative simplicity and concentration. His choral works – leaving aside their effectiveness as propaganda which does not interest me – have impressive musical force. And what is most impressive is that without falsifying the present nature of musical developments – within the atonal evolution – his music has an extraordinary thematic plasticity and harmonic coherence, revealing the composer's quality of aural lucidity, facilitating the ease of performance and assimilation of this music by the masses to whom it is directed. The aggressive manner which some choirs cultivate "to sing in the streets", the parody of choral singing by means of effects with the mouth closed and some *bim, bam* bell-effects, are given an intensity of musical expression and a persuasive force that silences all objections. Musically, at any rate, they fully convince you.

Die Massnahme – a collaboration between Eisler and the poet Brecht – is a work for choir in which four soloists engage in a dialectic with each other and the choir, supported by a small ensemble of wind instruments and percussion. This was sung by a choir of workers who had rehearsed it during their free time over a period of a few months. The impression the work made – according to those present – was wonderful. H. H. Stuckenschmidt, one of the most reliable German critics, even stated in the *Berliner Zeitung* that it was the revelation of a work of *prophetic* character. Although such a statement may be somewhat daring, take note, all the same, if not of the prophecy, certainly of the name of Hanns Eisler.

10 Bartók[53]

Amidst the disturbingly grey aspect of Barcelona's concert season, there is at least one beacon of light. Thanks to the invitation of the Associació d'Audicions Intimes, the Hungarian master, Béla Bartók, is coming to Barcelona. From these pages, I take pride in paying homage to this great musician, one of the few whom young musicians all over the world recognize as a peer figure and teacher.

If we drew a basic map of the contemporary musical situation, we would find that the Bartók colour occupies one of the most extensive areas: and that also affects the "hue" or character of a map which we are accustomed to see in terms of personal and idiosyncratic colourings. It's surprising how much Magyar influence relates to the Andalusian region and makes its colour more bold. But that's another subject. For the moment, let us consider this eminent musician in his own right.

In the flowering of musical composition so far in this century, the profiles of three figures who are spiritual leaders for new music stand out: Schoenberg, Bartók and Stravinsky. There is something over and above the temperamental and racial differences separating these three masters that links them closely. One could say that all the paths they have opened up since the beginning of the century amount to the entire territory modern music has so far covered.

The three of them share the same roots in romantic and impressionistic tendencies of the last century. Following what might be called a *fauve* period, which characterizes the works of the three of them at approximately the same time, they also arrive – albeit through different routes – at a *Neue Sachlichkeit* (New Objectivity), in which they return to organizing musical forms on a rational basis.

Naturally, their personal differences and variations are very important at each stage, but their intentions are directed towards the same or similar goals. Initially, what occupies pride of place is harmonic and expressive "colour"; in the second phase, it is rhythm and timbre; finally, polyphony and a kind of constructivism.

Works of such wonderful tectonic beauty and splendour of substance as Bartók's most recent String Quartets – the Third (1927) and Fourth (1928) respectively – are major landmarks in the evolution of contemporary musical techniques: the ultimate degree of progress and maturity that new music has so far attained. Nothing further beyond that has been achieved. On the one hand, Schoenberg's work still reveals a stronger and more meticulous structure, and again Stravinsky has already stirred up such controversy, it is as if ships are on fire and need to be rescued. Such daring is applauded, if not emulated by the younger generation, who are content to let these three masters deal with the challenge. That is, roughly, the present situation.

As far as Béla Bartók is concerned, there is an element which is as important as his extreme position on the musical map and that is the depth of his roots in the popular music of his native land.

Musical folkore began influencing "art-music" in different countries in the latter part of the last century. But from the very beginning (cf. Mussorgsky and Rimsky-Korsakov), two tendencies appeared that produce very dissimilar results. One values popular song more for its indigenous colour than for the melodic ingredient whose essence can be the basis of "composed" music. These musicians use folk-music as raw documentary material. Their procedure consists simply of quotation and imitation, through a language packed with characteristic melismas.

The other tendency attributes to popular music the same "natural" value that painters and poets find in the real world of phenomena, or in the very same life that they paint or describe. If we were to compare popular music with a landscape, for example, it wouldn't be just a matter of *faire ressemblant,* of making mirror copies, but rather, it's about capturing its spirit and revealing the sensitivity of the artist's response when faced with the model. This is the case with Bartók, as it was with Mussorgsky, Debussy and – up to a certain date – Stravinsky.

This means that artists are free to approach their models with whatever technique they choose, however advanced it might be. It is evident therefore to what degree Bartók's atonal music was the profound and exquisite expression of the Hungarian soul: and that it has, at the same time, value as universal music. This marvellous process of transubstantiation through which Bartók's music absorbs the folk-culture of his home country and turns it into musical essences representative of modern art-music and its sonorities, responding at the same time to the advanced ideas in the unstoppable evolution of our Western tradition is, in my opinion, the most significant lesson that Catalan musicians should extrapolate from this Hungarian master.

* * *

Bartók at "Audicions Intimes"[54]

Béla Bartók's visit to the new and friendly section of the Associaó de Música da Camera amounted to a brief courtesy call during which he talked about insubstantial topics. It is regrettable that this cultured selection of our Philharmonic audience from Barcelona should not have had the opportunity to encounter any of the truly characteristic and representative aspects of Bartók's compositions, those through which this composer has achieved high status in the most advanced sector of contemporary music.

I don't think that meeting Bartók will have made much impact on our progressive *amateurs*, as the works presented were not a good representation of the composer, but that in fact they were liable to confuse an audience that has so far has only heard only tiny snippets of modern music.

Indeed, Bartók the daring pioneer of new music is not found in the piano compositions of his first period. Here, an excessive concern for colour and the picturesque disturbs the composer's concentration and dilutes the musical substance to the detriment of the internal unity. It is a shame that the special advocacy provided by the composer himself as an interpreter could not have been applied to the most substantial part of his music – that part which needs it most. It was obvious that none of the works in this programme needed such special advocacy. They present no problems that could not be solved easily by our excellent Catalan pianists. The most substantial work in the programme – one that can be recommended to those pianists who still don't have it in their repertoire – was undoubtedly the Suite Op. 14. The *scherzo* and the final *sostenuto*, especially, are excellent samples of Bartók's "absolute" music, and oddly enough remind us of his other admirable works such as the Second String Quartet – which, incidentally, has gone round the world ten times over, but still hasn't reached Barcelona.

The five Hungarian popular songs have been harmonized by Bartók, using completely modern procedures that don't gloss over but rather enhance the wild freshness of the melodies. The refined Russian singer Vània Sokolova sang them with the ingenuity of expression required for popular songs. The melodies by Russian composers, however, could have done with a little exquisite touch.

Amongst the most agreeable surprises of the *soirée*, we should single out the magnificent *Canzone* by Azzolino Bernardino della Ciaia, an Italian of the seventeenth-century, probably, who has been totally ignored: Bartók, himself an excellent pianist, offered us this in a brilliant transcription. The curious theme of this *Canzone*, which shows contrapuntal and fugal mastery, is a true rarity in musical literature. I only know another example – by Lortzing, cited by Pfitzner – of such absolute rectilinear thematic structure. A score with an elevated style, sonic architecture of powerful dynamism created out of a virtually "abstract" theme, in itself "inexpressive". We must thank Bartók for having resuscitated this score.

11 Ildebrando Pizzetti[55]

Amidst that great stirring of ideas affecting music in the last 25 or 30 years, the chapter corresponding to the Italian *rinovamento* is one of the most interesting. The hypertrophy of descriptive "programme" music – and what was worse, the "realism" of a more recent date – had been matched in Italy by a gradual drying up of symphonic and instrumental music. The operatic wave flooding all Europe was claimed to be musically representative of the country: and the collapse the tradition of pure instrumental music had suffered seemed to signal a total exhaustion of Italian symphonic accomplishments.

But a reaction did not take long to come about. A *pleiade* of musicians that, at the beginning of the century, had absorbed French impressionism, set itself the task of regenerating Italian symphonic music, re-establishing contact with the great uninterrupted tradition of the *settecento*. The renewal was espoused by these musicians – Pizzetti, Malipiero, Casella and others – from the start reacting against the double tendency mentioned above. It was manifest as an avid assimilation of rejuvenating ideas coming from abroad – from France, from Russia, from the Central European countries, mainly – and, on the other hand, a concentration on the great national models of the period that we could call Pre-Neapolitan period.

This desire to reawaken links with the past is so powerful amongst these Italian musicians that it amounts to a real archaelogical fervour. In fact, nearly all of them are, in part, musicologists: nowhere else than in Italy can you see so many young musicians co-operating with scientists in the critical editions of musical monuments of the past and making new transcriptions and adaptations by themselves. Hence, perhaps, the odd mixture of anachronistic mannerisms and refinements, of impressionist asceticism and sensualism or, to say it with a musical simile, of Gregorian modes and a "Russian" scale that often gives a heteroclitic air to modern Italian repertoire.

In a musician like Ildebrando Pizzetti – who signed some works of his youth in the old manner, using the pseudonym Ildebrando da Parma – this mixture of elements emanates from a strong personality. And although they are not quite fused into a new and personal unity, they still manage to show a composer's noble and serious temperament which grants him a prominent place among the leading figures of contemporary Italian music.

With the three orchestral preludes to the Sophocles tragedy *Edipo re* (1903), the prelude to his opera *Lo Straniero*,[56] the *Rondo veneziano* (1929) and the suite from his incidental music to D'Annunzio's *La Pisanella*,[57] Pizzetti offered us – in the third concert of the Orquesta Pau Casals – a retrospective of the evolution of his work up to the present. This programme gave us once more the occasion to verify that all specific qualities of the music conceived on stage change their character when transferred to the concert hall.

A multiplicity of episodes that would strike us at the theatre for their appropriateness in a stage-context or their illustrative vitality appear to us in the concert hall as dis-articulated musical events – without precedent or consequence, unforeseen and with no bearing upon the future – that go by without uttering a "see you later". In a similar way, one can observe how the most dramatic, theatrical, even scenographic examples of incidental music, appear unfocused at a concert, and betray intentions which without doubt would serve the theatre admirably well, make an impact that is artificial and declamatory.

But what is most tiring is the prolixity and the slowness of a musical development that obeys an extrinsic principle, insufficiently well-justified by the actual composition. This means that the most powerful passages involving the genesis of ideas end up foundering in the short or the long run – generally in the short run – through the excessive extension of episodes following one another in a divagatory sequence.

This programme certainly did not allow one to formulate any definite judgement of the music of Pizzetti, whom we would like to see at the Liceu with representative works such as his operas *Debora e Jaele*[58] or *Lo Straniero:* these cannot be ignored any longer by a theatre that nowadays wants to promote the modern Italian lyric repertoire with dignity.

12 Baltasa Samper[59]

Most opportunely, Maestro Casals re-introduced, in his last spring programme, the symphonic *suite* called *Cançons i danses de l'illa de Mallorca*, by Baltasar Samper, who has lately obtained in Paris a brilliant and well-deserved reaction amongst audience and critics alike.[60] The performances of this work, already heard on several occasions in Barcelona, had this time a special interest for it was directed by the composer himself, who managed to bring out the powerful implications of a score, a warmer emotiveness and a personal accent of singular vigour and effectiveness.

This colourful and luminous music by Samper would have greatly pleased Felipe Pedrell. It makes us think that the element of orientalism – which revitalized the music of some European nations towards the end of the last century – may still bear fruit in Catalonia: but this time it comes to us from Majorca, for from this Majorcan-born musician we can expect, perhaps, the ripest harvest.

Samper has in his blood the exotic modality of the Golden Island of Majorca, just as there was, in the work of Rimsky-Korsakov – with whom, keeping a sense of proportion, we could make a parallel – a degree of orientalism that was endemic. In Samper, it is full of all the possibilities denied to the musician – like, say, Cyril Scott – for whom orientalism is result of a deliberate aesthetic attitude, a product of culture rather than of nature, deep down a mere desire for exoticism – the sort that was going to rapidly degenerate into a scenographic style like that of Russian ballet.

Without aspiring to a rigorous symphonic unity, Samper managed to unify the themes he used – popular melodies of a strong character and an admirable beauty of line – into a spacious rhapsodic form which allows all the resonances of poetic evocation to unfold which each theme carries with it. This is better achieved, in my opinion, in the first and last movement than in *Calma a la mar*, where the composer, seduced by the richness of material in his hands, relaxed his formal control giving rise to a sense of imbalance in its proportions. Were one of the central episodes more similar in character to be sacrificed, this movement, otherwise the most evocative one of the suite, would probably acquire as much intensity as it would lose length.

The orchestration, limpid and precise, plays very confidently with all the colours of an impressionist palette in which the explosions of the brass, the incisive timbres of the oboe and the cor anglais, and the high-pitched register of the piano and flutes go well together and make a strong impact when performed by accomplished instrumentalists.

13 Some Composers from Madrid[61]

We are greatly indebted to the organizers of the Associació de Música de Camera for having brought to Barcelona eight young composers from Madrid who represent the latest developments in Castilian new music. Gustavo Pittaluga,[62] who introduced his colleagues at the Ateneu Barcelones and Juan José Mantecón,[63] the spiritual leader, so to speak, of the group, warned us during this meeting not to expect a homogeneous school that tied its members to an aesthetic doctrine or to commonly identifiable techniques.

There is an overt consensus amongst these composers against prejudice or bias in their approach to all kinds of music, past and present: they share a reverence towards all those things that have impressed their sensibility. Alongside this is their rejection of anything that undermines their belief in the transcendental seriousness of art; and their tendency to put art on a pedestal is fundamentally something they share with the Romantics. Hence their general orientation towards music that has the clearest structural features – notably the varying forms of the eighteenth-century suite, as opposed to the dialectics of sonata-style development.

Another consequence of this preference is a marked concern for "style" rather than "the thing in itself" – to use Schoenberg's words – and therefore, the ready acceptance of a number of formulae that retain feelings of musical tonality: something that many modern composers distort or gently satirize in order to satisfy a need for dissonance (or *feismo* – we might say in relation to Juan José Mantecón). It is impossible to deny that the latter is something which we all try out as a way of leaving a fingerprint: either that or drawing attention with pastiche of the fashionable kind found in Stravinsky's *Pulcinella*.

Julián Bautista[64] was undoubtedly not well represented, either by *Azul*, from his piano suite entitled *Colores*, or by his orchestral work, *Preludio para un tibor japones*: we were unable thus to experience the essentially Madrid style that Gustavo Pittaluga had declared to be characteristic of this composer. This latter work, did, however, suggest a refined impressionist, with a tendency, perhaps, towards *pointillisme*, especially in his endless sequence of pentatonic motifs, colourfully varied to form a kind of curious rosary of kaleidoscopic colours.

Works by Juan José Mantecón – eg *Danza del atardecer* and *El osor triste* from his *Circo* suite – have, just like the composer himself, a singular quality hard to express in words: possibly, the nearest term would be *charme*. In his music there is voluptuous abandonment, a characteristic *morbidezza* which gives it a curious attractiveness, aside from moments of pure lyricism and genuine emotion. Mantecón's music is highly sensitive.

One only regrets that a spirit so lucid and refined as his should not concentrate more powerfully on containing a tendency towards profusion which, though it never lacks the composer's characteristic *charme*, damages one's impression of the whole, when the composition is an extended one – hence, working to the disadvantage of the manifest qualities of his original talent.

Rodolfo Halffter[65], in his two *Sonatas de El Escorial* and his Suite for orchestra, displays himself as a conscientious artist and master of technique. He is perhaps the one composer in this group who has reached the greatest refinement and consistency of style. His exceptional care as regards detail and the tectonic clarity of his music seem effortless, such is his fluency and sense of rhythmic flow. The Scherzo of his Suite is one of the most colourful and accomplished of his works. The Elegia has a depth of feeling that inspires great confidence in the future development of this artist.

A Suite for string orchestra by Fernando Remacha[66] had the form and style of an eighteenth-century concerto grosso, but was personal and modern in conception. Its dynamism was fully achieved by the composer and the performance demonstrated its special skill.

Gustavo Pittaluga is without doubt the artist with the most vital spirit within the group. The dances from his ballet *La Romeria de los Cornados* revealed an exceptionally gifted musician with a positive motivation. Although in some respects his musical voice is still unformed, his musical invention has a spontaneity and verve which may lead one to regard Pittaluga as another Chabrier or Albeniz. What I missed in the way of a special "Madrid" style in Bautista, I certainly found in the music of Pittaluga, especially in his *Escena* and his *La Danza del Chivato,* in my opinion the most successful pieces of the suite. Pittaluga's orchestration has character and imagination, is full of ideas and sharply defined colours, all executed with precision, elegance and grace. His was the success most talked about here: and if this musician manages to avoid the traps of sheer fluency, we can expect some extremely interesting works from him.

Rosita García-Ascot,[67] a pianist of exquisite refinement and sensitivity who arouses increasing admiration, revealed herself in her *Suite* as another composer of rare finesse and integrity. The influence of Manuel de Falla, her teacher, is obvious in her music. But transformed by her instinctive and agreeable temperament, it has something intimate, special, personal and an incomparable charm. Although it showed expertise in instrumentation, I preferred by far the version for piano, whose sonority was more faithful to the intimacy of the music, reflecting more deeply its emotion and poetry.

Salvador Bacarisse[68] is the most enterprising and exploratory of this *pleiade*. His Concertino reveals a musician eager for dissonance – the zest of music – and tricky experiment. This composer may be a bit too absorbed by matters of harmony and is not so demanding of himself when it comes to melody. It could be deliberate: an accumulation of difficulty in the sequence of problems he sets himself, resulting in a hierarchy, finally, of objectives. In any case, there remains a discrepancy between the harmonic basis of his music and the quality of his ideas. The one is not sufficiently justified by the other. However, Bacarisse's talent and sensitivity are apparent enough, making us want to know more of his output and follow his evolution as a composer with great expectancy.

Three dances from Ernesto Halffter's ballet *Sonatina*[69] closed the programme: a work already fairly well known in Barcelona, where he has repeatedly drawn applause for his magnificent *Sinfonietta*. Without doubt, he is one of the most gifted musicians in the group, the most mature, with a well-defined personal idiom. His music has a self-conscious, well-considered elegance and judging from performances of his work he seems irreproachable. Style matters most for him: he seems rather less concerned about content. But here his impeccable taste is apparent: for when he uses old formulae currently in vogue, he always demonstrates a modern sensibility and plays off the old against his own original talent.

I should like to say to the Castilian composers that we already consider them to belong to our musical scene and feel enriched by the perceptions and hope that they present. From now on the doors of our concert halls should always be open to them.

Ernesto Halffter[70]

In the penultimate concert of the spring series, Maestro Casals offered an overview of the already abundant works of the young Spanish musician Ernesto Halffter, not so long heard alongside the Madrid composers from Madrid in a concert promoted by the Associació de Música de Camera.

As well as a re-hearing of the Sinfonietta and of the fragments of the ballet *Sonatina*, this programme offered the attraction of two first performances: *Automne malade*, a setting for soprano and instrumental ensemble of the beautiful poem by Apollinaire, and *Dos canciones,* for low voice piano, to verses by the young Andalusian poet Rafael Alberti – and, finally, the world premiere of the final dance of the opera *La muerte de Carmen*, that Halffter has recently completed.

We can again note the singular elegance and grace of his melodic vein, so easy that his music could often seem to be result of a light and happy improvisation. His marked preference for the rhythm of dance, swaying, winged, and a way of threading the symmetries and repetitions to achieve a restrained, economic format, accentuate further this impression. The most captivating aspect of his talent is, perhaps, the "character" of the spontaneous thematic ideas, his naïve tenderness that often shines like a sincere smile through the studied eighteenth-century shaping of the discourse.

On the other hand, in Halffter's music one can perceive certain harmonic inertia – mainly evident in the voluptuous emphasis on which he relies, depending on an elementary tonal foundation – revealing a kind of form that is more static than dynamic. That is why the dance-movement which generally predominates, rather than being made the basis of an overblown composition, should instead be articulated by a collection of brief gestures with appropriate cadences: for in instrumental repetition and variation the composer displays an extraordinary sensual refinement.

New musical publications[71]

Three works by young Spanish composers have just been issued by publishing companies abroad. The composers in question – Xavier Gols,[72] Roldolfo Halffter and Gustavo Pittaluga – have just come to the notice of our musical press, such that they have already merited the attention of foreign publishers on the lookout for new and worthwhile figures.

It's worth noting that in this country, there doesn't seem to be the necessary commitment or confidence to create a significant publishing house that would take on the printing and dissemination of a number of potentially valuable scores by local composers: foreign publishers are more interested.

There are two sides to this issue: one obviously reflects poorly upon the quality of an our own publishers; the good side is that our composers have succeeded in standing up against the competition for attention abroad. The latter we should applaud, while calling for the mobilisation of effort amongst publishers to co-operate with outside companies. Apparently, this is the implication of Union Musicale Franco Espagnole, the company whose catalogue has just been enriched with the names of Pittaluga and Halffter.

Pittaluga, a young composer from Madrid, needs no introduction, as he was observed amongst the most promising when the colourful and seductive excerpts from his ballet *La Romeria de los Cornados* was heard this winter in Barcelona. His piano composition *Homenaje a Mateo Albéniz* is a transcription of a composition originally written for guitar. The problems of transcription are so well solved that you wouldn't have guessed – unless the composer had pointed it out – that it had not originally been written for the piano. It is a simple piece of elegant and discreet modernism, more evident when performed than from the look of it on the page.

The thematic outline is the basic cadence of a popular prelude for the guitar. Its imaginative flights do not take the music to any extreme, oscillating between a simple, folk-like melody and a florid line, full of mordents and ornamental notes of the kind beloved of "galant" composers of the eighteenth century. A modern touch is evident in some delightful dissonant friction within a simple tonal harmonic framework made up exclusively – oddly enough – of perfect triads, only spoilt by some over-insistence on the interval of the ninth within most harmonies, which becomes monotonous.

The form of the composition is rigidly straightforward, almost mechanical. The small phrases are jutaxposed, fragmented, sometimes crudely, like the design of a decorative poster composition without shades. The triple repetition, merely transposed to different keys, of the initial musical plan has a simplicity that seems not justified – a solution that borders on banality. Of the three repetitions, the central one appears the most interesting. There is an elegant ellipsis of lengthily outlined thematic ingredients that reveals a fine judgement by the composer – if you take the view that composition is in part elimination. It is in the seductive variation, rather than the more expansive one, that we can discern the quality of this composer's thought. But a talented musician like Pitaluga must be more self-demanding: we give him the credit to become so.

Rodolfo Halffter: *Sonatas de El Escorial* (1931)[73]

The main aim of Rodolfo Halffter's *Sonatas* is to reduce form to its essential skeleton, freed from all rhetoric, charging it with a kinetic energy that gives it the operational perfection of an engine, in a rectilinear progress from beginning to end, without fluctuations of *tempo* or dramatic highlighting of specific themes. It must be said that the work has enjoyed great success.

Its presentation in short movements, consistently throughout the whole composition, gives rise to a mono-rhythmic character maintained with almost mechanical fluency until the end. This music does not require "themes". An initial rhythmical figure is enough: a terse motivating force that is self-generating. What this movement embodies is less important than the sensations aroused by the irresistible energy which propels it. The "theme" – we could say – is movement itself.

This music depends more on its dynamic quality than on the expressive and expansive force of a theme, the poetic vigour of the melodic inventiveness. It depends on a driving *élan*, a pure kinetic energy. It is to this aspect that the composer gives the bulk of all his effort. His favourite technical procedures are the repetition of a motif and the unusual mechanism of sequence. The result is cold, metallic, impassive, "objective" music. This character is already indicated by its title.

No indication of psychological or expressive connotation heads the composition. But rather, simply, metronomic indications of tempo, like compass indications. *Rubato* flexibility of movement or *sforzato* accentuations, by nature essentially expressive, are not tolerated by this music. The only nuance which it allows in the course of the movement is also indicated in its most moderated form. There is no unreserved *ritenuto*; only an *appena ritenuto* is acceptable: and come to think of it, one could do without these also. The unity and constant driving motion of each cycle are emphasized.

As far as performance is concerned, Rodolfo Halffter's music is remarkably meticulous. The linear writing, fine and expressive, nearly always involving two real voices, firmly outlines the direct progress of the modulation against a roughly defined diatonism, which is peppered with "false notes", or slightly heterophonic. The form is clear, balanced, sober and concise.

Its substance, however, is hardly expressive and not very personal. The deliberate copying of a style which is more rococo than classic – neo-classicizers truly breed terminological confusion and subversion! – takes him unconditionally too near to *pastiche* so as not to overwhelm the personal physiognomic traits of the musician with archaic mannerisms. His idiom, deeply conventional in this sense despite the modern piquancy of the linear dissonance, gives the composition a character which is more that of a rhetorical exercise than of an original creation. I never understood how it is possible that a talented musician – whether as a sacrifice to the fashionable "neo-classicism" so obsessing everyone – could willingly abstain from what offers the maximum pleasure for him and for us: invention, original melodic creation.

Halffter's suite, and especially the *Elegia* which we heard last winter during the collective presentation of the new group of musicians from Madrid, seemed to me to be, in this context, a much more authentic portrait of the heart-warming and thoughtful musician that Rodolfo Halffter is. From his prolific yet refined explorations, we can expect work of positive value. This is what the *Suite* seems to indicate.

IV Music and Drama

14 Opera (1930)[74]

Everywhere, the symptoms of a renewed crisis in the Opera House are multiplying. Even the foundations of our great Teatro del Liceu are currently trembling. One might almost welcome any obstacles that might hasten this crisis at home. But let us not deceive ourselves. The difficulties for large opera houses are not new: indeed, they are even prosaic. They have nothing to do with the *ritorna all'antico* of the reactionaries who try, especially in Germany, to adopt an archaeological criterion, exhuming the forgotten operas of Verdi, Handel and others: that is no solution.

The so-desired, so-necessary renewal of the lyric repertoire has failed: and remember that the international "repertoire" has merely 80 box-office-proof works, and that the national repertoires – since not all the works have the same prestige in all countries – are not even half that number. The Handel revival, latterly proclaimed with so much optimism, has become a *fausse couche*, as Schoenberg showed not long ago. Verdi's *Simon Boccanegra*, with a new libretto by Franz Werfel, has (with all due respect) also been unsuccessful in Vienna.[75] Pessimism deepens each day as many people believe that indigenous opera as an art-form is flagrantly at variance with the spirit of our times – is a sick patient without a cure.

Nevertheless, there has been recently one fact of significance. During the last 15 years, chamber music has been the genre attracting the most interesting and productive developments in contemporary music: and these developments have gravitated towards the theatre. The criticisms of unproductiveness, of lack of talent, or of the failure of new music in the face of the stylistic demands of the musical theatre, are refuted every day by a proliferation of convincing new pieces. Ernst Krenek's *Johnny spielt auf* was, already a few years ago, the first audience success for a piece dealing with the modern musical situation. Stravinsky's *Oedipus Rex*, *Renard*, *L'Histoire du soldat* and *Mavra* are conquering all the stages of the world. Berg's *Wozzeck*, Hindemith's *Neues von Tage* and Milhaud's short chamber operas complete the picture of success in the new musical theatre. Works of the most representative musicians of our day have been premiered. Schoenberg has made minimal concessions to the theatre with his innovatory musical language, but he has renewed the *buffo* genre with his opera, *Von Heut auf morgen*, recently premiered in Frankfurt. Krenek pursues the idea of the "great serious opera" again with his *Leben des Orest*, premiered in Leipzig; Kurt Weill, meanwhile, continues his own way with the *singoper*, provoking, with his *Mahagonny*, one of the major scandals in theatrical history. Compared with what happens here, it is worth noting that most of these works have already been performed an amazing number of times. Weill's *Dreigroschenoper* (an opera about the poor) beat all records with 500 performances in two years. If this is the death of the contemporary opera house, what would life be?

The problems of the musical theatre are tackled in these works with a revolutionary impulse that understandably caused scandals amongst audiences accustomed to the aesthetics of *The Ring* and of *La Bohème*. The collaboration between composer Weill and poet Brecht, above all, has introduced a new concept of theatre. *Mahagonny*, following in the direction begun with *Dreigroschenoper* and *Happy End*, initiates a form of epic theatre nearer to a stage *ballade* than a musical drama. The music does not act as motor for the performed action, nor does it explain all the vicissitudes in the plot: it simply gives a rigorous musical meaning to the moments of rest, the situations in which music can delay the dramatic development. The composition of *Mahagonny* is a sequence of closed scenes that represent successive states, staggered stages of the "story" that is being recounted. The succession of these images in movement and the dynamism of the music produce a kind of dramatic evolution in the same way that, in film, the succession of pictures, of fixed stages, projects the movement and action on the screen.

15 Music and film (1930)[76]

Music offers the medium of film probably one of its most dangerous pitfalls, due to the "slow motion" effect which the sung word imposes on the development of the dramatic action. So much so that, when speaking of film, everybody clearly thinks that it should have nothing to do with opera or operetta. Neither for its themes, nor for its technique, can the realist art of the cinema copy the lyric theatre, which has manifestly its own conventions. Whether it be called *dramma per musica*, *opera seria* or *opera buffa*, the lyric theatre contains only pseudo-action and pseudo-movement. Remember that the time taken by the music to develop its forms exceeds greatly the time that the spoken word needs, so that one has to reduce and simplify the dramatic action of a libretto. As music becomes dominant in opera, the action becomes schematized to the point of being reduced to pure illusion. Conversely, when the plot becomes complicated, the music has to give way – hence, *recitativo secco*, with the music following the spoken dialogue, so that the audience can follow the thread of what is happening on the stage.

The widely debated question of whether in the musical theatre the music or the drama should be supreme is one that hardly needs to be considered in film. Music in film has a necessarily subordinate role. Overall, it may from time to time enliven the impact in an epigrammatic manner, but generally it can count only on a small part of the audience's attention. It has to act on the subconscious of the listener – as a counterpoint to a flexible visual melody, which it can deepen quite immeasurably. Out of what we might call its "solos", the music in a film has to find a technique that permits it to capture the imagination of a "spectator" rather than a "listener" audience.

There is no way to foresee, of course, how music that has an 80 per cent inattentive audience can achieve its aims. We might suppose that the "utilitarian" tendency, the simplification of means proclaimed by neo-classic music today will make good use of film. There they might simply feed the apathy of youth by restoring historical criteria, rather than following a difficult path forward that has neither the sympathy of the masses nor the trust of the critics.

What cannot be doubted is that neither the techniques of sound reproduction through the microphone, which limit the possible range of musical colours, nor the marginal role granted to music in film, will tolerate the opulence and massive texture of Romantic music: they demand, on the contrary, a transparent, almost black-and-white sonority, a clear polyphony of well-defined lines.

Presumably, the simplification that film demands from music will indirectly influence current musical aesthetics, just as the arrival of opera – and I do not believe this parallel to be exaggerated – helped, unexpectedly, the evolution of the madrigal and pure instrumental music. Not, however, in the sense of looking back, as the creators of opera in Florence imagined, when they emulated Greek drama; nor, also, in the way that those who, since the Armistice after the First World War, have tried to counter the evolution of modern music with a more comfortable neo-classicism, advocating a return to the values of Clementi, Scarlatti and Bach for the next 25 years or so. There is no way today we can return to an eighteenth-century-style simplicity, which was a response to a particular and irreversible state of sonorous materials: our simplicity will be achieved at the end of a path that music has yet to explore, having got rid of the crutches of tonality.

Film with a music soundtrack asks us to accelerate this development, as every application of music to a useful purpose draws it out of an esoteric realm in which too easily it is confined, when left alone. This "application" of music to film is unlikely to be made according to a Wagnerian recipe, with music as the prime means of expression, drama defining the purpose of that expression. None of that. It is sufficient for music to keep its distance.

Adding "noises" to music, on the other hand, opens doors to a distinctive cine-phonic genre: perspectives that might be a little puzzling, maybe, given the memory of Marinetti's futurist noise-aesthetic. We must tread carefully here. However, with all our reservations, we should accept that there is all the immense repertoire of acoustic impressions of an "extra-musical" order that attack our ears all the time, and constitutes an almost unexplored territory, untested as to its aesthetic value to the musician.

Finally, there is no doubt that capturing the human voice on film will offer the actors and singers a critical mirror one hundred times more efficient than that they have available on discs, and needless to say, than the response of journalistic critics. In utopian terms, this might engender a new culture of diction and intonation, with God knows what results. The utopian aim might be to modulate the sound as the person recording wishes, the same way that the camera modulates or interprets optical reality, making choices according to a subjective viewpoint.

Certainly, the current achievements of film with music soundtrack are not very considerable, indeed it is still in its nappies, babbling its first syllables with Bunuel-Auric-Cocteau's *Le sang d'un poète*,[77] which we hope to see soon in Barcelona: but we can take for granted its magnificent future. Its technical possibilities are its strongest guarantees. The machine, inanimate element at the start, once assimilated by the artist, becomes an organ of his sensitivity; the machine becomes the music. One should only recall the comparatively recent evolution of instruments in relation to the forms of musical composition.

16 The Duenna (1949)[78]

What first attracted me to *The Duenna* was its setting in Seville. It is true Sheridan did not trouble himself about local colour. Seville was probably a mere stage-convention to him, not meant to be taken more realistically than Shakespeare's Illyria or his seashore of Bohemia. But Seville is full of a wealth of associations for me: its colour and atmosphere; its social climate, wealth and fashion rubbing shoulders with beggars, gypsies and picaresque rogues; extreme cultural refinement with the vigour of the common vernacular; lightheartedness and tormented pessimism side by side; wild superstitious beliefs mingling with intense religious feeling – all this was food for music. Sheridan's setting vividly suggested to me images of eighteenth-century Seville, where the Brethen of Deadly Sin – laymen dressed in monks' habits – would be strolling through the streets at night, chanting *memento mori* and exhorting sinners to repentance. In fact, I felt this so strongly that to create this atmosphere of the streets of Seville at night with adventure and death both round the corner, as it were, I have given my opera a dumb-show introduction which is dominated by the chanting Brethren.

It was above all the beauty of Sheridan's English, however, the sparkle and elegance of his dialogue which I found irresistibly attractive. There is, I think, some affinity between Sheridan and the imaginative humour and wit of the Andalusian people and their polished turn of speech. Sheridan's characters were therefore credible to me as Andalusians. This coloured my whole feeling towards the play and allowed me to portray the characters in the musical key suggested by the Sevillian stage.

Sheridan's lyrics lent themselves admirably to musical setting. But it was especially his prose that proved unfailingly stimulating, whether I wished to turn it into recitative, into *arioso* or even into set pieces treated as formal musical units, as I have done occasionally. Despite the absence of metrical pattern and rhyme, his sentences always move with a musical impetus and verve that readily accept and sustain larger *cantabile* lines and balanced musical forms.

The setting of the serenade, "The breath of morn bids hence the night", with which Antonio, a young impoverished gentleman, serenades Dona Luisa, daughter of the wealthy Sevillian nobleman Don Jerome; the duet that follows for Dona Luisa (who is roused by the serenade and appears at the window); and the dialogue in accompanied recitative between Don Ferdinand, Luisa's brother (in love with Dona Clara) and his friend Don Antonio, when he tells him of the reception he received in the middle of the night, when he forced his way into Clara's room and tried to persuade her to elope with him; and the *arioso*-style dialogue that forms a small set-piece duet for the Duenna and Dona Luisa at the beginning of the third scene of Act 1: these are all different examples of the way I was able to treat Sheridan's lyrics and prose dialogue.

As an opera libretto, *The Duenna* presented several difficulties which could only be solved by occasional modifications of the layout of the play. Apart from cutting subsidiary scenes and some of the dialogue in order to reduce the libretto to the normal length of an opera, I made only two important alterations of Sheridan's text. In the first place, I felt that it was not possible to begin the opera, as Sheridan does, with the long monologue of one of the menservants, a character who has practically nothing to do with the main plot and is allotted only a few sentences in the rest of the play. (For the same reason, by the way, I dropped the character of Don Carlos and substituted Father Paul as Isaac's companion and guide in Seville.) Neither did it seem practicable to begin the opera with the serenades sung by Don Antonio under Dona Luisa's window. These obviously wanted some introduction, careful timing and adequate background.

Therefore, to provide by way of an opening a number of contrasting tensions that would create an atmosphere of the streets of Seville at night, with adventure and death both around the corner, I introduced the chanting Brethren of Deadly Sin. When the curtain goes up, Don Antonio is seen tuning his guitar, his servant and bodyguard watching him. After a few bars, the mournful *memento mori* is heard from the distance, growing louder as the chanting Brethren approach. To avoid the encounter Don Antonio and his servant recede to the back of the stage. The Brethren pass by and their chant dies away into the distance.

Hard on their heels follow a pretty strumpet and an old bawd, both dressed in black, looking like two figures out of Goya. Don Antonio comes forward and warns the girl of the presence of her natural enemies. She turns round and briskly retraces her steps, followed by the bawd. After this dumb-show introduction, Don Antonio serenades Dona Luisa and the scene closely follows Sheridan till the end when, in order to achieve a dramatic close, the Brethren reappear and abruptly interrupt the serenading.

The biggest problem in the writing of an opera is the problem of musical form. While closely following the course of the dramatic action, the music must have structural coherence for considerable periods of time. In addition, it must of necessity follow the laws of its own development and at certain moments must lead by steady progress to a climax. Therefore, when Sheridan did not supply a dramatic climax when a musical one was required – eg in the Finale of Act 1, where Sheridan ends with a simple trio – the Chorus is introduced (promenaders, people of fashion and finally a swarm of beggars) and, in order to heighten the tension of the situation, Don Ferdinand (in search of the missing Dona Clara) reappears, which puts his sister Luisa in a predicament. The climax is reached when Ferdinand, seeming to recognize

Clara in the veiled Dona Luisa, is prevented by Father Paul from approaching her as she runs off with Don Isaac.

These are the only major alterations to Sheridan's text. Later on, for instance, in the second scene of Act II, when Isaac and the Duenna (whom he still believes to be Dona Luisa) have agreed to elope and sealed their pact with a kiss, the situation, both for dramatic and musical reasons, called for a love-duet. As Sheridan did not provide me with a lyric for such a piece, I looked for one in his *Collected Poems* and, to my delight, found exactly what suited my intentions in the charming poem, *The Kiss*, beginning with the lines:

> Hurried seal of soft affection
> Tenderest pledge of future bliss.

This delicate and tender lyric sung by the old harridan and the cunning Isaac will produce, I think, the *buffo* effect intended without being musically underlined in the least.

As regards the problem of composition and musical form as a whole, I must limit myself to stating what has been my chief aim in setting Sheridan's play. I have endeavoured to achieve the strongest possible articulation of symphonic continuity through the constant interplay of four distinct symphonic principles. Namely, the arias or ensembles treated as formal musical units, yet not entirely detached or self-contained; secondly, the accompanied recitative to speed up the action and carry the plot forward; thirdly, *scena*-like developments in *arioso*-style to follow dramatic incident step by step; and lastly, spoken dialogue either underlined or punctuated musically, or backed with static musical patterns in the manner of melodrama.

The Duenna – Revised (1951)

In revising *The Duenna*, the experience gained through the BBC broadcast performance two years ago has been of great value to me. I also like to hope that I have profited from the criticisms of my work received on that occasion. The most helpful critical contribution came from Sir Steuart Wilson,[79] who took the trouble of sending me an extensive *catalogue raisonné* of desirable improvements, giving me chapter and verse for each item. All in all, I have thus had something very tangible from which to work. The result of such a revision might properly be regarded as an author's criticism of his own work. I would not claim any special validity for that. Indeed the reverse might be true. The critical mind operating *in* poetry, T.S. Eliot maintains, "the critical effort which goes to the writing of it, may always be in advance of the critical mind operating *upon* poetry, whether it be one's own or someone else's".[80]

Moreover, the crucial point the question of the stage-worthiness of the work is one which, I believe, could not be settled one way or another through a broadcast performance. And while the point is not settled, the work is obviously still very much *sub judice*. At which stage it is no doubt wiser for an author to keep his peace, however much relevant evidence he may think he could contribute.

On the other hand, it is obvious that the "sightless" broadcast performance of an operative work puts it to a limited test, most exciting in one direction and incomplete in others. Inevitably, a stage performance will subject it to a very different order of strains and stresses. A revision considering the experience in the first medium only is therefore bound to be provisional.

Why, then, do I go on with such good reasons for stopping short here and how? I'm afraid I don't really know. Except that the peculiar tension of a contradictory state of mind may be the only reason for my doing anything at all.

Most composers, I think, would admit that the broadcasting of a musical work is, in the literal sense of the word, an ordeal. Sound thus disembodied seems to force one's attention (and not always quite naturally, I can't help feeling) into a considerably modified focus, as compared to one's listening in the concert hall or theatre where the eye is allowed to associate. Listening by oneself in seclusion, as distinct from listening collectively, as part of an audience, may also affect it, and perhaps more than we realize.

On the whole, radio listening would seem to make for an aesthetically more detached, cool and rigorous, if sometimes narrower, kind of listening. And I suspect that in the concert-hall my willing ear is aided by the concurrence of other wills. Not necessarily, or not always, in the sense of greater discrimination but certainly in the sense of warmer enjoyment.

However, it is a fact that the microphone often embarrassingly spotlights more than was meant to meet your ear – if I may so mix my metaphors. One would never want to write anything that was not really meant to be heard; but one is sometimes tempted to speculate on proverbial shortcomings in performance, such as indistinct articulation in opera singers.

To take one case, I confess that the reiterated repetition of words in set pieces – Mozart's, for instance – has never disturbed me in the least. Yet on listening to the broadcast I am much embarrassed by the same thing in my own set pieces. Perhaps it all simply goes to show not how slack opera singers are apt to be in matters of enunciation, but how carelessly one listens to words in opera. For better or for worse, the microphone will not allow one to do so. Christopher Hassall has now helped me to correct this fault by providing me where necessary with additional lines to Sheridan's lyrics.

When first setting Sheridan's original lyrics, however, I had found this repetition of lines, for musical reasons, absolutely unavoidable. It is easy to see that both the occurrence of set pieces and their actual length are dependent, on the one hand, on the character of a dramatic situation at a given moment and, on the other hand, on general requirements of overall structural design. Sometimes, Sheridan's lyrics were too long; something they were not wanted at the particular moment where they occurred, owing to the ratio that has to be observed between the importance of a given character in the plot and the frequency of his *solo* opportunities; in either case the solution was easy, unwanted lyrics could be shortened or omitted.

But when the reverse happened, when Sheridan's lyrics were too short for the musical proportions a given "aria" *had* to have, or when no lyrics were provided where the situation cried out for a solo piece for a given character, then there was clearly nothing for it but to make do with the text in hand and firmly put musical requirements first.

I have already mentioned the unsatisfactory nature of the solution in the first case, when simple lyrics were too short, and how we have now tried to put it right. When the second case arose – a lyric wanted where none was provided – I was able in one instance to find a couple of suitable stanzas in Sheridan's Collected Poems – *Fugitive Verse* – but for the rest, I had simply to base my set pieces on the few sentences of plain dialogue available. I did not find the absence of regular metrical patterns and rhyme to be in any sense a hindrance to the musical shaping of such "prose-numbers". Rather, on the contrary, it seems to me that prose is even more congenial than verse to the contemporary conception of musical form, at any rate I feel it to be so in this particular case. Provided the prose sentence is well shaped in itself and contains no – in the pejorative sense – *prosaic* words, it offers the composer, it seems to me, considerably more flexible material than a metrically controlled stanza whose fixed symmetries and subtle interplay of assonance and rhyme are apt, at times, to become something of a liability or to worry one's conscience if, as not infrequently happens, they have to be disrupted for some specifically musical reason.

Examples of such prose-numbers in the score: the cabaletta between Dona Luisa and the Duenna, "if we succeed ..." (Act I, Scene III); Don Jerome's *arioso* later on, "But the choice on one side ..."; the Duenna's aria at the end of the same scene, "So speed you well ..."; Don Jerome's main aria, "Aye, her beauty will affect you ..." (Act II, Scene I); or Father Paul's solo number, "You forget who I am ..." (Act III, Scene I).

The alterations which, for strictly dramatic reasons, I felt it necessary to make in Sheridan's play were a far more difficult task. The excision of subsidiary scenes was a delicate operation with a plot that has so many twists to it. This and the systematic pruning of the dialogue at once reduced Sheridan's text to a little more than half. But the real stumbling-blocks were the opening scene and the three Finales. The very opening offered two pitfalls at once. Between an uncomfortably close paraphrase of *Notte de gorno faticar* for a minor character and a plump opening with a Serenade for the principal tenor, the choice appeared wholly uninviting. There seemed to be nothing in it but to delay the beginning to the Serenade and do something useful with the time thus appropriated.

Two objects presented themselves as worth pursuing. In the first place, having made up my mind to use under certain conditions plain spoken dialogue, traditionally accepted in comic opera, I thought it desirable to establish this at once, as a sort of ground level as it were. Hence the stage-business of the broken guitar-string and ensuing dialogue. Then, as a further motivation of the delayed serenading and, at the same time, musically viewed, as a kind of rising slope leading imperceptibly from speech to song; the appearance of the strolling Brethren of Deadly Sin chanting their *memento mori*. Strumpet and Bawd following sharp on the Brethren's heels are again meant to fulfil a double purpose to imply further and contrasting stage-incident, as well as transition, on the musical plane, from the sombre *memento mori* to the climate of the Serenade.

I have mentioned that it seems necessary to me to attach certain conditions to the use of plain dialogue in comic opera. It is not only that the pull from speech to song and vice-versa always feels so uncomfortably jerky. To my mind the main objection to this use of plain dialogue seems to be that, without doing something about it, plain dialogue simply does not integrate with the rest of the sound-picture and awkwardly sticks out as an alien impediment. Without, that is, some degree of leading, lacing, framing dovetailing or backing, it does not seem possible to coax it into fusion with the sound-scheme as a whole.

An example will perhaps make my meaning clearer. I would like to compare plain dialogue in such a context to the natural grain or texture of the canvas – or whatever other material it may happen to be which Miró sometimes allows to *show through* in his paintings. The places where this occurs do not make a hole in the picture because they seem to be pictorially as much controlled, balanced and organically integrated as anything else on the rest of the surface.

Some of the cuts made in the present revision are meant for radio only; the first appearance of the Brethren has thus been omitted. I should like to see it restored on the stage, where I feel the chant of the Brethren to be the right frame for the first scene as a whole; from the very beginning I have always seen it thus *burlée de noir*. Most of the more important cuts affect the longer set pieces and ensembles. I was reminded of Coleridge's startling remark that there can be too much poetry in a long poem – and so, possibly, too much music in an opera! A difficult, but indeed vital viewpoint to arrive at for either poet or musician. The revision of the recitative has been mostly a matter of small adjustments and compressions aimed at correcting faulty timing, which occasionally tended to interrupt or slow down what was intended to be quick-fire dialogue.

The most absorbing problem in opera is, no doubt, the problems of form. In Schoenberg's conception, form constitutes the social aspect *par excellence* in the complex matter of musical organization. It would be obviously premature for me to discuss it here. As Eliot remarks in connection with the problem of "meaning" and "communication" in poetry: "the poem's existence is somewhere between the writer and the reader."[81]

There are two further, subjective points I should like to make. In the first place, I do not feel that my choice of Sheridan's play as an opera libretto calls for an apology. Indeed, it may well amount to something bordering on an offence against the *Zeitgeist*, for all I know, to have dared to offer an entertaining and agreeable comedy in *the commedia dell'arte* vein, considering that discomforts of subject-matter as well as of style seem to have become so indispensable an ingredient in the pleasure we take in the work of the contemporary artist. But I honestly do not see how I could remedy that.

My second point refers to what Gide has called *la quatrième unité*, the unity of one's audience. I cannot think of a better illustration of my meaning than to confess how deeply stirred I felt on coming across Dr Johnson's famous passage which opens with the pregnant words, "I rejoice to concur with the common reader".[82] This is a feeling that has been alive in Spain through many centuries. Students of Spanish art and literature know that the opposition between "popular" and the "highbrow" has never been allowed in Spain to lead to a real divorce, not even in such extreme a case as that of the poet Góngora.

17 Music and Ballet

It is generally agreed that it is quite possible for a creative artist to produce good work in spite of inadequate or even questionable theoretical tenets; and that, conversely, the soundest and most plausible views in the theoretical field are by no means a guarantee of good creative work. It would certainly seem that all the artist's theorizing on his own craft had best be taken with a pinch of salt. The fact is that between creative activity and theoretical speculation there is a tremendous gap which none of us – whether artist or theorist – can possibly bridge. This all springs from the fact that the creative state of mind is basically different from the critical state of mind.

In an admirable lecture on the *raison d'être* of criticism given at a Symposium of Music at Harvard, E. M. Forster formulated the basic difference between these two states of mind in these words: "Think before you speak is criticism's motto; speak before you think is creation's."[84] Of course, it is possible to shake a grain of truth out of every inverted platitude; yet I do believe that this is not one, but a perfectly true statement of fact. What it amounts to is really this: the artist knows what he has said *after* he has spoken and not before. That this must be so of necessity will be readily admitted if one accepts that the prime stimulus in the creative process can legitimately be summed up in Valéry's words: "*Je veux me faire une surprise à moi-même*".

This sense of surprise, essential to creation, precludes distinct foreknowledge and even (to a greater extent than is commonly supposed) deliberation. From all this you will realize how ill-equipped the artist must find himself when he attempts to discourse on matters which, in his ordinary experience, are for very good reasons most of the time beyond his ken: and what a shock it must be to find oneself one day literally "holding forth in ignorance".[85]

As an art-form ballet undoubtedly exercises a powerful attraction on the musician. Dance is after all one of the twin roots of music. The other root is the word. In music to steps, or dance, and music to words or song, we see the beginnings of all music. We can trace these origins even in the most highly organized forms of instrumental and vocal music. The very names of a great many musical forms still remind us of this: *Ciaccona*, *Passacaglia*, *Bourrée*, *Minuet*, *Aria*, *Couplet*, *Lied* and so forth, with examples of cross-fertilization in forms like Rondo or Ballad.

Time measured in equal beats and the even or uneven distribution of accents in rhythmical patterns were probably among the earliest intuitive discoveries of man. Mimicry and expression by gesture are probably as ancient as articulate language. The shaping and form-giving principle in both is Rhythm. Rhythm *is* where we begin, or rather where awareness begins. With the heart-beat and the rhythm of breathing the very principle of music is linked with the human body, with man's physical frame. I sometimes regret that our Western musical terminology has neglected to take over two Aristotelian concepts which were familiar to Byzantine musicians. They called the conjoint intervals – that is to say the intervals of the minor and major seconds – *somata*, ie bodies. This distinction between *somata* and *pneumata*, bodily and spiritual intervals, as it were, is not so capricious as it might seem at first. According to this division a series or chain of seconds like our diatonic scale, for example, could be regarded as entirely somatic, ie corporeal or physical.

Such a view, I think, makes perfect good sense.Take any given melody, a piece of Gregorian plainsong, for instance, or a hillbilly tune. According to this view, we would regard those parts of the tune which are made up of chains of seconds as the material part of the tune. It is with the other intervals, with the leaps or *pneumata*, that the spirit is breathed in, as it were. This again seems quite unobjectionable. And by the way, it gives you a perfectly clear and reliable criterion for judging the true quality of a tune.

In a really good tune you would expect to find a nice balance between the material and spiritual components, that is to say between *soma* and *pneuma*. Should it ever occur to you to analyse a tune on these lines, you will discover that the simplest melody, if it is any good, is organized so to speak on two levels. On the surface, you will find the groups of intervals (conjoint or leaps, or both) which constitute minute cells adding up to motives, units of phrase or, as I like to call them, musical images. Underneath, in a second layer, you will discover the interesting fact that the main notes of the motive or, more often still, the main notes of the successive motives, betray a tendency for arranging themselves in chains – ascendant or descendant – of seconds. These, then, are really the bones of the tune, and every good tune has bones, must have bones, sturdy, well-shaped bones round which the animated flesh of the tune will grow.

Consider further the role of the *pneuma* in the melody. If the leaps or big intervals in your tune happen to follow too obviously the patterns of common chords, this will account very often for the effect of shallowness or triviality of such a tune; it would mean, according to our theory, that the spirit is not blowing where it listeth but is, so to speak, weighed down to earth. You know, of course, that the common chord derives from a natural phenomenon: the spontaneous division of the full length of a vibrating string or column of air in its two halves, three thirds and so forth.

I should like to consider further some aspects of contemporary music in the light of this distinction between *soma* and *pneuma*. Imagine the balance between the two elements destroyed and the scales heavily tipped in favour of the large intervals. From our previous definition you would expect a musical idiom that stifles the *somatic* and over-develops the *pneumatic* elements to take on an increasingly abstract, almost disembodied character. That, as a consequence of this, such music should overcome the phenomenon of harmonic gravitation towards a bass and present, on the contrary, a phenomenon of levitation, as it were; this would also fit into the picture. Neither would you be surprised to find a depreciation of a hedonistic approach to music and a disregard for the sensuous qualities of sound going hand-in-hand with the same process. Such a process has in fact taken place and is characteristic of some tendencies in contemporary music.

I should point out a disturbing thought at this juncture. One might ask: is it possible that mind could be the enemy of beauty? If a musician happens to be passionately in love not only with the soul but with the body of music as well; in other words, if he believes that one does not conceive music with one's brain and heart alone but also with the solar plexus, hips and thighs and the tips of one's toes, you will not be surprised that he should regard ballet as an almost ideal outlet for the exercise of this many-sided activity.

The question now is: what, from the musician's point of view, are the real assets and the unavoidable liabilities with which ballet as an art-form confronts him. First of all, ballet appeals and offers singular opportunities to the *dramatist* in the musician. Ballet in our time is a highly developed form of stage-craft. It is *theatre* in the most genuine sense and in one of its most exhilarating forms. As an instrument of dramatic expression it has a swiftness and directness of attack, a streamlined economy, in comparison with which opera must seem ponderous, slow and awkwardly heterogeneous.

Of course, ballet too is a complex art-form requiring the co-operation of at least three crafts if one leaves out the scenario-writer who, although it does not seem quite fair, usually has to take a back seat and is regarded more or less as the Cinderella of the combination. For my purpose I must naturally concentrate upon the relationship between music and choreography and disregard the other factors – decor, costumes and stage-lighting which otherwise would be very much worth considering, not only for the important part they play in the whole but especially in their relation to music.

Ballet, then, can be regarded as an art-form eminently congenial to the musician who approaches it from the point of view of its possibilities as Theatre and Drama. True, this view is diametrically opposed to that of many lovers of ballet who care mainly for pure dancing and perhaps nothing much else besides. For them, ballet is, of course, more of an abstract art-form than a specifically dramatic one; and it would seem quite consistent to regard the dramatic content or the story of the ballet as largely irrelevant, and even music as an entirely subsidiary factor. In principle I have no quarrel with the purists in so far as their attitude simply expresses predilection for one form of ballet rather than for another, that is to say, a partiality for pure dancing, or abstract ballet rather than for the *ballet d'action* or the ballet which tells a story.

Clearly, the enchantment of pure dancing and abstract ballet is akin to the pleasure of absolute music. In a purely aesthetic sense it must perhaps rate the highest. Released from the trammels of plot, representation and meaning, dance can soar and inhabit its proper delectable sphere of form and movement inscribed in pure duration, where time does seem to have a stop. Beautifully self-explanatory and self-sufficient works like Ashton's *Symphonic Variations* or Balanchine's *Ballet Imperial* do not have to look for a *raison d'être* beyond their intrinsic nature.

Yet it cannot be denied that the pleasure given by such a spectacle as a whole has a quality of cool aesthetic detachment that, in the last analysis, leaves one with a faint feeling of frustration, because the very presence of the human person on the stage inescapably arouses expectations which are not fulfilled. As soon as the dancer appears on the stage it seems impossible not to attach meaning to his gestures and evolutions, and we catch ourselves quite involuntarily stringing sequences together, assuming some purposeful design and making up some sort of story as we go. I believe that this is a psychologically true fact and I am not sure that one may dismiss it as irrelevant or as a nuisance with the same justification that one will dismiss a similar sequence of associations intruding upon the mind of the listener in the case of pure chamber or symphonic music.

Regarding the dramatic conception of ballet, the basic fact is that *in the theatre the human interest is paramount*. This means in the first place that dancing is inseparable from the impersonation, and that among the factors involved in ballet-making the dancer has supremacy. But it means also that *in the theatre the spectator is himself involved in the spectacle*, indeed he must be placed at the very centre of the picture and hold all the strands in his hands.

The case against symphonic ballet, on the other hand, is so obvious and so overwhelmingly strong that it need not detain us long. Its only chance lies in its conception as an abstract ballet, because at least the absurdity of superimposing a story on a self-sufficient work of absolute music is then obviated. Clearly, symphonic writing and symphonic form in the classical meaning of the word can be dramatic in essence but not necessarily in the theatrical sense. As a matter of fact the recapitulation or re-statement of the main groups of musical ideas in the concluding part of classical sonata form must make nonsense of any attempt at fitting it with an equivalent and parallel dramatic development on the stage. A dramatic "recapitulation" is a contradiction in terms.

Admittedly, the case for the defence is stronger with works like Berlioz's *Symphonie Fantastique* which carry their own "programme" or, I should say, with almost the whole of Tchaikovsky, whose music, whether a programme is intended or not, has anyhow that curious quality of "eloquence" that seems so constantly to reach beyond itself for concrete utterance in word or gesture. Besides, the typically rhetorical organization of Tchaikovsky's symphonic structure, with its wave after wave of sequential repetition and its reliance on cumulative effect, is in reality comparatively simple. It leaves the listener's mind so much at leisure that it can bear much more easily the superimposition of a parallel train of thought or visual images which it seems in any case to be soliciting so persistently.

Now I believe that what really matters is not so much the constant touch as the *decisive contact*. I know from experience that it is quite possible to set to music a whole poem of which one has taken in no more than one single line in a flash of intuition and not even bothered to read the poem to the end after that; because if the coincidence has happened at a deep enough level, if the musical mind has struck one of the main arteries of the poem (and the intuitive flash would probably not have occurred otherwise) it cannot help being led blindfold through the whole (provided it *is* a whole in which all parts communicate) and branch out in true identity through all the fibres of the poem's living body.

But for all that I must say I do regret that so far I have never had an opportunity to work in close touch and from the very start with the painter as well. I know that I can take suggestions from the painter's work which will influence my music, and therefore cannot help thinking that this might also work the other way round. For instance, I remember that while my ballet *Don Quixote*[86] was in the first stages of production, it was decided that the different scenes should be separated by drop-curtains to allow for the necessary change of decor. I was asked to write interludes which would cover the interval and act as links between the scenes. One of these drops – by the painter Edward Burra – precedes the scene in which Don Quixote is lowered into the subterranean cave of Montesinos. I saw the painter's sketch for this drop *before* writing the interlude. And *after* I had written it I discovered that I had been entirely governed by the painter's idea.

Massine's ballets based on Brahms or Beethoven symphonies and the Ballets Suedois' or Lifar's experiments in dancing without music, that is to say with percussion effects only, poles apart though they are, will probably have to be classed in the same tetralogical department in ballet history. On account of Massine's choreography, symphonic ballet can undoubtedly claim great historical importance, but from the aesthetic viewpoint it must be considered an aberration.

* * *

In his autobiography, Stravinsky tells us that during the first stage of production of one of his early ballets he worked in constant touch with his collaborators; they were all present at every rehearsal and they generally ended the day with a fine dinner washed down with good claret.[87] As Arnold Haskell points out, the significant phrases here were the *constant touch* and the *fine dinner*.[88] It sounds ideal, no doubt, though it can also be done more modestly on mere cups of tea and the briefest of contacts. Still, the pre-war methods seem most reasonable and convincing. During the composition of my ballet *Pandora* with Kurt Joos there was certainly constant touch, but no dinner.

With Antony Tudor, on the other hand, who I hope is going to be my next choreographer, we have already had a fine dinner but no constant touch as yet. As for Ninette de Valois, who is responsible for the choreography of *Don Quixote*, we had no more than a couple of sessions and nice cups of tea.

One of the backdrops in the ballet represents the well or shaft leading into the cave. It looks on the curtain like a series of concentric rings in different colours with, in the focal point (as seen from above, looking down the shaft) the figure of the Knight dangling from a rope halfway down, and the barber's basin (which the Don wears as a helmet) seen as the centre and hub of the picture. Now the musical composition of the interlude this backdrop covered happens to be a triple canon based on alternating phrases which bite their tails, as it were, and so "go round and round"; and in the centre of the canon is a sort of *cantus firmus*, the theme of *Don Quixote* is heard first on flutes and bassoon and later on the muted brass (see Ex. 1, p.98), exactly the painter's idea rendered in terms of sound which, as I have said, I did quite unconsciously at the time and only discovered afterwards.

I mention this as an example of the mutual and positive "give and take" which is the basis on which the artists concerned in the production of ballet ought to work from the outset and through all the phases of the production. It must also be accepted in the restrictive sense that one of the partners has sometimes to give way and take upon himself limitations imposed by the requirements of one of the other partners. This need not be irksome in the least. On the contrary, the true artist rejoices at the cropping up of artistic necessity of this order: he has learned to draw strength from the limitations.

In practice, the partnership between the artists concerned in ballet-making may work in various ways. The starting point will usually be the choice of a suitable subject. The idea may originate with any of the partners; it may be a general idea which will only gradually unfold and acquire definition in the actual growth of the work; or it may be (as is naturally the case with *ballet d'action*) a synoptic outline of a dramatic story or scenario which choreographer and composer will have to discuss in every detail, timing accurately all its episodes.

Undoubtedly the most hazardous way to start a ballet is for the composer to write his own scenario, complete and fixed in every incident, and then present it with the finished score to the choreographer. This is what I did with *Don Quixote*. Disaster can only be avoided on two conditions. The first is the musician's ability to see his subject truly and genuinely in terms of the possibilities and requirements of the dance-theatre. The second is his willingness to take his inspiration not from the literary aspect and associations of his subject seen as a pageantry and from the outside, but from within the movement of the dance itself – from dance as impersonation – letting rhythm, phrasing and expression flow from this *somatic* and *pneumatic Einfühlung* with the dancer.

For imagining movement there is nothing like performing it oneself. The

Spaniard says: *el movimiento se demuestra andando*, to demonstrate movement you walk. I would say: you dance. I have actually phrased and accurately timed all the major action-episodes in *Don Quixote* by performing them myself – which, by the way, must have been a rather poor show, balletically speaking, to judge from the impression it made on my wife, when she sometimes surprised my acrobatics. Nevertheless, this is how I believe I got phrasing and timings right. Naturally I did not perform to Miss de Valois, this would have been beside the point, but my own exercises had given me the "feel" of every sequence and I knew that I had given the dancers music and rhythm into which they could slip as into fitting garments.

Yet this is only one half of the musician's task. In addition – and leaving entirely out of the picture all the problems the music has to tackle in order to organize itself in its own right – it must also paint its own decor, light the stage, establish a mood and, above all, it must also *impersonate*. The word itself could not be a happier one as an expression of what it stands for. *Persona* originally applied by the Latins to the actor's mask, means literally *that which sounds through* (*per-sona*, *per sonare*) the sound behind the mask, in short, the *pneuma*.

Apart from Dulcinea, who plays a double role because she is a dual being – firstly a country wench of flesh and blood, and later a pure figment of Don Quixote's imagination – the characters which have to be impersonated can be divided into two groups. On the one hand, Don Quixote himself, with all the fantastic beings that people his feverish mind: monsters, giants, Arcadian shepherds, legendary Knights and so forth, all set in a dream-like world; and on the other hand, Sancho, priest and barber, muleteers, innkeepers, galley-slaves, realistically set against the background of the bleak plain of La Mancha under the blazing Spanish sun. This naturally postulates a twofold musical approach (I do not like to call it two *styles* since, if style is the man, no man can have two). But it is clear that the contrasts, his and Sancho's, had to be expressed commensurately in terms of music.

The problem of Don Quixote's impersonation is in itself a twofold one, since the Knight of La Mancha is by no means a madman pure and simple, but a most subtle mixture of sense and folly, a compound of sweet reasonableness and delirious hallucinations. All these reflections are afterthoughts. None could have prompted by itself a single musical idea. There was nothing for it but to get into the Don's skin and impersonate him. I should like to focus here on Don Quixote's theme, in order to illustrate the conscious and unconscious processes in the growth of a musical idea.

I remember that from a number of sketches for Don Quixote's theme, which I kept discarding almost as soon as they had been jotted down, I finally picked on one which seemed to have about it more of a likeness of the Knight of the Sorrowful Countenance than the others. When I looked at its more closely I gradually became aware of the fact that, under its grave and dignified air, I seemed to detect something vaguely familiar, yet elusive, an indefinably ironic touch which I had not consciously intended. It suggested to me a singular mixture of the genuine and of the spurious, of truth and make-believe. This puzzled me for a long time but as it also appealed to me very strongly I went on with my work and put the theme through its paces for most of the first scene: then suddenly it dawned upon me that the puzzling familiarity was with a strange little tune which, in my home town in Spain, is played on a primitive reed instrument as the march music for the huge cardboard-headed giants heralding the approach of religious processions as they move slowly through the crowded streets. These giants are tall, over-lifesize figures (perhaps familiar from the Carnival at Nice, but known through the south of France and all over Spain); they are carried on light wooden structures by men who remain hidden under the rich drapery of the giant's garments.

Now the way my Don Quixote theme reflects the strange little tune I am speaking of is rather similar to those puzzle-pictures you may remember from boys' magazines. One picture would represent for instance a tiger-hunter in the jungle and the question asked was: where is the tiger? You turned the pictures this way and that, you looked at it upside-down, until at last you discovered the spot where parts of the design, maybe of the trees or the hunter himself or both, combine and add to something which indeed looks uncommonly like a tiger. It is a picture hidden within a picture. In the same way my strange little tune is hidden within my theme. I was very happy when I made this discovery. After all, Don Quixote is the Knight of the hidden images. Sancho could only see windmills where Don Quixote saw the giants as well. Moreover, I felt that there was perhaps a grain of poetical truth in the fact that my sad and dignified Don Quixote theme should have these unexpected overtones of awe-inspiring wonder and disbelief, which in my childhood memories are linked with the vision of my home-town's cardboard giants. I knew I could draw from this source. It made me also realize that I was looking at Don Quixote through Sancho's eyes, as it were. In short I had found that my attitude to the Knights of La Mancha was frankly Sancho-esque in this mixture of belief and disbelief; and *this* being the point where Don Quixote's secret estimate of himself probably coincides with that of his Squire's. I felt assured that I had got the character rightly and properly focused.

But I had made another and more important discovery before all this had become clear to me. Analysing my theme I found that it was unusually rich in notes, I mean in notes of different pitch. It consists actually of 20 notes out of which there are nine that are of different pitch. That is to say, out of the total number of 12 different notes which our chromatic scale affords, my theme contains no less than nine. This discovery prompted me to pick out the nine different notes in the same order in which they appear in my original theme and join them together in a row or series, so that they would reproduce in its essentials the *substance* of my theme, in the abstract, as it were; that is to say purely as a sequence of intervals stripped of all concrete rhythmical configuration. To obtain an entirely satisfying correlation between my original theme and its abstract double it proved necessary at certain points to repeat three notes already contained in the series, thus bringing the total number to twelve notes in all, nine different and three repeated ones.

To have used my original theme as a Wagnerian *leitmotif* would have been much too static a principle for the impersonation of my character. To have used it in the sense of Berlioz's *idée fixe* might often have led to too much distortion, producing an effect of caricature which I wished very carefully to avoid. So, while with my original theme I could represent Don Quixote objectively, as seen through Sancho's eyes as it were, with the twelve-note series or abstract double of the theme I could, so to speak, slip inside my character and impersonate Don Quixote from within.

The use of my twelve-note series in the variation and polymorphous combination technique created and developed by Schoenberg offered practically unlimited possibilities of invention of musical images of every description which would naturally all be formed of the very substance of my theme, however various in patterns and character, in the same sense as all the Don's hallucinations proceed from the pranks and changing patterns of his central delusion in the matter of Knight-errantry. Finally, the fact that my twelve-note series containing only nine different notes and three repeated ones must be regarded as an incomplete or deficient series from the Schoenbergian point of view had in itself, I felt again, a grain of poetical truth. I did not deliberately plan it thus; it was given to me in and with my original theme which, as I said, had been one among many discarded ones that had come spontaneously to my mind from the first.

Not always quite knowing what he is doing, the creative artist may sometimes perhaps do better than he knows. This much is certain at any rate; in whatever situation, he can only be guided by the one over-riding consideration, which is *serving the dramatic idea*. This service may at times seem like a menial task. For instance, personally, I loathe having to write battle music. To illustrate a fight not much more than loosely organized conflict in sound is required; yet the simmering and boiling over in the orchestra has to be worked out: and when the blows fall, the appropriate noise is expected. Obviously the only decent way out is not to treat any situation as a purely local event and lonely child of circumstance, but so to direct the main stream of thought against the obstacle that it will strike it out of its own momentum, just as a swift current will strike a rock in mid-stream.

Choreographer and painter are of course in the same boat and have sometimes to endorse similarly awkward obligations. I remember for instance how bitterly Miss de Valois complained to me about the necessity of having repeatedly to dress and undress Dulcinea on the stage. "This is terribly unballetic", she exclaimed and I couldn't agree with her more wholeheartedly.

Before setting out on his adventurous journey, Don Quixote ennobles in his deluded mind a peasant girl from a neighbouring village with whom he was supposed to have been in love in his youth. He elevates her to the rank of

Mistress of his Thoughts and gives her the euphonious name of Dulcinea. Dulcinea, therefore, must first appear in the likeness of a strapping wench and then, to illustrate what goes on in the Don's mind, she must be transformed in full view of the audience into the ideal figure of the peerless Dulcinea.

To express choreographically this transformation the scenario prefigures the apparition of the country girl at the climax of Don Quixote's brainstorm in the first scene. After her solo dance, there appear the legendary Knights Amadis of Gaul, Palmerin of England and Orlando Furioso accompanied by their ladies Oriana, Urganda and Angelica who perform the ceremony of enrobing and crowning the wench. When in her new garments she is finally lifted on the shields of the Knights and the whole group fades away, she has become Dulcinea, the image of an enthroned Immaculate Conception.

Similarly, in the final scene when Don Quixote recovers his soundness of mind and his end in sanity and defeat has to be portrayed, the legendary ladies have to perform in reverse a ceremony of disrobing Dulcinea, to let her reappear in the rustic garb of a poor peasant girl, as she is now finally seen by the vanquished and disillusioned knight.

Obviously, these proceedings of en-robing and dis-robing are unballetic because they cannot really be danced and must therefore be something of a nuisance to the choreographer. But they are unballetic in the same sense as my task of illustrating a stage-fight must be considered "unmusical".

The truth is that every artist who has to convey a plot and make its mechanics intelligible and meaningful in terms of his own craft is bound to find himself sometimes in such straits. This is where the dramatist in the dance-theatre may well envy his colleague who knows of no such fetters in the domain of abstract ballet. Yet the real dramatist will not fight shy of such difficulties. Any amount of trouble is worth facing for the sake of a successful presentation of a dramatic situation: in other words it must be faced that a dramatic point can sometimes only be made at the cost of the balletic *pointes*, a case of *point-counter-pointes*.

Just imagine, for instance, what a despairing task it must be for the choreographer to make his Don Quixote dance carrying spear and shield as he sometimes must. Yet the way Miss de Valois solved the problem and not only redeemed the lance choreographically but even took it as a challenge for startling balletic invention – as she did also in the cave scene with the rope on which Don Quixote swings about the stage in fascinating, seemingly elliptic curves – this is truly a victory of balletic imagination over the material encumbrances sometimes inherent in the mechanics of plot representation.

Don Quixote: a synopsis (1956)[89]

The curtain rises as a fanfare-like figure is heard on brass. After six bars, the muted trumpet states Don Quixote's theme:

Ex. 1.

and the first Act Drop, depicting the Knight's sad face against a background of his hallucinations, becomes visible. The theme itself represents Don Quixote, the man of flesh and blood.

However, there remains the "ideal" of Don Quixote – his "dreamworld" dominated by his obsession with knight-errantry. The musical treatment is designed to assist the distinction, in the theatre, between the interior world and the "real", naturalistic environment in which Don Quixote finds himself. Thus, while the "complete" Don Quixote theme functions as a kind of *leitmotif* for the Knight himself, throughout the ballet, a serial extract from it is employed to define the world of his imagination. This twelve-note series, nine notes of which are different, may appear in its original, inverted, or mirror forms.

The **opening scene** is set in a bare room and shows the sleep-walking Knight, wrapped in a sheet and brandishing his sword. A strangely wistful tune first played on the cor anglais signals the entrance of the Don's idealized love, Dulcinea, in the person of the country girl Adonza. Three ladies – Oriana, Urganda and Angelica – enter, with the legendary knights – Amadis of Gaul, Palmerin of England and Orlando Furioso – and "enrobe" Aldonza. She has become Dulcinea and as she stands on the raised shields of the knights, she takes on the appearance of a Spanish Madonna, clothed in blue, red and gold. The group then leave and the music changes to a *scherzando Allegretto* as Sancho, who is to be the Don's squire in his journey of knight-errantry, enters and helps his master put on his armour. Housekeeper, Niece, Priest and Barber express their warnings and disapproval in a *pas de quatre*, but to no avail: the Don and Sancho sally forth.

The second act backdrop shows master and squire riding in the bare, sunbacked plain of La Mancha. Priest and Barber cross the stage in front of the drop as if pursuing the two adventurers. This recurs in all the following interludes.

Scene 2 shows a wayside inn where muleteers and wenches are enjoying a high-spirited dance. The entry of Don Quixote (and his theme) throws the dancers into confusion and overwhelms the *seguidilla manchega* rhythm of the music.

Now follows Don Quixote's nocturnal Vigil of Arms. At its mid-point, his dream-image of Dulcinea appears and a variant of her cor anglais theme may be heard in the gently swaying movement of the strings. The flutes distantly echo the opening fanfare of the work. After this quiet interlude comes the fray with the muleteers – one of whom the Knight has chastized in return for a supposed insult. Next the Don undergoes a mock ceremony of knighting by the innkeeper, whom he takes to be a great lord and castellan of a fortress (for that is how he views the inn).

Scene 3 opens with the famous adventure of the windmills, whose jerky, robot-like movements are first suggested by the angular phrases of bassoon and bass clarinet. Two shorter episodes follow. The first (marked *allegretto triviale* in the score and notable for the interplay of piano and solo piccolo) concerns the Don's conquest of a barber's basin, which he believes to be the legendary Mambrino's helmet. The second is a lyrical *pas de deux* representing a tale told by the Don to some goatherds, about a "Golden Age" shepherd and shepherdess. The scene closes with a second "main" adventure, balancing the one with the windmills. The Don frees some galley-slaves from their chains, but they thank him by stoning him to the point of death.

Scene 4 is actually a dream sequence of Don Quixote's, but supposedly takes place in the underground mansion of Montesinos. Burra's backdrop for this act strikingly represents the cave as seen looking down the well, and the orchestral interlude reflects the formal pattern in its close canonic writing. The music for the actual cave scene is a mysterious chaconne, based on a seven-bar ground. The Don has arrived in time to witness the woeful daily procession led by Lady Belerma, who bears the heart of her lover Durandarte on a cushion. Montesinos introduces the Don to the figure of Durandarte, who is lying on his tomb. But Durandarte stares coldly at his visitor, and then dismisses him with a curt gesture. The Don has barely recovered from the shock of this reception when Dulcinea enters in her "natural" role of the peasant girl Aldonza. The Don kneels in homage, but the girl skips around frivolously and then produces a petticoat, which she waves at him irreverently, thus signifying her willingness to part with it for money. Quixote, appalled and broken-hearted, clambers out of the cave. The chaconne is over: a *maestoso* statement of Quixote's complete theme, combined with its serial extract, tells us plainly that this is the beginning of the end: the Don's faith in himself, his ideal love and his mission of knight-errantry, has begun to crumble.

During the interlude, the Priest and Barber reappear accompanied by the three *quadrilleros* of the Holy Brotherhood Police. When the curtain rises, the enraged Don Quixote is seen shut up in a huge cage, the prisoner of his pursuers, who dance triumphantly before him, while Sancho looks on in helpless misery. To sad and tender music (*allegretto placido*) a procession of mourning widows, orphans and maidens dance gravely in front of the cage, expressing their commiseration. The group of Don Quixote's persecutors, who have been driven off by the gallant Sancho, now return, retreating in fight before Sancho, who is now assisted by the legendary knights. The combatants disappear again offstage and the three ladies from the first scene lead in a figure heavily veiled in black: it is Dulcinea.

The ladies unveil and disrobe her and she is revealed again as Aldonza. She dances once more to her wistful tune, which acquires an added poignancy in this new context since it comes to express Don Quixote's ultimate disillusioned awakening to "reality" as it appears to the sane. The "bars" of the cage vanish and Don Quixote steps out just as Sancho arrives, flushed with victory, to liberate the captive. He entreats his master to take up arms again, but the Knight brushes him gently aside and the pair drift apart. The Knights, Ladies and Golden Age shepherds step in between them and finally screen them from each other.

The stage clears, leaving only the shepherds (whose music is heard once more, but in a new key), and Don Quixote, who is lying on the couch from which he first set out. After this brief lyrical interlude, Sancho, Priest and Barber, Housekeeper and Niece gather round the couch, whilst the "real" figures encountered by the Knight during his adventures dance past as if in sorrowful parting. The Don takes the basin, which Sancho has been wearing, and gives it back to the Barber; and then, after a moment's hesitation, he gives his beloved sword to the Priest. As he lies down again, Sancho is overcome with grief and tries to rouse him. The opening brass fanfare is heard again and the three knights, with their ladies, enter carrying the "transfigured" Dulcinea on their shields. Sancho rushes from the couch and kneels before her, with a gesture of impassioned appeal.

V New Horizons

18 Schoenberg, twelve-note music and serialism

Schoenberg in Barcelona (1932)[90]

Arnold Schoenberg is one of those rare personalities that appear from time to time in the course of history, who both announce and develop in their work a radical change, a profound mutation in the thought and sensibility of a whole era. This transformation had already been begun in Schoenberg's first pieces, more than a quarter of a century ago. It has been since completed with disconcerting speed. The works of his maturity already speak a totally new language. They embody with absolute purity a concept of music that emanates from a spirit and sensitivity radically different from that encountered in the past. However, for us, Schoenberg's contemporaries amongst the public of 1932, the transformation is still dormant or has only just begun: hence the discrepancy between Schoenberg and his age. It isn't new in history that genius should be prodigiously ahead of its time. Nor is it surprising, therefore, that he has been long misunderstood. It is relevant to remember Cocteau's dictum: "When a work seems to go ahead of its time, it is simply the time that stays behind." One might say that the delay has been marked in our geographical region: for Schoenberg's music has been late to reach Barcelona; and it has been preceded by a lot *against*, about the fame of his "difficulty".

We cannot avoid the fact that there are in truth "difficult" writers, and that Schoenberg is one of them. The difficulty of this difficult writer comes, probably, from the nature of the ideas expressed; and maybe also from the way of dealing with them. Even though in the case of a musician like Schoenberg, the latter is clearly a consequence of the former; that is to say, that the nature of the ideas implies the way of exposing them.

It would be naive to try to "explain" Schoenberg's music. The technical side, in the first place, is of no interest to the audience. Words also cannot explain the music. Music would not be music if it could be explained through words. One can't reach Schoenberg's music from the outside – to try and arrive through technical analysis. There is just one way: to listen, to listen and to listen; simply that. Until the veils drop from people's eyes; until the deafness of the internal ear ceases and starts to feel, despite its unprecedented novelty, Schoenberg's music; the beauty of its melody, the prodigious art of its structure, the superb clarity and soberness of its forms, the genius of its constructions, the greatness of its conception, its spirituality, its ineffable emotionality.

However, much of or more than the technical revolution which Schoenberg has produced, so Protean is the diversity of his work, its content, its expression, that it has always disconcerted the critics. To pigeon-hole Schoenberg is impossible. He has eluded all labels or formulae.

From the ultra-romanticism of *Gurrelieder*, a vocal-instrumental symphony of massive dimensions, to the "constructivism" of the Chamber Symphony Op.9 , the "impressionist" refinement of the Five Orchestral Pieces Op.16 and *Pierrot Lunaire*; from there still to the expressionism of the dramas *Erwartung* and *Die glückliche Hand*; or the objectivity of the Wind Quintet Op.26, the classical serenity of the Serenade Op.24 and the Suite Op.29, the pure spirituality of the String Quartet No.3, or of the Variations Op.31 for orchestra ... what a fabulous richness, what a variety of styles, what a diversity of forms of expression! And what a profound originality of spirit, always true to itself throughout all that diversity! An originality already evident, clearly, in the first works of his youth, like *Verklärte Nacht, Pelleas und Melisande* and the Lieder Op.8 (which we shall shortly hear in Barcelona), in which the composer still uses traditional vocabulary and technical procedures. Always uncompromising originality: hence the opposition of the masses, yesterday as well as today; although today it seems to us almost inconceivable that those youthful works could irritate the audiences of 25 years ago. But today we merely appreciate to what extent with the novelty of their melodic, rhythmic and harmonic conception, Schoenberg was contradicting already the listening habits of pre-war audiences. We can't understand it any more, simply because so much contemporary music, assimilating and disseminating Schoenbergian innovations, has familiarized our ear with a whole range of new sonorous relationships, dissonances that must have shocked the ears of earlier listeners, incapable of understanding their meaning through lack of experience.

The ear is the most conservative of the senses!

Never, on the other hand, has a "revolutionary" been more profoundly linked and in mutual sympathy with the past. There's a notable story about Schoenberg in this regard. Called up during the war, it bothered him greatly when his soldier colleagues talked to him about music. He wanted to be a soldier. Nothing more. One of the questions that most used to irritate him was: "Are you that much discussed composer that has caused a musical revolution?" One day when an officer asked him in front of the whole company, Schoenberg replied, "Now I cannot deny it. But I must explain how it happened: someone or other had to do it; and as nobody else had the courage, in the end I volunteered." An innovator in the opposite direction, really, and endowed with an enormous sense of responsibility. But also, genial intuition and powerful intelligence in the service of an artist of incorruptible conscience.

A conversation with Schoenberg (1931)[91]

About a month ago, Schoenberg settled for a while in Barcelona. He loves the country, the weather, the people, everything of ours that he has encountered up till now: to the extent that he aims to return every year to spend some time with us. We need hardly conceal our pleasure if this came about: above all, if his stay in our country benefited his health, as seems likely.

I do not pretend here to have interviewed him. Given that it is Schoenberg, I do not dare! I owe him too much gratitude and know how to admire and worship him too profoundly as a disciple to be able to betray him as a reporter. I can't see himself in the absurd situation of that actual interviewer whom Schoenberg one day welcomed with the words, "Please start by telling me what I should say, and then I will try to tell you myself." But I can give you some glimpses of the conversations I had with him in his small villa at La Salut, Barcelona, where there is a large window with a splendid view overlooking the urban landscape. Sometimes slightly veiled by fog and a bit chilly, sometimes, at noon, in the sunny tennis court, between sets, our talks on those autumnal days brought back memories of my periods of study with Schoenberg in Mödling, Vienna and Berlin.

Schoenberg disappoints and completely bewilders the journalist, for his opinions are not "sensational". This should be particularly understood, maybe, in a man who, because of his work, is the most "sensational" figure in contemporary music; work which has not only said the last word to our generation, but seems likely to save its full revelatory power, its genuine and definitive "sensation" for future generations; especially when present generations, wary of how unpopularity digs its heels in around the greatest musician of our time, have decided to move away from him, to follow paths that lead more directly towards success.

Having dealt incidentally with this matter of young people's tendencies today, Schoenberg said to me: "I found it very odd that, after the War, a lot of young people, showing a surprising lack of 'practical sense', started following me. Nowadays, however, I find less strange the fact most of them have at last acquired enough practical sense to know the time is ripe to put me right. I congratulate myself, because I like to walk alone. And, being my pupil, you know already how I have always insisted in warning those that approach near to my 'danger zone'."

In fact, Schoenberg has managed to discourage some young people. Maybe this is a good thing. The majority, for whom discouragement is more astutely appropriate, in enabling them to find an easier path, has already found a way of escaping from a difficult situation; and today, in opposition to Schoenberg, they preach the restoration of old historical styles and practice an ingenuous game called "neo-classicism".

'Back to Bach and Handel', I hear them say! 'If only those musicians could notice the great difference there is between Bach and Handel!' If there has to be a return, I wish that at least they would make up their mind for Bach or for Handel. If this return would be to Bach, at bottom I would agree with it, and I would even promote it myself. But I'm afraid that if I taught these 'returning' musicians everything they need to know in order to compose like Bach, then composition would flow for them. That is what I hope, at least!

Regarding this old style which young people want to utilize nowadays, and the return to tonality and even to strict diatonicism which they preach, there seems to me a strong objection. Although in Europe, in the art-music of these last centuries, there were no such antecedents so that one could easily imagine a rigorously diatonic music, that is, based exclusively on the seven notes of the scale. But one could, strictly speaking, also abolish modulation. Because with the smallest modulating deviation the chromaticism we want to condemn would burst back in. For what reason do diatonic composers of today close their eyes to this question?

For my part, I can say that the compositions thus made which I have had the chance to listen to, do not agree at all with supposed diatonicism. On the contrary, to my ears, the dissonances in this music sound horrible, because they have no relationship with the rest. They have the effect of grease stains on a white waistcoat.

What significance do you give to your technique of twelve semitones?

I ought really to be surprised that you of all people should should ask me this question. For you must recall from our composition lessons that I am able to clarify more important problems than that one and like doing so. If you are after an answer for the public, I should say that, regarding twelve-tone technique, understanding is only possible for people who have enough knowledge about the general technique of our art, and not, simply, the usual dilettante notions of the Conservatoire. For the latter what I have to say now will continue to be an enigma for a long time.

What I mean when I say that, in composition with twelve tones it is the same way as in tonal music. In music with seven notes, the harmony is just an 'inversion' of the melody and vice-versa, the melody an 'inversion' of the harmony; with the only difference that instead of seven notes being used there are twelve. But, be it seven or twelve, everything, harmony or melody, proceeds from the same series. Now, the question of whether it is appropriate to underline and emphasize a tonic centre is not a question of aesthetics or taste, but merely one of capacity of understanding.

I'm sure of one thing, that no 'brain owner', like Beethoven, could doubt that another 'brain owner' could move whoever it affects. Regarding this, I, who know the effect my music provokes in me when I compose it, don't feel the smallest anxiety faced with the future.

Reminiscences of Schoenberg (1955)[92]

The man who revolutionized contemporary music was nothing of a revolutionary himself. In a special number of the magazine *Musikblatter des Ansbruch*, produced in Vienna in 1924 for Schoenberg's 50th birthday, Hanns Eisler, a former pupil, went so far as to call him a "reactionary". This is a surprising criticism, coming, as it does, from a communist, but it is nonsense too, apart from its doubtful orthodoxy.

The dig at the master was no doubt provoked by the fact that in his then most recent works – Serenade Op.24, Suite Op.25 and the Wind Quintet Op.26. Schoenberg had returned, at least nominally, to the use of sonata and other traditional forms. But how far his treatment of these forms corresponds in fact to traditional notions of form organization (Op.25 and 26 are pure twelve-tone compositions, by the way) that is quite another matter. The plain truth is that to that typical segment of the middle- and upper-middle-class of the days before and after 1914 who sported the intellectual hardening of the arteries with stupendous pride of prejudice, Schoenberg had been the *bête noir* almost from the beginning of his career, and shared alike with his friends and contemporaries, the "rebels" Kokoschka, Karl Kraus and the architect Adolf Loos, a full measure of neglect and contempt.

Schoenberg felt a deep reverence for the masters of the past. Their works were his constant terms of reference, both in his own creative work and in his teaching. Seldom can an innovator have scrutinized more heart-searchingly every prompting that bid him to defy accepted convention and venture into the unexplored. I remember that analysing his Three Piano Pieces Op.11 – one of his first "revolutionary" works – he once pointed out how often he had had to pause in the very act of writing down some of the more unusual sound-combinations, startled at the radicalism of his own spontaneous thought: and, rubbing out, he tried to take off the edge and tone the thing down, only to find, on re-reading his work the next day, that there was something palpably "wrong" in the passages thus emended and they would only sound "right" when he was able to restore the first notation.

Yet, as Schoenberg wrote in 1949, "very few critics have been able to discern to what extent the permanent laws of music are being observed in those works, or disregarded, or simply adapted to new circumstances; and all that has been happening is a process of growth and evolution in no way more exorbitant than such processes have always been in the history of music." On the other hand, it is only too plain that without some degree of "exorbitance" there would be no evolution at all.

It was an important event in Schoenberg's career when, in 1925, he was offered the succession to Busoni's chair at the Prussian Academy of Fine Arts in Berlin. The Academy was the loftiest cultural institution in Germany at the time. Its members held the rank of Senator: and with the dignity of the office went a truly munificent stipend as well. To Schoenberg this meant complete security at last, the end of the long, lean years. It was an appointment for life, too – which didn't of course prevent the Nazis from sacking him as soon as they came to power. The Chair, moreover, was a potential sinecure in the sense that, according to his contract, Schoenberg need not have taken any pupils at all in case the candidates for the so-called *Meisterklasse* did not seem to him promising enough. The choice of pupils was entirely up to him. He was supposed to reside in Berlin for periods of six months at a time, chosen at his pleasure, and teach such pupils as he had accepted. For the rest he could live wherever he chose and concentrate entirely on his own creative work.

When Schoenberg went to Berlin to take up his appointment I had already been studying with him in Vienna for two years. The change from Vienna to Berlin was most enjoyable to me, given not only the difference between Vienna and Berlin in those pregnant Twenties, but also the difference between single and communal tuition with Schoenberg – the difference, that is, between being a private pupil of the master and being a member of the Meisterklasse. Irresistibly, I'm afraid, some of us felt at times a little pompous about that. As members of the *Meisterklasse* we rather looked down on the undergraduate population of the Charlottenburg Hochschule für Musik. In fact, we very much played up to our higher academic status as *Meisterschuler*. In retaliation, the Hochschule referred to us, I believe, as *die Meistersinger von Schoenberg.*

The Berlin of the middle Twenties hardly bore any resemblance to the topsy-turvy Berlin of the years immediately after the First World War, and the crazy inflation, when the underworld sat at the West End cafés and the population of the Reich's capital seemed to consist mainly of spivs. From the squalid, catastrophic city of those chaotic years, Berlin had become a brilliant metropolis, almost overnight, with characteristically German powers of recovery. For a brief period, stretching from the mid-Twenties to the seizure of power by the Nazis, Berlin was a cultural centre of the world. Even Paris looked a little dim by comparison then.

Musically, at any rate, Berlin was undoubtedly on top. It had three permanent opera houses: the Staatsoper Unter den Linden recently engaged the young Erich Kleiber as *Generalmusikdirektor*, with Fritz Stiedry and later on Leo Blech as his second in command; the more popular Stadtische Oper in Charlottenburg had Bruno Walter, with Fritz Zweig and later on Stiedry as permanent conductors; Otto Klemperer with Alexander Zemlinksy, George Szell and Karl Rankl were at the new Kroll Oper. Furtwängler was the permanent conductor of the Berlin Philharmonic Orchestra; Kleiber conducted the symphony concerts at the Staatskapelle. The Hochschule für Musik, whose director was Franz Schreker, had among its teachers people like Artur Schnabel, Carl Flesch, Piatigorsky, Curt Sachs and the young Hindemith.

Berlin had a spate of world premieres of new works during those years: Berg's *Wozzeck*, Milhaud's *Christophe Colomb*, Janacek's *From the House of the Dead*, Schoenberg's *Erwartung and Die glückliche Hand*, his Variations for Orchestra, Music to Accompany a Film Scene, Six pieces for *a cappella* chorus, Berg's Chamber Concerto, Bartok's Second Piano Concerto, Stravinsky's Violin Concerto, and his *Oedipus Rex* were the highlights. The theatrical world, too, was at its most brilliant. With producers like Piscator, Jessner and Max Reinhardt, the accent was on the new and experimental. To keep up with all that was going on at the time was hard in more ways than one.

The Academy regularly sent some free tickets for the *Meisterklasse*, but there were never enough to go round. Personally, I had the good luck to make friends with an extraordinary personage at the Spanish Embassy, Colonel Valdivia, who was most popular in Berlin society circles and was known to everybody as Herr Musik Attaché. A constant visitor at the house of the famous Berlin hostess Frau Louise Wolf, of the concert agency Wolf & Sachs, the Colonel always had plenty of complimentary tickets and I was dragged along everywhere. In return I had to go home with him after shows and act as his patient audience into the small hours, while the Colonel performed exuberantly on an electric pianola.

In the world of the visual arts and letters, the painters Pechstein, Carl Hofer, Beckmann, poets Brecht and Klabund were the people *en vogue*, with their avant-garde magazines *Der Sturm*, *Der Anbruch* and *Der Querschnitt*. The music review *Melos* had been founded by Hermann Scherchen in the early days of the postwar period. Those were also the years of the expressionistic experiments in dancing, with Mary Wigmann, Laban, Kreuzberg and Palucca. *The Blue Angel* with Emil Jennings and Marlene Dietrich was the great UFA film of the time. They were the years of the first impact of jazz on the Western world. Ragtime, foxtrot, Shimmy, Blues and Charleston were the rage. The reign of the saxophone and the percussionist had begun. Kurt Weill with his *Dreigroschenoper*, *Mahagonny*, and *Der Zar lasst sich photographieren* and Ernest Krenek with *Jonny spielt auf* and *Leben des Orest* cashed in on the craze. A smart society of *nouveaux riches* had sprung up: the type was portrayed by George Grosz and Christopher Isherwood's *Goodbye to Berlin* introduced it to English readers; they were a sham-sophisticated middle-class crowd trying terribly hard to be "modern" and to feel wicked. They flocked everywhere and loved to be bored expensively in unspeakably dismal night-clubs. Above all they loved to be shocked. Rarely can the business of *épater le bourgeois* have been carried on more profitably. Piscator's social satires were all the rage. No other climate could have produced such works as Hindemith's *Neues von Tage* or Schoenberg's *Von Heute auf Morgen*.

Berlin was a bewildering maze of cross-currents in those years: the socialistic Volksbuhne organization: the first impact of politics on art; Hanns Eisler's mock-lyric *Newspaper Cuttings*, setting personal column adverts; or his marching songs for workers; the Bauhaus influence with its functional *Neue Sachlichkeit*; or Fritz Jöde's *Jugenbewegung*, the activist amateur musicians for whom Hindemith wrote easy pieces and *Wir bauen eine Stadt*; Weill's cantata on Lindberg's first crossing of the Atlantic; a movement – this *Jugendbewegung* – which in later years Krenek amusingly ridiculed *as die Blockflötenkultur* – the beads and tweeds folk, or the civilization of the recorder, as you might say.

Seen in retrospect all this seems pretty incongruous as a background to Schoenberg's existence during those years. But then, with the possible exception of *Von Heute auf Morgen*, there was hardly ever any relation between Schoenberg's work and outward circumstances. When, in 1931, he came to stay for a long period in Barcelona, I happened to meet Falla a few days before Schoenberg was due to arrive. When I told Falla he commented, "Well, I hope that your lovely Mediterranean landscape may have a good influence on him; perhaps he will write some more 'tuneful' music here." To which, when reported to him, Schoenberg retorted, "Why, to write good music, my back room in Berlin with no view at all is good enough for me, I think."

It cannot be denied that Schoenberg's personality was somewhat overpowering. His manner was not exactly engaging, in the social sense, but very much so in the other, the challenging sense of the word. It was certainly less of a nervous strain to meet him in the Berlin *Meisterklasse* – corporately, as it were – than it had been to meet him individually, as a private pupil in Vienna. Many years later it came as an amusing discovery and as a relief to hear that even Alban Berg had never quite been able to shake off that awesome feeling Schoenberg inspired, although their relationship had for a long time been that of devoted intimate friends rather than that of master and disciple. This was so strong with Berg that he would not be beyond inventing some harmless fib in order to stay away from some of the Saturday afternoon parties at Schoenberg's villa in Mödling, where a few friends and pupils were asked. We had tea and then some chamber music was played.

One of the most horribly awkward moments of my life occurred at one of these parties. I want to tell it because it throws such an unusual light on Schoenberg and shows a quality in the man with which he is hardly ever credited. Present on that afternoon were Webern, Berg, Rudolf Kolisch and, I think, Fritz Rothschild and also Frau Steuermann (wife of the pianist Edward Steuermann) and two or three other pupils. At one moment the conversation came to centre on Stravinsky. Nearly everyone had had his say. The criticisms were mostly unsympathetic and rather harsh. Then suddenly Schoenberg turned to me – who had not been dreaming of opening my mouth – and asked my opinion. It took me completely off my guard and I was thrown into considerable confusion, linguistic and otherwise. I don't remember what I said, I only know that I must have fumbled most wretchedly, but I spoke up for Stravinsky. There was a long, embarrassed, agonizing silence. I was stunned myself. I felt as if I had been using bad language in polite society. If the Danube had happened to flow under the wide-open window of that room, I am sure I could not have resisted the temptation. Schoenberg broke the silence: he took up his viola and they sat down to play, I think it was a Haydn quartet. Then a most unexpected thing happened: Schoenberg got up and went to the library, he took out the miniature score of the Haydn and came over and offered it to me with a smile and an expression of kindness I shall never forget. He would never know that at that moment he had saved my life.

Yes, he *was* an intimidating person to meet and on each occasion one literally had to brace oneself up to it. I remember the state of trepidation in which I went down to Mödling for my first interview. I had rung the bell, the door opened, and before I knew what was happening I felt the thrust of a huge dog who had leapt at me and planted its paws on my chest. In the back – just a little shorter than the dog on its hind legs – I could see Schoenberg standing, short, stocky, a bronzed face with dark burning eyes, a Roman emperor's head. I don't think I shall ever forget that dog. It was a formidable looking fellow, yet in reality it was an incredibly gentle creature. Somehow I have never been able to dissociate Schoenberg from his dog in that first impression.

One realized, of course, that the long years of fierce antagonism and denigration of his work had hardened the man and must have over-developed his combative instincts. But what made an ordinary human relationship with Schoenberg so difficult at times was probably his almost complete lack of a sense of humour. He was fond of joking, and he could see a joke all right and enjoy it, but one never felt quite, quite sure. At any rate, it was never quite safe to come forth with a joke oneself. On the other hand, he had plenty of wit. He was a master of the caustic epigram. His witticisms often had the crack of the whip and I am sure they made him more enemies than his music ever did.

One of his biographers, H.H. Stuckenschmidt, deplores as a serious drawback Schoenberg's lack of a sense of humour – actually the word he uses is *Leichfertigkeit,* levity, but sense of humour is obviously what he means. "It is a very German fault in Schoenberg's nature", Stuckenschmidt writes, "that he was incapable of treating anything as if it were a bagatelle."[93] Very possibly. But is there really any point at all in deploring the want of levity in Schoenberg's nature: isn't that to misconceive his nature altogether? There just seems to be no room at all for levity in this type of man. Schoenberg had a terrific sense of mission. He was a man of faith; his was not a quietistic, but a dynamic, non-conformist, militant faith, wrestling with doubt. In some ways he reminded one of Unamuno. He too was a tortured soul. So was Swedenborg, of whom both Schoenberg and Unamuno were constant readers. There was also something truly quixotic in his burning sense of mission, which to me was absolutely fascinating. And it seems so fitting that his earthly career should have been a long series of defeats in public, from each one of them he emerges in our eyes not the lesser but truly the greater figure.

During lessons Schoenberg talked a good deal, rationalizing everything that could possibly be rationalized, trying all the time to go to the heart of the matter and show you what to expect there, what to look for. Sometimes he would say, "I'll just show you." He would take pencil and paper and start sketching whatever it was he wanted to show. No word was spoken then, one just looked on. It was in this way that I had some of the greatest and most vividly illuminating experiences with Schoenberg as a teacher.

It was fascinating to watch how his mind worked, the amazing speed and even flow of thought; to observe the occasional hesitations or corrections, suddenly to realize the reason for the correction and how many moves ahead he had been thinking; to be able to follow with one's eyes the actual morphogenetical process and sequence of events; to see how the thing grew; the order in which the various elements appeared, their interplay, their re-percussions and metamorphosis; in short, teamwork of chance, choice and deliberation.

It was a breathtaking adventure.

Reluctant revolutionary: on studying composition with Schoenberg (1961)[94]

Schoenberg detested being labelled a "revolutionary", and for a good reason: he never actually *revolted* against the past. He simply grew out of it by degrees, inevitably, almost reluctantly.

His often quoted remarks: "This book I learned from my pupils" (the opening sentence in his *Treatise on Harmony*) or "A true artist learns from himself alone", might easily be taken as little more than autobiographical asides. In a sense they epitomize Schoenberg's whole attitude towards the complex matters of teaching and of learning how to compose music.

It is difficult to think of any innovator who was less theoretical. This lack of "theoretical" enthusiasm alone sets him apart from the true-blood revolutionary. Paradoxically, the man who did in fact revolutionize the technique of musical composition, at the beginning of the century, was essentially intuitive and, what is more, an ingrained traditionalist. Schoenberg's sense of belonging to a tradition and of working in the main stream of that tradition is alive in every phase of his evolution, even at his most boldly innovative. His teaching reflects the creative artist's guiding ideas and the peculiar bias of his mind.

Classroom analytical work was almost exclusively based on the great masters of the German tradition. The object of the analysis was to try to grasp how a master-mind had coped with a given compositional problem. The sum of insights gained would lead eventually to the formulation of "principles". These in turn would be tested against a great deal of fresh evidence.

However, the whole approach was in reality far less systematic than I make it appear. Characteristically, Schoenberg always avoided the word "system" and preferred "method" with reference to twelve-note technique. Clearly, what he was concerned with was a *modus operandi*, not doctrine. This accords perfectly with the idea he had of his role as a teacher. He thought of himself as a craftsman teaching his craft. The ideal manner of doing this, he often said, must have been the way in which a great painter of the Renaissance worked with his pupils in the studio.

Of course, this is not altogether possible in music, and with a master so intolerant of copying and repetition, it could hardly have worked. But this difficulty emphasizes the basic weakness of all composition teaching: the concentration on analytical method. When occasionally he reversed the process and, to illustrate a point, he started to compose before one's eyes, an entirely different world seemed to open up, and the experience was enlightening out of all proportion to the actual matter in hand.

"Aesthetics" was another topic to which he gave a wide berth. Neither "style" nor "form" were abstract categories to him, nor were they matters of absolute privilege in which the artist is responsible to himself alone. They were closely linked with the idea, paramount to him, of comprehensibility. Form, he used to say, is the expression of the artist's concern to make himself intelligible. Communication was for Schoenberg the all-important end. What makes communication difficult, in his case, is the subject-matter. With the techniques of communication – including (emphatically) twelve-note technique – he took the proverbial endless pains of genius.

As a personality there was something truly formidable, almost unapproachable about Schoenberg. The musical world had for long treated him with neglect or with contempt; the small world of the Viennese Schoenberg-circle surrounded the master with an atmosphere of awestruck reverence, and both, probably, had helped to develop in him a defence-mechanism that was apt to make him flare up aggressively at the mere suspicion of provocation. Even in repose, the burning eyes in that ascetic face and the faint expression of disdain in the peculiar shape of his mouth had an extraordinary power of intimidation.

But I also remember the image of a relaxed and happy Schoenberg in Barcelona, when he came to stay for the best part of a year, in 1931. He liked the country and the people and, unsurprisingly, no one seemed in the least intimidated by him. To be taken as an equal by other people, with perfect naturalness and, at the same time, warmly and considerately, was obviously a novel experience for Schoenberg. He responded with delight, on occasions even expansively.

I remember him once executing a victory-dance after a match with a former Spanish tennis-champion; I have a photograph of a smiling, levitating Schoenberg, well over two feet off the ground.

19 On composition with twelve notes (1954)[95]

There will probably always be as many different ways of handling the twelve-note technique as there are original composers who use it, possibly even more. For, as H.H. Stuckenschmidt justly remarks, the "rules" are no harder to learn than those of chess, "but one can only become a good chess-player by long practice".[96]

Schoenberg's creative originality can already be recognized in the unexampled variety of his own handling of the serial technique, but not only or even principally in this. Rufer's questions to composers are wisely inspired by Schoenberg's warning against orthodoxy. In fact, seldom can a great innovator have been less dogmatic than Schoenberg. So nothing could be more mistaken than an attempt to set up a canonical definition which, though it may be applicable to one or other of Schoenberg's creative periods, would lead to the impression that his serial technique was uniform and homogeneously simple. The unifying power which is the inner core of the serial law not only allows but enforces variety; through a comparatively uncomplicated network of constructive channels, a constant flow of infinitely varied forms is set up. In a word, what matters is the understanding of a creative process, not the copying of a "procedure".

The new departures, sometimes important ones, which Schoenberg's serial technique made in his successive works, remind one of a spiral or circular development, rather than development in a straight line; the development turns in complete revolutions round a centre, from which all the possibilities which the basic idea provides are systematically explored. This gives rise to a "polarity" which counteracts the principle of the unalterability of the order of the notes within the series, by the principle of systematic or free permutation within definite note-groups. In Schoenberg's opera, *Von Heute auf morgen* for instance, both halves of the series (example 2, p.115) appear as early as bars 3–4 (double-bass), 5–6 (harp) and 7–8 (the Man), in permutations which are in fact identical with the scale-like arrangement of the hexachords on which the series is based.

The legitimacy of this treatment is clear: it rests on Rameau's principle of the harmonic identity of the different inversions of the triad, as different aspects of the same sound-concept (a conception which we express in the symbol of the figured bass). This principle naturally retains its validity for any kind of combination of notes. Its use in serial technique, as a freedom of permutation within chords of three, four or six notes or other note-groups into which the twelve-note series can be subdivided, is legitimized *a priori* by

Ex. 2.

Schoenberg's axioms of the unity of "musical space", in which the horizontal and the vertical are treated as being aspects, identical in substance, of the musical "object".

Important consequences of this new principle (which so far as I know has not yet been appreciated theoretically) can be found particularly in the *Dance round the Golden Calf* from *Moses und Aron*, the Violin Concerto, the *Ode to Napoleon* and the Piano Concerto. Its importance can hardly be overemphasized.

In a discussion on obscurity and intelligibility in modern poetry, T.S. Eliot speaks of the chief use of the "meaning" of a poem: "To satisfy one habit of the reader, to keep his mind diverted and quiet, while the poem does its work upon him; much as the imaginary burglar is always provided with a bit of nice meat for the guard-dog."[97] In my view the use of serial technique fulfils a comparable function in the creative process of the composer. It is not possible to reach the unconscious by frontal attack. The complex intellectual work which serial organization imposes on the composer fulfils among other things a similar function of diversion which allows free play to the unconscious. The limiting effect of which serial technique is accused can thus be counteracted to an incalculable extent. Above all, "*par une système de gênes bien placées*" the serial law re-introduces compulsion and necessity, and thereby also a positive measure of freedom.

20 Tonality in twelve-tone music (1952)[98]

"Atonal", that tiresome word, was originally just a journalist's gibe, probably, like "cubism". It came into current use towards the end of the 1914 war and we see it taken up, apparently, without qualms, by composers and critics alike. We have all been bothered with it ever since. And now there is no hope of ever getting rid of it. It has become history. At the same time, it is disquieting to realize that this tampering with terminology threatens to become a habit. "Athematic" is the latest arrival. It is difficult to see what is the point in blunting yet another useful word, although there is, of course, one thing it does positively indicate and that is an admission of failure to account adequately for whatever it is meant to describe.

However, since "atonal" was first used in connection with some early works of Schoenberg and his disciples Berg and Webern, it will be of interest to know what Schoenberg thought of it. That is made perfectly clear in a footnote he adds to the third edition of his *Harmonielehre*:

> To call any kind of tone-relationship "atonal" is as inadmissible as it would be to call colour relationships "a-spectral" or "a-complementary". There is no such antithesis. Furthermore, we have not yet even examined the question as to whether that which links these chords together does not constitute, precisely, the tonality of a twelve-tone series. This might quite well prove to be the case ..."[99]

It is an illuminating remark. *The tonality of a twelve-tone series* ... the two notions had never been brought together like that before. Their conjunction was entirely new and unforeseen. It amounted to what must in fact be regarded as a bold hypothesis which, some of us nowadays think, subsequent developments have proved correct.

Let us try to view the picture as it would appear to an observer, say, in 1921. New developments had been taking place in music from the first decade of the century onwards, for which the champions of atonality, not surprisingly, had no positive interpretations to offer.[100] It had merely been observed that new chords had been appearing which could not possibly be traced back to any of the standard forms of tonal harmony (piled-up thirds); that the concatenation of these chords could not be described or understood as in any way realizing a harmonic function which would imply a tonal centre; that this very centre itself seemed to have vanished for good; at any rate it was not decisively to be felt anywhere, nor could its existence be shown with any theoretical conclusiveness. It had been noticed, furthermore, that melodies were being written which used remarkably many notes of different pitch (eight, nine, sometimes up to twelve different notes) joined in chains of intervals such as could not possibly be referred to any known scale and were therefore not amenable to harmonic treatment in any tonal sense.

More than this, the convention of the key-signature had been dropped altogether, so that music had even ceased pretending to be written in one particular key. Lastly, it had become increasingly evident that musical form presented entirely new aspects at all levels, and that the old notion of a more or less vastly magnified cadence could nowhere be taken for an articulating and shaping force any longer. In short, it was abundantly clear what new music was not. In the circumstances, it was perhaps not surprising that "atonal" should have been thought to sum up the state of affairs well enough after all.

Admittedly, it was, still is and may remain extremely difficult to describe any of these new developments in a positive sense. If you ask a research scientist point blank what it is he is trying to find out, his reply might give the impression that he doesn't really quite know himself: and yet every step in his research seems to have been planned and carried out with painstaking accuracy. True, there is also a kind of feeling in the dark. And there is system as well as purpose in the search, even if both are hard to define. Oddly, or perhaps significantly enough, it is the artist's speculative faculties which are most likely to lead him astray.

There is an amusing gallery of Czechoslovakian theorists in Alois Hába's *Neue Harmonielehre*,[101] each in historical succession postulating a further stage in the widening field of harmonic relationships within the tonal system. Hába himself caps the series with a thesis of his own which affirms that "each tone can be linked with or related to any other tone: each interval, each chord (of however many notes) can be linked with or related to any other interval or chord within any of the possible systems" (ie the diatonic, chromatic, quarter-tone, or any other system). It cannot be denied that there is a certain beauty in the sheer comprehensiveness of the proposition. But coming down to earth, doesn't it simply mean that "everything is allowed"; that you may do exactly what you like? Indeed, it is difficult to see what else it can mean. And as for a positive definition of "atonality", this is probably the nearest we shall be able to get to one. It was a liberation from traditional formulae all round, in harmony, melody and form; it was freedom to flit even from system to system if you were so minded.

In every period of strongly-marked transition there is probably a phase of anarchy which dissolves and disorganizes, thereby providing "fresh randomness". It may well be that a certain store of randomness is vitally necessary and that we cannot risk letting it run too low. The whole "atonal" episode might, therefore, be regarded as a tremendous adventure providing fresh randomness, on a perhaps unprecedented scale, so that a new system of order could grow out of it. It is only too clear, on the other hand, how oppressive the "weight of too much liberty" can be. Where anything is possible at any moment, nothing can ever happen *of necessity*. There is the flaw. And to restore this element of "necessity" was one of Schoenberg's constant aims throughout his atonal period.

Let us review the steps leading from atonality to the fully developed twelve-tone technique. In comparison with the highly articulated structure of the diatonic scale, the chromatic scale is invertebrate. It has neither beginning, middle nor end; it is really something of a tapeworm. It lacks all formative potentiality and provides no structural principle beyond what one might call "cohesiveness" through smallest interval-transitions, which is of small account anyhow. Obviously, it could never supersede the diatonic scale as a basis of composition.

All the same, the tendency in composers to treat all the notes of the chromatic scale with absolute freedom is clearly gaining ground. It shows itself in the already mentioned fact that the new melodic line has begun to use more notes than those contained in any one scale. Melodic lines with eight, nine, sometimes twelve different notes are indeed becoming more and more frequent. At the same time there is a growing disinclination, especially on the part of Schoenberg and his disciples, to repeat in any given phrase a note that has already been used, thus preventing this note from taking on special importance from the very fact that it reappears at different points of the phrase. There is nothing "cerebral" or even deliberate in this. We must not think of it as a precept arbitrarily promulgated and then obeyed. On the contrary, composers had obeyed it instinctively long before they became conscious of doing so.

The same tendencies can be observed also in the field of harmony. Trying to find an explanation for the fact that certain progressions which broke all accepted rules of harmony were nevertheless felt to be plausible and "natural", Schoenberg suggests that "such progressions seem to be regulated by the tendency to include in the second chord only notes which were not present in the first one", a remark which, by implication, almost postulates the twelve-tone technique already. He then adds: "I have also observed that octave-doublings would outweigh the others and become a kind of root-note, which is surely not intended."[102] However this may be, what I want to emphasize is, firstly, that the avoidance of note-repetitions in the melodic line and of octave-doublings in chords did originate in practice and not in precept; and secondly, that the two are in reality one and the same thing making itself felt in the two media. The whole point is that the susceptibility to note-repetitions and doublings once again anticipates the twelve-tone technique which alone can explain and justify it: it reveals a new feeling for balance in terms no longer of the "horizontal" or of the "vertical" alone, but in terms of the structural unit of the twelve-tone cell in which the function of each note is unique.

One final thing: the freedom with which composers were using all the twelve notes of the chromatic scale, combined with the fact that this scale in itself was intrinsically unsuitable as a theoretical or practical basis of composition, seems to leave only one alternative, namely, some way of organizing the twelve notes other than the scale. From this to the tone-rows or "series" of the twelve-tone technique is clearly only a short step. Of course, it is easy enough for us now to see that the idea of the "series" was the logical and inevitable outcome. Yet it must be stressed again that it was not arrived at through theoretical speculation, but that in practice it took Schoenberg a very roundabout way to reach it.

Late on in *Harmonielehre* – whose first edition, it must be remembered, was published in 1911 – Schoenberg makes the following statement:

> I believe that a further development in the theory of harmony is not to be expected for the present. Modern music, which makes use of chords of six notes and more, seems to find itself in a stage corresponding to that of early polyphonic music. It is probably going to be easier to discriminate in matters of chord-structure by something similar to the figured-bass system, than to arrive at a clear understanding of the functional significance of chords by the method of tracing them back to degrees of the scale. It seems – and this will probably become clearer as time goes on – that we are heading for a new epoch of polyphonic style, in which chords, much as in early polyphony, will be the *resultant* of part-writing, that is to say, they will be justified entirely by the melodic lines.[103] [italics mine]

Clearly, harmony was at a discount. It was felt that Rameau's extraordinary pronouncement: "Harmony alone can rouse the passions. Melody saps them of their vitality." was no longer true, but rather the reverse.

In 1924, Schoenberg went to Italy to conduct some performances of *Pierrot Lunaire*, and I remember him saying this on his return:

> One of my Italian critics pointed out that there is not a single concord in the whole of *Pierrot Lunaire*. I have not the faintest idea whether this is true or not. But I do know that if there is one such concord, it will be found to have been introduced and 'resolved' with the same care that the old masters took over discords. This is a question of part-writing (*Stimmführung*) to us: harmony as such does not enter into it – *Harmonie seht nich zur Diskussion.*

In the course of the conversation he added:

> The reason why we must not use any of the traditional chords without the greatest precautions: why, in fact, I think we had better do without them altogether, is not difficult to discover. Our new musical language is in its early phase of development; promiscuity with elements of the older system at this stage could, therefore, only obstruct and delay its natural growth. But when it consolidates itself the time will come, no doubt, for the re-integration of many elements from the older system which for the present we must firmly discard.

Both statements struck me as memorable.

Harmony does not enter into it: what the statement in reality amounted to was the dismissal of harmony as a constructive principle. It was a momentous decision for Schoenberg to take. To be fully appreciated, the story of the break must be read in works like the Five Orchestral Pieces, Op.16, *Erwartung*, Op.17, or *Pierrot Lunaire*, Op.22, all written between 1908 and 1914. The audacity of the conception and the sleep-walking sureness of touch in the execution still take one's breath away.

It is in fact no longer possible to give an adequate harmonic analysis of these works, because they are no longer "harmonically" conceived. It is no longer possible to pinpoint a harmonic skeleton and express it neatly in figured-bass symbols, because, in slipping its cables, harmony has shed all sense of static rootedness and assumed a new mode of being of which the distinctive note is its essentially *kinetic* nature: all is now flux and transience, "*sans rien qui pèse ou qui pose …*". The traditional notion of harmony as "sound-perspective" has vanished in Schoenberg as completely as geometric perspective has disappeared from contemporary painting. Indeed, the whole concept of "harmony" has exchanged the specific, technical meaning it had in the musician's vocabulary for one which comes quite close to the general meaning with which it is used in the other arts. A new harmonic consciousness arises, infinitely more subtle and complex than before. How the imagination plots its courses in these uncharted expanses we do not know: all we can say is that it seems to take its bearings by the light of immediate experience.

If melody was now to assume the role of supreme formative agency, it was essential that it should develop its own means of promoting co-ordination and coherence far beyond what had been felt sufficient in "harmonically" conceived music. It was this which led to a revival of interest in pre-homophonic methods of composition, and above all, to the contemporary Renaissance of counterpoint, which dates from Schoenberg's works of this 1908–1914 period.

The two points to be emphasized here for the direct bearing they have upon the conception and genesis of the twelve-tone technique are, first, the clear realization of the fact that it is the *fixed character of a given series of intervals*, independently of rhythm, which constitutes the essence of strict canonic imitation; because interval relationships are inviolable, while metrical proportions and rhythmical pattern admit at least of variation in size (and by implication, this also postulates the essential identity of all the forms of the series – direct, crab-form, mirror and mirrored crab-form – as simply different aspects – of one and the same series). The second point, more important still, refers to what we must recognize as a unique feature of the canonic subject, namely, it begins the only type of musical thought which, in its purely melodic entity, *implies its own complete system of accompaniment* in the form of a fully articulated polyphonic structure. Taken together and generalized, the two points add up to the following notion: *a fixed series of intervals* (independent of metre and rhythm) *as an abstract form of musical thought implying its own complete system of accompaniment*. This is almost a definition of the main idea in twelve-tone technique: it shows its canonic roots and constitutes clear evidence of its kinship with strict imitative contrapuntal style. It also illustrates the meaning of Schoenberg's remark in a letter to Slonimsky: "I was always occupied with the aim to base the structure of my music consciously on a unifying idea, which would not only produce all the other ideas, but would also regulate their accompaniment as well as the chords, the 'harmonies'."[104]

The "method of composition with twelve tones related only to one another" – as Schoenberg called it – is just what it says it is: a method of composition. It cannot, therefore, be too strongly emphasized that it is entirely and exclusively the concern of the composer. It does not concern the listener at all. Above all, the listener must not believe that, if only he knew more about it theoretically, he might find twelve-tone music less difficult. This is a hopeless delusion. He will find it easier to listen to only if he hears more of it, often enough. He must, of course, learn how to listen to it, but this will only come from listening itself: and he must remember that it is the *music* and nothing but the music which matters. It must particularly be stressed that the listener is not supposed to detect the "series" on which a given piece of twelve-tone music is based, as if it were Ariadne's thread: or to follow the ways in which it is woven into the sound-fabric. That, incidentally, can only be discovered by analysis, and although listening and analysis have certainly something in common, they are basically antithetical mental operations.

To insist, however, that twelve-tone technique is no concern of the listener, is not to say that he is not affected by it. The fact that the listener may remain unaware of the specific effect it has upon him does not in the least detract from the reality of that effect: just as there can be no doubt that an intelligent listener who is yet entirely ignorant of the principle of tonality may still genuinely enjoy, and even form a valid aesthetic judgment of, a piece written, say, in C major.

For this is the real issue: the twelve-tone technique must be understood and appraised as a new principle of tonality. Whether we agree or not with this view will, of course, depend upon the degree of generality we are prepared to attribute to the idea of "tonality". We must define it. Tonality, I suggest, is an all-embracing principle of correlation based upon an *a priori* arrangement of our tone-material: this arrangement to be understood as an instituted order in which the value attached to any single element is relative to and emanates from the whole. Any method of composition which strictly adheres to and is ruled by such an order can be properly said to manifest the principles of tonality. Tonality, therefore, can manifest itself in many different ways. What has hitherto been called "tonality" by autonomasia, that is, the order based upon the diatonic scale and the common chord was accurately defined by Tovey as "the harmonic perspective of music".[105] We have seen that with the abandonment of harmony as a constructive principle, the notion of "sound-perspective" also disappeared from atonal music. In twelve-tone music the principle of tonality manifests itself in the strict adherence to the *a priori* arrangement of the twelve notes as shown in the given "series" and, consequently, in the fact that the "series" is the key by which to determine the values attached to any notes and their relations. Thus, any arrangement of the twelve notes, any series – except, for the reason already mentioned, the chromatic scale – may be taken as the "tonal order" which will rule for the whole duration of the work. The series, ie the "tonal order" may change from work to work, but the principle involved remains the same.

If we are to understand how, from the listener's standpoint, an order which he does not grasp intellectually may all the same condition his listening, it is perhaps necessary to regard the mental activity involved in listening to music as embracing probably several simultaneous levels of awareness. If one comes to think of the bewildering complexity and lightning speed of the mental operations involved in the process of decoding an inpouring stream of sensorial stimuli and translating it into aural images, it is perhaps not unreasonable to assume that music is to any normal listener what mathematics can be to a child prodigy that can perform intricate operations of mental arithmetic, literally in a flash. It seems natural that the internal regularities, the subcutaneous net of connections, the logic and sustained consistency produced by the organizing principle of tonality, must register at a comparatively dim level of consciousness; they would clearly throw everything out of focus if they could make themselves conspicuous and occupy for an instant the close-up plane of our attention. It is, no doubt, at a level below the threshold of full consciousness that we would expect such a general law as the principle of tonality to be operative.

In addition to this, the closely-knit texture produced by the cellular organization peculiar to the twelve-tone technique also assumes, or is capable of assuming, that other connective function which in tonal and atonal music exercises itself through the tissue of motive-relationships, also sometimes loosely referred to as "thematic unity". This works probably at a higher level of consciousness than the general law of tonality, yet need not necessarily – must not, perhaps – be grasped intellectually to be fully effective. These, I suggest, are two of the ways in which twelve-tone technique is expected to affect the listener.

It will therefore be clear that he may truly let the composer take care of it. In other words, the composer must needs talk grammar, but grammar is not what he is talking about, or what he expects the listener to be consciously attending to.

How, it may be asked, does a composer choose and fix on a particular series? There is probably more than one answer to this question. In the first place, there seems to be no valid reason why the choice should be settled *a priori* on purely theoretical grounds. Since the number of different series we can obtain through permutation is of the order of hundreds of millions, naive detractors have assumed that the choice must necessarily be arbitrary: you put the twelve notes into a hat, shake the hat, extract the notes one by one, and abide then by the chance order of the drawing. Few composers would admit, I suppose, that this is their own way of settling the question, yet the suggestion is by no means as ridiculous as it sounds. It caricatures, by simply showing it up in crude isolation, the inevitable element of chance which is an essential ingredient in all creative work. So much so, that to most composers, I imagine, the question of deliberate choice of a series need not arise at all, the element of chance being wrapped up in the very process of invention. I mean that the series is sometimes given outright, sometimes foreshadowed in its main outline in the first, spontaneous creative thought – *der Einfall.* The series will then be read from the context and, when necessary, adjustments will be made to settle for good the question of the consecutive order of the twelve notes. There is nothing essentially different in this from the adjustments one has to practise sometimes on a fugue subject in order to make it fit the requirements of double and triple counterpoint.

Whichever way the consecutive order of the series is finally arrived at makes no difference at all to the next step, which is the really important one: the *nature* of the series has to be understood, its properties have to be discovered, its "genius" has to be apprehended. It must be realized that the internal structure peculiar to the series will favour certain lines of development, while discountenancing or even effectively barring others: this individual quality of the series – its grain, as it were – has a far-reaching an influence upon my subject-matter and mode of treatment as the nature of the sculptor's or the painter's or the engraver's material can have upon their respective styles and techniques.

According to its structure a series[106] can be shown to belong to one of three possible types: (a) series whose antecedent (notes 1–6) is reproduced by transposition in theconsequent (notes 7–12) either in the same order or in crab-form, or else in a new permutational form (this is a comparatively rare type: about one series in ten belongs to it): (b) series whose antecedent is inverted in the consequent, again either in the original or in the reverse order, or else in permutation (about one series in four belongs to this second type): and (c) asymmetrical series, that is, series whose antecedent and consequent are structurally different (more than half belong to this last type) – example 3:

Ex. 3(a).

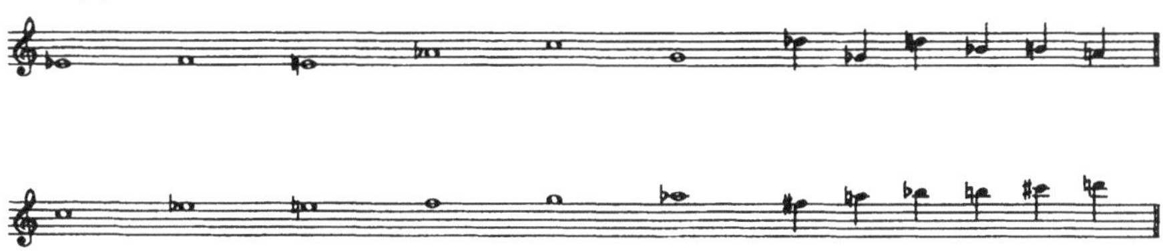

Ex. 3(b).

Ex. 3(c).

Schoenberg has consistently favoured series of the second type, for two main reasons: firstly, because it always has a mirror-inversion (thought not at an invariable interval, as seems to have been implied) which can be deployed together with the direct form of the series, without producing octaves or unisons: in other words, the antecedent of the mirror-form contains all the notes of the consequent of the ground-form though, of course, in a different order, and vice versa. The second reason for the privileged position of this second type of series is that it casts a wider net of relationships with transpositions of the ground series than either of the two other types, this plane of relationships corresponding fairly closely to key-relationships in the old tonal system. (The series of Schoenberg's Wind Quintet Op.26

Ex. 4.

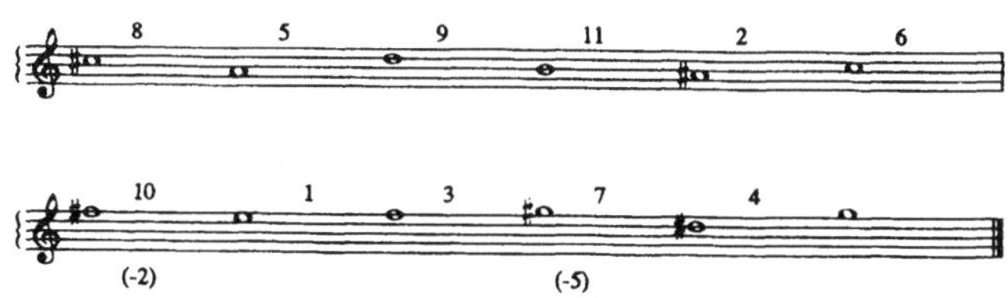

has also its mirror-inversion fulfilling the conditions described, though not a fifth below, but a minor ninth below the ground series – example 4, above.)

From the standpoint of the composer, the immediate effect of the application of the twelve-tone technique to composition, and especially the effect of its two main rules: the continuous rotation of the series in any of its four forms or transpositions of them, and the inviolability of the consecutive order – these give the tone-material, which atonality had "softened" and reduced to a state of over-plasticity, a new, exhilarating quality of resistance, hardness, almost intractableness. The nature, the "grain", of the series wants to be obeyed. It is no longer possible to do "anything you like" or exactly as you like. By "re-introducing compulsion and restrictions, *par un système de gênes bien placées* – necessity has come again into its own, and with it a positive measure of liberty.

Some critics seem to think that twelve-tone technique imposes a rigid egalitarian system, where it is not possible or admissible for any one note to attract more attention than any of its neighbours. Not at all: fundamentally all the twelve notes are equal in the sense that none can claim the position of a tonic or a centre, but in practice, some can be "more equal than others", in George Orwell's phrase, whenever there is a musical reason for it. Even a very small amount of analysis ought to make this clear: one could take as an extreme example the bagpipe-drone G in the *Musette* from Schoenberg's Suite Op.25, for piano – example 5:

Ex. 5.

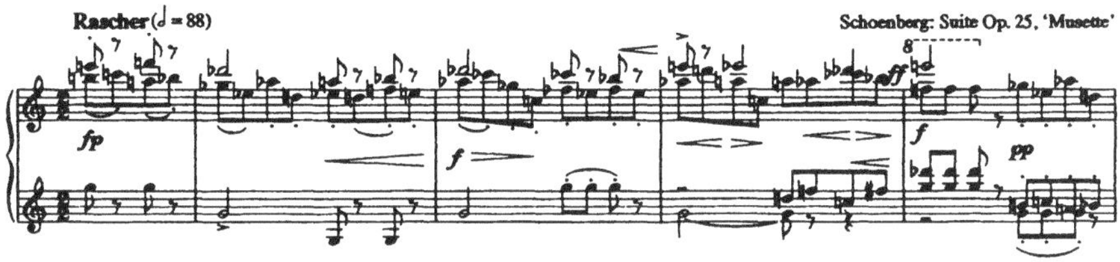

It must not be forgotten that twelve-tone technique is just over a quarter of a century old and in full evolution. It would be idle to speculate on how it may develop in future. But something useful can perhaps be learnt from the measure of evolution we can already observe in Schoenberg's own work. It is quite evident that Schoenberg made in his own work a very full survey of all the possibilities his central idea contains. This process of exploration did not for long proceed in a straight line, but turned often upon itself in complete revolution comprising even sporadic returns to composition in the old key-system.

It is possible to divide the ground covered into two fields, roughly speaking, which come under opposite poles of attraction. The one pole could be said to stand for increasing radicalism, the other for an inalienable sense of tradition: the one would stand for the vital necessity of "experiment" and *renouveau*, the other for re-integration of vital elements from the past and, in a general sense, for the indispensability of *routine* for survival. I would place in the first field works like the Variations for Orchestra Op.31, the String Quartet No. 4, or the String Trio; the second field would be represented by works like the comic opera *Von Heute auf Morgen*, the *Ode to Napoleon*, or the Piano Concerto.

Von Heute auf Morgen presents for the first time, so far as I know, the following remarkable feature: the law of the consecutive order of the twelve notes of the series, hitherto regarded as inviolable, is sometimes deliberately disregarded: and this happens not only at a later stage of the work, where it might be assumed that the series had sufficiently established to allow for digressions, but quite early on, and before the series could possibly have registered at any level of consciousness. Example 2 presents the first four bars of the opera; the series of *Von Heute auf Morgen* is the one given in example 3b (page 123) above as an instance of a series of the second type.

It will be noticed that, in bars 3 and 4, the bass six notes of the consequent of the mirror-form are in an entirely new order. Still more remarkable, however, is the fact that the new arrangement of these six notes is the one that comes closest to scale-form: it is, indeed, one of the 80 different hexachords possible from the combination of our twelve different notes.[107] This hexachord naturally implies a second, complementary hexachord, containing the other six notes; and since, as already shown, the series belongs to the second type, we must expect this second hexachord to be a mirror-inversion of the first. And in fact, it appears in the next bar of the score, in place of the consequent of the ground-form of the series. These and similar variations of the serial order appear on every page of the work.

This raises an important question: how are such deviations from the twelve-tone canon to be judged? I said previously that the rule of the inviolability of the consecutive order of the twelve notes of the series was being deliberately disregarded by Schoenberg. This is not quite true. He is not just taking liberties with the serial order: what he is doing is something quite different. Our example goes to show that he treats either of the two halves of the series as interchangeable with its corresponding hexachord – which postulates a relation of identity between the two interchangeable units. Now this is undoubtedly correct and must be allowed to rest on the same principle in which Rameau claimed the identity of a triad and its inversion.

In effect, whether the triad appears in its root-position or in its first or second inversions, it is still the same chord, though under different aspects – a fact which we acknowledge in the figured-bass symbols by which we express the chord. And Rameau's principle holds equally true of any chord of more than three notes as well.

All these variations affecting the position of the notes within the unit, whether it be a triad or a hexachord are, of course, the result of permutation. And this, in my opinion, is precisely what is shown in *Von Heute auf Morgen*, namely the acceptance of the principle of permutation (within antecedent and consequent) based on a recognition of the fact that beyond the actual series there is an ultimate ground, an abstract archetype – represented by the coupled hexachords – of which the individual series is only one *aspect*, that is, one of the possible permutations. The hexachord-dichotomy is the division of the series generally favoured by Schoenberg; but what holds true here would apply equally in the case of a series regarded as consisting of three tetrachords, nor would division into unequal groups make any difference. To sum up: the identity of the series will be maintained in spite of permutation, provided that this takes place exclusively within the constituent units (hexachord, tetrachord etc), in other words, as long as these constituent units maintain *their* identity and place.

This seems to me to confirm the view that the fundamental idea of the twelve-tone technique is in fact a new formation of the principle of tonality.

It is important to realize, however, that the treatment which strictly observes the given consecutive serial order is by no means divorced from the permutational treatment I have been trying to outline. They do not exclude each other: they can, in fact, co-exist. The latter can even sometimes be made out, *in a figurative sense*, within the former. For instance, the device (constantly used in the strict treatment) of breaking up the series into complementary groups, sometimes leads to one of the parts, generally the principal one, arriving, through more than one rotation of the series, at a deployment of the twelve notes in a pseudo-permutational order. (Schoenberg[108] gives an example from his Wind Quintet, where the rotation is absolutely regular, yet the bassoon part – taken separately over the nine bars of the example which comprise three rotations – deploys a full series in the following pseudo-permutational order: 12, 11, 10–3, 2, 1–6, 5, 4–9, 8, 7. Or again, series of the second type have, as we have seen, a mirror-inversion whose antecedent will contain all the notes of the ground series' consequent, and vice versa, but in a different order, that is to say, in *de facto* permutation of the order of the ground series.)

From the standpoint of the permutational treatment, the original consecutive order of the series (as given in the first germinative idea or as adopted after adjustments) can be allowed a privileged position as *thematically* significant, and be used, as Schoenberg says, "in the manner of a motif". Thus the two treatments can go hand in hand, and the prevalence of the one or of the other will be determined by the degree of stress one wishes to lay on thematic connections altogether.

The crucial evidence for the compatibility of the two modes of treatment is to be found in Schoenberg's Piano Concerto. The series – the right hand part in the solo piano (example 6)

Ex. 6.

– is deployed in its four forms successively: direct, crab-form of the row, crab-form of the original and mirror-form, drawing a superbly arched *cantabile* line over the first 39 bars. From the first bar onwards, however, the series is doubly related: on the melodic plane it carries forward the thematic line in strict serial order, while in each bar it draws complementarily for its accompaniment upon the *rest* of the hexachord, in free permutation, so that several rotations take place on the textural plane for each rotation taking place in the top line. Consequently, an analysis on the principle of the strict serial order alone will have to put up with a number of loose ends, whereas if one accepts the principle of permutation, everything falls into pattern at once.

Distinguishing between the two modes of treatment, we might say that serial technique is to the permutational technique what *strict contrapuntal style* is to the *free melodic style* of homophonic music. The brief life-history of twelve-tone music would thus seem to reproduce on a miniature scale the salient phases of the historical evolution of Western music, just as the human embryo is said to pass in its development through the salient phases of man's biological evolution.

Strict serial technique would seem to be more congenial to the artist who is concerned rather with the "mathematical world of ornament" than with the "representational" world – the artists, that is, whose deepest thoughts are expressed in a constructional treatment of the tone-material. The artist of the opposite type, on the other hand, might conceivably feel that it is possible to have a surfeit of *esprit de géométrie*; that homogeneity of texture and technical treatment may further the cause of unity without necessarily achieving it; that unity, after all, may be achieved even with disparate materials (which would seem to be one of the more engaging problems to set oneself); in short, to hammer away at cause and effect all the time does not seem a vital necessity.

It seems possible to relax with happy effect. Digression from the main line of argument need not be wasteful. Even to explore a blind alley here and there may have its right and delightful place in the overall design. Above all, this type of artist will find it needful to remember that in such a well-policed state as the twelve-tone commonwealth, everything "irregular" has an added fascination, and that randomness and irrationality are at a premium, since once crowded out – unlike nature, which, it is said, invariably finds a way back – they are apt to stay out for good, which would be a pity.

21 Developments in twelve-tone technique (1956)[109]

Twelve-tone technique has produced achievements of the highest order, especially in the works of Schoenberg and Webern, as we all know. Nonetheless it cannot in itself be regarded as having reached its full growth in the works of these composers alone. On purely systematic grounds it stands in need of further development. I propose to indicate in what direction things seem to me to be moving; needless to say, I can only speak of what I understand (or think I understand) of my own experience.

The matter can be summarized as follows:

I use, together with the twelve-tone series, a correlated set of proportions expressed in numbers. The series is regarded as a miniature code for the combinatorial operations concerned with pitch structure. The proportion set is the steering device for all time structural operations. In this capacity it is the source of rhythm and articulation at all levels of form organization and, in the last resort, it rules form as a whole.

In composition, I now use the complete serial field. The field-order is based on the model of the original series, the sequence of transpositions following (so to speak) an acrostic-pattern which reproduces at super-ordinate time levels the interval structure of the original series. The rotation of the transpositions is ruled by the progression of the time set.

The expression currently used in American for the Schoenbergian twelve-tone series – a *tone-row* – strikes me as most literally accurate. The central meaning of the word "tone" is obviously pitch. In scientific usage, as pure or sine tone, it is uniquely defined by pitch, ie by one single frequency rate. Tone, then, is pitch.[110] Now Schoenberg's tone row is, in fact, exclusively concerned with pitch. Duration and, therefore, rhythm and, therefore ultimately, form, are left out of the picture. The way Schoenberg uses the series in composition also shows that he never envisaged it as anything but a principle of pitch-organization.

In *Style and Idea*, he indeed mentions *rhythmization* and *phrasing* as incidental to the pitch structural operations, as freely imposed on them from without, as it were.[111] In short, Schoenberg did not attempt to correlate pitch-structure and time-structure. His method has no time-structural criterion of its own, and for this reason he never felt any inhibition about using sonata and other traditional forms.

Some of his more recent critics have rashly concluded from this that the method proposed by Schoenberg is in fact incapable of establishing temporal relations from within. If this were true, it would of course follow that it is also incapable of developing "form" from within and is thus forced to borrow from outside, from other styles, its notions of rhythm and modes of form organization.

This view is mistaken. The critics in question seem to have overlooked one important detail, namely, that the Schoenbergian tone-row does in fact offer in itself the necessary and sufficient basis for pitch and time correlation. To realize that this is in effect so, we have only to remind ourselves that pitch too (in the last analysis) is *rhythm*. We define pitch as the frequency rate at which a particular sound-wave recurs. The phenomenon constitutes obviously a simple, regular rhythmical sequence. We might say that the ear has in reality two different ways of grasping rhythm: (a) rhythm *qua* pitch – which is almost qualitative, and (b) rhythm *qua* duration or, more exactly, *qua* sequence of varying durations, which is clearly quantitative. In other words, we do not actually have to count the complete number of 440 vibrations for one full second in order to be sure that the pitch in question is central *a*. It registers as such, instantly, with the immediacy with which qualitative impressions strike us.

Nevertheless, although we need not count the 440 vibrations, we certainly can if we want to, and we know that our impression is *de facto* produced by a medium vibrating precisely at that frequency rate. On the other hand, we compare durations by reference to an adopted time-unit and by actually or subconsciously counting beats or sub-divisions of beats. In short, it is evident that, regardless of the mood of apprehension, both pitch values and duration values are based on number, since they are measurable.

Number is, then, the common basis of pitch and time. Pitch-values can therefore be translated into duration-values, and vice versa. It is thus possible to derive from any given twelve-tone series a correlated set of duration values. The two, pitch-set and time-set, will stand in equivalence relation. Jointly they constitute the necessary basis on which the integration of pitch-structure and time-structure becomes possible. This is to say that the time-set in addition to being the source for all rhythmical or poly-rhythmical configuration – in the same way that the pitch-set is the source of all melodic, harmonic or polyphonic configuration – must also rule articulation at all levels of form organization. It follows that form as a whole can develop and regulate itself truly from within, since its growth will be directed step by step and at all super-ordinate time levels by the steering operations of the time-set. In other words, form thus obeys laws which are immanent and is therefore in no need of external props for constructive schemata borrowed from outside.

It is perhaps well to remind ourselves at this stage that what we are talking about is, after all, means not ends. In these days of fierce partisanship it is, I think, more necessary than ever to stress the *relativity* of means. I, for one, refuse to believe that salvation depends on your creed. While twelve-tone technique is, to my mind, the most satisfactorily developed and potentially versatile tool the composer of our time has at his disposal, it strikes me, nevertheless, as downright silly to disparage or deplore the use of other techniques which other people may find congenial. I will frankly admit that I do not really expect to be bowled over tomorrow by a new piece written in C major; all the same, I see no reason for ruling out the possibility categorically.

On the other hand, I see even less reason for ruling out the possibility of being bowled over by a piece that, while using the twelve notes of our chromatic scale, would organize sound in a way that could truly be said to owe nothing whatever to the principles of twelve-tone composition. To be quite candid, that *would* surprise me a little; after all, we do not live in a world of watertight compartments and, since *tout se tient*, I could sooner imagine a C major piece handling the seven notes of the diatonic scale combinatorially and managing to establish tonality without the aid of functional harmony, or something of that sort.

Returning to the problem of correlating pitch and time on the basis of a given twelve-tone series, what it amounts to is reducing the set of pitch-values to number or, more exactly, to a set of proportional magnitudes which, in turn, can be translated into a series of time values according to any chosen scale. Reduction to number is measurement. The sky-line of the series is measured (in semitones or whatever metrical unit we may choose) as successive point-elevations above the lowest note taken as a horizon, as it were. For reasons I need not go into now, the lowest or horizon note is not necessarily the one which to the eye appears to be the lowest on the stave on which the series is written out. A purely theoretical concept, namely a couple of complementary hexachords (what Milton Babbitt calls a source-set) underlies the actual series. The sky-line is then simply one of the possible permutational unfoldings or deployments of the underlying couple of hexachords.

It is more logical therefore to adopt as horizon-note the lowest note of the first hexachord. Now since the figure zero can neither be multiplied nor divided, it would obviously not do in a proportions set which we want to be the matrix of time structures on various scales or time levels. Consequently, where the horizon-note actually appears in the pitch-set, we shall take advantage of the indeterminacy of the Schoenbergian tone-row in respect of the precise octave, ie by the figure twelve instead of zero. Thus a twelve-tone series like the following:

Ex. 7(a).

of which the underlying pair of hexachords is:

Ex. 7(b).

gives the following proportions set (calculating in semi-tones from C):

6 1 2 8 12 4 / 3 5 10 11 7 9

which, in turn, can be projected into the temporal dimension according to whatever scale we choose, and thus act as a time-structure generator.

The mirror inversion of the twelve-tone series will of course produce an inversely proportional set which is actually a complementation (module 12) of the first time set, ie:

6 11 10 4 12 8 / 9 7 2 1 5 3

The retrograde forms of the series present no special problem, since we cannot move backwards in time. However, rhythmical structures can of course be turned back to front, as such, while moving on in the only possible time direction. Accordingly, the proportions set can also be run back to front, in correspondence with the retrograde forms of the pitch-set.

This is all that needs to be said concerning the basis of pitch time correlation. The couple; pitch-set, time-set is to be understood in the manner of an arbitrarily chosen system of coordinates, the "arbitrariness" being of course of the same kind as that invariably found in methods, canons or procedural rules in every sphere.[112] To argue about the intrinsic sense of the rules of chess, for example, would be evidently meaningless; the point of the rules lies in their being observed in the game and in their making sense in the observance.

Yet, it may still be asked, why add to the self-imposed limitations which (one would have thought) are already almost inhumanly stringent in the Schoenbergian method? Aren't you just stopping the last loopholes through which a certain measure of spontaneity and freedom of movement could still creep into the system? I might even be asked the following personal question: since you have argued elsewhere that "a certain store of randomness is vitally necessary and that we cannot risk letting it run too low", are you not being inconsistent when you propose a development of the Schoenbergian method amounting almost to a complete rationalization of the process of composition? The question is a serious one, not to be evaded. I will try to answer it.

Anyone who has the smallest experience of introspection must surely be familiar with the fact that thought, left to itself, the "stream of cerebration", as William James calls it, is in truth a fantastically erratic thing. We do not start it by an act of volition. We awaken to the realization that the process is in full swing within. Conscious thought, by contrast, is the effort to stem and oppose the natural incoherence of this spontaneous generation. We have discovered that we can only achieve it by a well-organized system of obstacles, *par un système de gênes bien placées,* as Paul Valéry has put it.

Logic is the most powerful obstacle the mind has found to curb its natural bent to divagate, extravagate and turn round in circles. It is a mistake to suppose that methods, prosodies, precepts of composition and all self-imposed rules, however stringent, are conditions of an inhibited creative activity. On the contrary, they are conditions of completeness; they are the means of asserting against the dark of the mind the other lucid side, where intelligibility begins, and without which it is questionable whether even what we call perception could take place at all. I am paraphrasing Valery who, speaking of method in general, adds: "These constraints may be purely arbitrary; it suffices that they effectively hinder the natural course of spontaneous thought fortuitously propagating itself from incident to incident." In short, the true purpose of method, as Valéry tersely puts it, is "*l'invention contrariée et bien temperée*"[113]

"*L'invention contrariée*" is evidently what Schoenberg's restrictive rules are aimed at. Constraint is the whole purpose, the very *raison d'être* of the method. From which it is easy to see how little the meaning of Schoenberg's idea has been understood by practitioners of a so-called "free twelve-tone technique". Yet to recognize that a system of constraints has a positive and not, as is so often assumed, an inhibitory function, answers of course only the first part of the question. The second part concerns the preservation of spontaneity.

Without question, the autonomy of conscious thought has its limits, and spontaneity is of the essence of the mind. Fresh randomness is provided unceasingly. From chance to chance and amidst the welter of inessentials, of baffling detail, of valuable but unique traits not immediately relevant, it also presents us with the happy coincidences, the strokes of luck, the sudden flashes which, as Schoenberg once put it, are more than one could possibly have thought of. Implicit in the very effort of intellectually grasping and ordering this welter of immediate experience is, no doubt, the danger of sacrificing the irrational, the wayward to the system. Intelligence can undoubtedly be narrow-visioned. Whitehead has said that "to some extent, to understand is always to exclude a background of intellectual incoherence ... But deeper understanding [is] ever confronting intellectual systems with the importance of its omissions."[114] The problem of safeguarding the vital flow of spontaneity is indeed a problem of the "deeper understanding".

It is obvious that the strengthening of our methodological controls postulates a vitalizing of the powers at the opposite pole. And, conversely, more living-room for the anarchist demands a commensurate increase in the rigour of our system of constraints. We are faced, here too, it seems, with the problem, nay with the drama, of coexistence. It has to be lived through, and solved (or spoiled) in the process of living it through. But it is the hazards involved that help to make creative work truly an adventure of the spirit.

I have previously referred to the actual twelve-tone series as a miniature code for the combinatorial operations concerned with pitch structure. On these I need not insist, since the principles involved are fairly well- known by now. Yet my notion of the series of a "code" differs from Schoenberg's interpretation in a fundamental way which I must try to explain.

To my mind the claim put forward by Schoenberg that the series "is meant to function in the manner of a motif" raises a conceptual difficulty. If "motif" be understood according to its current meaning in the musician's vocabulary, then the claim (I think) is too concrete, and by prejudging the possibilities of the method's functioning, it reduces its degree of generality. Method imposes common relationships to all that happens, but cannot impose what that relationship shall be.

The notion of securing *Zusammenhang* or achieving patterns of connectedness through a network of motivic or, *a fortiori*, thematic correspondence belongs to a pre-dodecatonic mode of thought: or, from the opposite point of view, it constitutes the most precious heritage of the classic Viennese tradition. I agree, so long as we are not asked to grant the Viennese ideal something like categorical status, embodying principles whose validity would extend beyond the limits of a style which, like any other style, is of necessity historically circumscribed.

Modern psychology would probably support the view that apprehension is not an *additive* process. A whole is grasped as a whole in its very wholeness. It is not arrived at by concatenation of its separately distinguishable features. We can, of course, if we choose, inspect the structure of a complex whole and analyse it into its separable components. But this is neither the way it arises in the projecting mind, nor the way the apprehending mind grasps it. This view – essentially that held by Gestalt psychologists – has led to the rejection of the traditional associationist account of thought. To my mind this has a direct bearing upon Schoenberg's view of the series as 'intended to function in the manner of a motif".

It cannot be too strongly emphasized that for all the stress Schoenberg lays on the surface and internal tracery of his motivic ramifications, they never quite succeed in obscuring the fact that the specific operations of the pitch set, considered in themselves and apart from the "motivic work" they are made to do as well, constitute in reality what is vitally new of Schoenberg's contribution: an *ars combinatoria* which as a mode of sound-organization is entirely unprecedented. It has its own specific laws. The common relationship they impose on all that happens results in a tautological *double emploi* when, in addition, the old associationist "motivic working" operates.

No one man can do or see everything. It seems rather unintelligent to criticize Schoenberg for what he did *not* do. Deeply rooted as he was in the Viennese tradition, it is not that, while having the genius and the courage to cut the Gordian knot of the harmonic *imbroglio*, he recoiled from casting aside the principle of motivic-thematic relationship which had been the soul of classical form. He was, on the contrary, consciously bent on extending its range and making the principle all-pervasive, absolute. A paradoxical situation thus arises; we must come to the conclusion that where literally *everything* is thematic, *nothing* is.

But Schoenberg's critics have very rarely understood that it was only at this point that the next (in the literal sense, exorbitant) step could be taken, by which the old concept jumps out of its closed circle and enters a new orbit, thus opening up a new realm of possibility. The idea of obtaining an unceasing flow of diversity out of an unceasing recurrence of sameness leads straight to the notion of the series understood as a "code", ie stripped of any concrete motivic-thematic obligations.

In effect, why should any surface group of interval relations in the horizontal or in the vertical which the naked eye can pinpoint on the stave that spells the "code", be granted privilege or priority over all the potential relations which only the combinatorial operation of the code can actualize if we agree that the *ars combinatoria* is indeed the organizing factor in the new orbit?

To illustrate the manner in which I conceive the operation of the "code", I recall the counsel Leonardo is said to have given his pupils: "If you wish to paint an equestrian battle", (I quote from memory), "look for the spot of dampness on an old wall and gaze on it intently for some time; after a while you will suddenly see your battle emerge in firm outline from the chaos of the damp spot." There is a most striking element of truth in this. We have all had similar experiences when, for instance, lying ill in bed for long idle hours we have suddenly seen one of the flowers of the wallpaper-pattern start a train of metamorphoses which can hold one spellbound for a considerable period

The combinatorial faculty seems indeed to be one of the basic modes of mental activity. We seem to be watching here – at a liminal stage, as it were – the initial blending and interweaving of randomness and order. From the conviction that this is in fact the case, springs what I call my quixotic attitude towards the general operations of my serial code. Once firmly established and adhered to, the series is resistant. Being thus able to rely on the rigour of its constraints, I can afford to let the stream of cerebration take a free course.

Just as, Don Quixote's code of behaviour being so deeply ingrained – there being such system in his madness – he could allow Rocinante a loose rein at the crossroads. Whether his mount took him East or West would not matter, he could be sure to be led into trouble anywhere, since it was in wait for him everywhere. The only thing that matters is how he will deal with conflict when it arises. We expect him to tackle it in a manner fitting and true to his code; nothing else counts. When he does so behave, strictly and utterly in accord with his guiding idea, then not even defeat can diminish him in our eyes. Whether victor or vanquished is, in the end, irrelevant. The whole adventure has then a beautifully satisfying logical fit, as it were.

Mutatis mutandis, this is how my code is meant to operate. Something must be made to happen in music. My rigid series begins to throw up images. They are, of course, hidden images or (if you like) metamorphoses already of bare interval relations. The simple spelling of the twelve-tone series forwards and backwards in the correct order seems to me too much like copying the flower of my wallpaper-pattern. I attend only to its metamorphoses. To Sancho, windmills are windmills. But Don Quixote, *par excellence* the knight of the hidden images, sees giants where Sancho can only see mere windmills. The image engages in action. And it is in action that I shall be able to meet tests of the kind I have been trying to indicate.

But to return from metaphor to description, there is a further point concerning the hand-in-hand working of pitch-set and time-set which calls for explanation. As I said before, the time-set is correlated to the pitch-set as an equivalent series of proportions expressed in numbers. The principle of common relationship therefore obtains in both dimensions. Rhythmicization in the Schoenbergian sense, as freely impressed from without, is thus replaced by rhythmical invention developed from within, ie analogically and hand-in-hand with the combinatorial operations concerned with pitch-structure. To put it in a nutshell: my proportions or time-set goes back to the Greek idea of number as the father of rhythm.

In practice, however, rhythmical invention seems always to have proceeded largely (if not exclusively) from somatic rather than from intellectual inspiration: and psychologists may one day be able to explain why. For the moment the only possible attitude seems to be an empirical one, which may be expressed in the form of the idea: number proposes but the body disposes. In effect, number will suggest an incalculable variety of rhythmical structures of which the body, left to its own kinaesthetic devices, would indeed never have dreamed. So a vast new field of rhythmical configuration is thus opened up. Yet it seems to narrow down as complexity increases. And the limiting factor seems to be the bodily faculty of realizing the proposed structure with the immediacy with which sensorial impressions must register or "speak" to be grasped at all.

So far I have used the time-set as a principle of rhythmical articulation operating on two different time-scales simultaneously: the time-unit of the first being the smallest adopted subdivision of the actual counting beat; the time-unit of the second being a multiple of the beat, perhaps bar or some magnitude of that order. The progression of the time-set thus creates concurrent patterns of regularity, minute at the one end and of increasing range towards the opposite end.

For example, taking the figure six to be the first number in my time-set, the adopted small-scale time-unit to be the semiquaver, and the large scale time-unit to be the one full bar, then the number 6 will rule concurrently the following two different time-spans: on the one hand, rhythmical configuration on the phrase-length level, ie pattern (conjoint or disjoint) totalling a duration of six semiquavers in either equal or unequal values; on the other hand, it will integrate the whole sequence at the next super-ordinate time-level into one six-bar structure. I have purposely chosen a case of the simplest possible type in order not to obstruct the perspective by too much complexity in the foreground of the picture, because the next step is to show how the steering operations of the time-set rule the fanning-out of the structures into super-ordinate time-levels. To show this, it is necessary for me to take up now the last of my topics, namely the ordering of the total serial field.

By the "total serial field" is meant the original series plus its replicas at all transposition levels of the twelve-note scale. The replicas, however, are not taken in chromatic sequence, in successive semitone steps, but arranged in an acrostic-pattern so that the successive transpositions reproduce, over the total field, the interval structure pattern of the original series. The rotation of the transpositions is ruled by the progression of the time-set.

If we envisage now a composition as a whole in progress, we realize that it is to be understood as a train of events, a "becoming", *Geschehen* (as the Germans call it) which "stratifies" time into super-ordinate "layers" of time levels. The layers open up fan-wise from the start, each articulating itself within its proper range, and contributing (as a whole) to the articulation of the next higher level, where it becomes simply a member of the super-ordinate structure; and so forth, up to the highest level which is the whole, in the light of which the parts achieve their proper meaning. I say achieve, meaning to imply a two-way traffic, a give-and-take; a certain measure of immediate suggestion constantly going out from the individual part, but making sense only in the train of suggestion emanating from the whole. This, from a musician's point of view, is what we commonly mean by the word "context". Context, too, is a "stratification" where everything achieves meaning in the light of the next higher contextual level.

Let us now take a last look at the interacting of my pitch- and time-sets. At the lowest level, or bottom layer, my series begins its revolutions (comprising its mirror and retrograde-motions linked in continuous rotation). The musical configuration now actually arising is rhythmically articulated by the operation of the first number on my time-set. As I said earlier, the articulation is twofold at this level; in my chosen example it took place concurrently on the semiquaver scale and on the bar scale. The next higher level, ruled by the progression of the complete time-set, embraces one complete revolution of the entire serial field. The time-span involved here equals therefore in number of bars the sum of the twelve integers of my time-set.

The next higher level spans a fourfold revolution of the serial field, in one of the 24 possible permutations of the time-set in its original form, plus its inversely proportioned mirror, plus their respective retrograde forms. The total time-span here is of the order of a complete movement of (say) a symphonic work. Beyond this the 24 possible permutations in the sequence of the four aspects of the time-set cover a timespan more than sufficient for a complete work on the largest scale. This is, in rough outline, how I conceive the process of integration of pitch- and time-structure.

An analogy might perhaps help to illustrate my meaning. Take the following sequence: my heart beats (though not, I'm glad to say, in semiquavers); I breathe, on a different timescale – in fact, at the appropriately termed phrasing level; I am engaged in an action of some sort which has a beginning in time and is directed towards its appointed goal; my pulse, my breathing, the steps taken in the course of my action are all coetaneous, yet each of a different length and rhythmical order; and all the while day turns into night, the moon increases and wanes, the seasons alternate and so forth, and my action, from beginning to end, is inscribed in that manifold temporal frame; a continuous tide-like process, creating its own patterns of movement and its centres of stillness.

It would completely falsify my meaning to objectify my time-frame, to take it as a "thing", a tangible construction, armature or skeleton which one mounts and round which one lets the music grow. Not at all. My measurements are not to be understood as props but as principles; as principles which inform the growth of the musical form. The living shape is in no way predetermined by, but arises out of, my steering operations. Furthermore, sense and structure mutually condition one another but need not always be rigidly co-extensive. Similarly, to what the poets call free *enjambement*, sense may run on from structure to structure and thus, without destroying it, achieve a higher freedom on the very support of structure.

I have not yet found a truly satisfactory definition of form. Perhaps there is none. But the Scholastics' definition of the soul as the *form* of the body has always pleased me. I suppose logical positivists nowadays would make short shrift of the notion. All the same, it seems to me to send out a "beam" in the right direction. Meeting the definition for the first time gives a delightful little shock which turns the old pairing "form-content" topsy-turvy. "Form-content" would seem to be an adequate enough notion for (say) pottery, but in musical matters it has led, without question, to all the stultifying conclusions which dogged us in our schooldays and still do so in most of our textbooks. I suggest that what chiefly bedevils our arguments about form is the fact that we have taken the word as a noun instead of – as we should – as a verb. Our key-words, like railway points, are sometimes apt to sidetrack us. "Form", as a noun, sits on the dead-end of a line of thought. We ought to shunt it back and switch over to the verb-line, where it becomes active as "to form", "to inform"; not a vehicle any longer resting on a frame, but the moving power.

22 Alban Berg: obituary (1936)[115]

The death of Alban Berg awakens a sympathetic response among all of us who felt united with him through warm friendship and through a common link with Schoenberg, whose pupils amounted altogether to a kind of spiritual family. Even the most distant ones and those who were distant despite their geographical proximity – I am referring to his Viennese compatriots by whom he was not seen as a prophet – today agree unanimously that in Alan Berg, we have lost one of the leading musicians of our time.

Alban Berg and Anton von Webern, Schoenberg's first pupils – first in date and in status – have been, like their teacher, the great pioneers of the new music. They were the first to penetrate decisively into the unexplored regions of our modern musical systems, opening the most important gateway to contemporary musical evolution. Apart from its pure artistic value, the work of Alban Berg has an extremely outstanding circumstantial importance for having been the first manifestation of this school which silenced *en masse* the objections which opposed the legitimacy of the language created by the three Viennese masters. Berg's opera, *Wozzeck*, premiered in 1925 in Berlin under Erich Kleiber has travelled everywhere causing a sensation amongst its audiences.

In other words, a musical style until then branded as cerebral and esoteric, was tested in a theatrical context – the medium in which experimental music would be most exposed – with subject-matter of tremendous humanity: the tragedy of the poor soldier Wozzeck, based on the play by the renowned Georg Büchner. The result has an incomparable emotive and persuasive force.

The influence of *Wozzeck* has been broad in scope, illuminating and stimulating. By reputation, an anarchic dissolution of our musical system has suddenly become an intelligible language with immediate and irresistible impact. The high intellectual beauty of the organizational methods used in this music has been recognized: but everyone feels above all captivated by the fact that this unusual sound-world should express in an inexplicable although immediately persuasive fashion, qualities that are really those of *music*!

Apart from what proof *Wozzeck* offers as regards the value of the much-discussed principles of the Schoenberg school, it is obvious that the most secret and decisive factor of the world success of *Wozzeck* is none other than Berg's own sheer personality. In actuality, the mysterious power that an exceptional personality irradiates became evident soon after starting a conversation with this artist. Whoever saw him only once cannot forget his tall aristocratic figure, his beautiful artist's head and, especially the extremely lively expression of his gaze; and certain traits, in which you could find outstandingly harmonized some elements of masculine hardness with an indeterminate nearly feminine gracefulness. Alban Berg was a true great Viennese gentleman. His simplicity was made up of friendly tact and courtesies: he was one of the most sensitive and affectionate beings I have ever met.

Berg's early biography does not give the slightest indication of his likely achievement. Born in Vienna on 9th February, 1885, his 50th birthday last year attracted tributes within his own country and in the musical world at large. Apart from the trips he made to premieres of his opera *Wozzeck* all over Europe, he hardly moved from his beloved Vienna. Berg and Helene Nahowski enjoyed an ideal marriage, living in idyllic peace in a delightful house, welcoming to artists in the *cottage* of Hitzing, or near the Kärntern lakes in summer. He created all his works in this solitary place: the Piano Sonata (1908), the first songs, the String Quartet Op.3, the Three Orchestral Pieces, the Four Pieces for clarinet and piano, the *lieder* with orchestra on texts by Peter Altenberg.

Berg had worked on *Wozzeck* from 1914 to 1920. Between this opera and *Lulu*, on a libretto after Wedekind, we find also chamber works of great importance: the Chamber Concerto and the Lyric Suite. The concert aria *Der Wein* for soprano and orchestra on a poem by Baudelaire is already a kind of stylistic prelude to the music of his last opera *Lulu*. The Symphonic Pieces which Berg extracted from the opera as a concert suite have already been performed by many major orchestras. Only a few weeks before his death, Alban Berg had the satisfaction of witnessing the success of this suite at a Vienna Philharmonic Orchestra concert. It seems that the composition of the opera is finished; Berg could not finish the instrumentation, but the manuscript is so elaborate and detailed in indications that it will not be difficult to complete the score.

The last composition by Alban Berg, still unknown, will have been – some mysterious inescapable fate? – a *Requiem*. This work was written last summer. He owes its production to special circumstances. An American violinist, Louis Krasner, had commissioned a concerto for violin and orchestra. He had just started to think about the work when Manon Gropius suddenly died: an 18-year-old girl, an extraordinary being, daughter of Alma Mahler and intimate friend of the Berg couple. Berg was overcome by something of a fever-like frenzy, and – normally so slow in his production – finished the score of the violin concerto in six weeks! The theme of the composition is based around a chorale by Bach, *Es ist genug,* whose text heads the score. The text and, needless to say, the music are closely linked to the emotional upheaval that the death of Manon Gropius caused him. The score is dedicated "to the memory of an angel"; Berg finished it by the Wörther lake, not far from the house where Brahms had written 50 years earlier his only violin concerto.

The jury of the ISCM, gathered in Barcelona a few days ago to determine the programmes of the next festival, agreed to dedicate part of the first orchestra programme *in memoriam* Alban Berg. The works performed will in fact be the new Violin Concerto – its world premiere – and the Symphonic Fragments from *Wozzeck*.[116]

23 Webern

Webern in Barcelona (1932)[117]

The forthcoming appearance of Anton Webern in the Música da Camara concerts in Barcelona is an important event, worthy of attention. For he is one of the most profoundly original and distinguished figures in contemporary music.

The implications of Schoenberg's bold innovations led this clear-sighted, ardent creative spirit towards an unsuspected world of sonority: a uniquely hyper-sensitive art, of such extraordinary delicacy and subtleness of feeling that one marvels at the existence of a sensibility alert to their many dimensions and a technique capable of doing them justice.

Webern's compositional style has one outstanding characteristic – extreme conciseness. He needs only a few bars to outline a musical form of the greatest richness and organizational complexity, condensing the substance of a vast symphonic panorama. He needs only a few sonorities, a few rhythms, a few timbres magically combined, to evoke an atmosphere and feeling of fascinating intensity of expression. No-one has characterized his art more exactly than Schoenberg, when he wrote a foreword to the printed score of Webern's Six Bagatelles for string quartet Op.9:

> Although the brevity of these pieces is a persuasive advocate for them, on the other hand that very brevity itself requires an advocate. Consider what moderation is required to express oneself so briefly. Every glance can be expanded into a poem, every sigh into a novel. But to express a novel in a single gesture, joy in a single breath – such concentration can only be present in proportion to the absence of self-indulgence. These pieces will be understood only by someone who has faith in music as the expression of something that can be said only musically. They can stand up to criticism as little as beliefs of any kind. If faith can move mountains, disbelief can deny their existence. Faith is impotent against such impotence. Does the player know how to play these pieces, does the listener know how to receive them? Can believing performers and listeners fail to surrender themselves to one another? But what shall one do with the heathen? Fire and sword can keep them down; but only believers can be kept under a spell. For them, may this stillness ring!

The majority of Webern's works are written for diverse chamber groups, to which he also allies admirably the human voice – hence the prominence of the *lied* in his output. But Webern also links a mixed choir or vocal quartet with instrumental groups, as in, for instance, his two *Goethe Lieder* Op.19, for mixed voices and celesta, guitar, violin, clarinet and bass clarinet. Notable among his purely instrumental works are the pieces for String Quartet Op.5, his String Trio, Symphony Op.21 and, recently, his Quartet with piano and saxophone. To obtain a proper perspective of this singular musical personality, one should get to know his orchestral works, such as the Passacaglia Op.1, and Six Pieces Op.6 and Five Pieces Op.10, where Webern's sublime lyricism and incomparable sonic imagination find the most stunning expression.

Another of the most interesting aspects of Webern's personality is his work as a conductor. Schoenberg, conducted by Webern, reminds us of the Viennese classics Mozart, Haydn or Schubert; however, they have an indescribable modernity under his nervous and subtle baton. In Vienna, Webern has for two years been conducting the Arbeiter Symphonie-Konzerte (a similar institution to our Associació Obrera de Concerts) for two years; the Viennese association has also a great mixed choir, formed exclusively of workmen, with whom Webern has performed such works as Mahler's Second and Eighth Symphonies, Brahms' Requiem, Schoenberg's *Friede auf Erden* Op.15 and works by Reger, Kodaly, Hanns Eisler and other modern and classical composers. Anyone attending any of these concerts, which are sponsored by the *Sozialdemokratische Kunstelle* (Society for Art and Culture) will understand the profound educational and elevating activity in which Webern has been engaged: and it is time he was known and esteemed in our country as one of the masters of contemporary music.

Webern's *The Path to the New Music* (1961)[118]

The Path to the New Music[119] is a series of lectures given by Webern to a lay audience at a private house in Vienna in 1932 and 1933. They were delivered extempore and occasionally illustrated at the piano. A member of the audience took down the lectures in shorthand and this is how they have been preserved. The person who did so must have been a most accomplished stenographer, for they read like a genuine verbatim manuscript. In every word and turn of phrase, this is certainly Webern at his most spontaneous. The impression is so strong that one is irresistibly reminded even of matters of intonation. The characteristic accent-curve in Webern's individual manner of speaking makes itself felt in every sentence. In writing, in letters especially, this would result in a lavish use of exclamation marks, one for stress, two for emphasis, three for strong feelings, four for passion, five for rapture. The unique documentary value of a record that shows us Webern caught, as it were, in the very act of thinking aloud, is no doubt the most treasurable aspect of the publication.

As regards the content, anyone who would expect to find answers here to the sort of questions we would like to ask Webern today, is likely to be disappointed. No new light is shed on the fundamental processes of thought behind the work of the composer who has most profoundly affected the course of evolution in musical matters since the war.

In particular, none of the issues raised by the new echelons of contemporary leadership in connection with Webern's work are so much as touched upon. This may prove disconcerting to young readers who have formed a mental picture of their Webern from interpreting his scores in the light of statistical methods of analysis as propounded, for example, by the journal *Die Reihe*. The quantitative element is, of course, fundamental to all music. To a certain extent and purely intuitively, the masters have been conscious of it at all times. It has been left to our experimental age to discover the pitfalls of systematic parameter-manipulation. In this context, the Webern lectures, with their strong, almost exclusive emphasis on roots and tradition are a timely and potentially salutary reminder. Unfortunately, it is just this aspect of his message which, I am afraid, is most likely to fall on deaf ears.

Webern insistently reminds us of all that we tend to slur over and overlook in his work. So much so that a naive reader might be forgiven for pausing in bewilderment to ask himself: did Webern really know how revolutionary he was? He most certainly did. Of course, he would have repudiated the word "revolutionary" as emphatically as Schoenberg did – four exclamation marks.

Not that it matters, but it was never clear to me to what extent Webern's lifelong association with the Austrian socialist party may have rested on actual political convictions. His background, I suppose, could have been described as *gut bürgerlich*, the same as Schoenberg's, though a little more upper-middle-class. It is interesting how often the seed of far-reaching innovatory change happens to germinate in a social layer characterized by the more typically bourgeois virtues, conservatism, moderation, respect for traditional values, a sense of responsibility, a strong distaste for the wayward and madcap, and all that. Their common bourgeois origin is equally typical of the personalities of innovators like Marx or Lenin. It is as if the combination of conservative temper and exceptional powers of analysis and imagination would generate, in the very tension of opposites, the highest degree of will and vision necessary to bring about a major re-arrangement in any field of human affairs. The point here is that Webern's rootedness in classical working models and modes of thought, far from obscuring his own radicalism, explains it.

Webern's plan, in his lectures, is to show, along historical lines, the emergence of novelty in music; when, how and why things that had not been thought of, said or done before, happen to come about. By tracing the connections between new and old and by pinpointing the change-promoting factors, Webern hopes to underline certain regularities from which something like general laws of change might be deduced. Schoenberg's innovations in particular are considered in this light.

The idea is ambitious but perfectly sound. If the demonstration turns out to be something like a bird's-eye view of a very large subject, one can only regret, once again, that Webern should have been addressing a lay audience; a thoroughgoing inquiry was obviously out of the question. Only landmarks and highlights could be picked out. Even so, the ranks of his listeners seem to have thinned out rapidly, to judge from an ironic aside at the beginning of the fourth lecture.

To my mind a thrilling moment occurs when we reach the year 1908, the date of Schoenberg's piano pieces Op.11. "The times were ripe for the disappearance of tonality."[120] We are familiar with the facts and with the circumstances from which they originated. Less well known is the frame of mind in which these facts were faced when Schoenberg and his disciples first became conscious of their implications. Probably few young composers nowadays have the faintest idea of the anxieties, of the tremendous heart-searching the pioneers went through when matters did come to a head. And no wonder. The new means made available by the breakthrough have come to be taken so much for granted today, that almost any sense of struggle and personal effort in acquiring them has vanished. The young advanced composer now takes to them like a duck to water. They have become part of his genetic equipment. Nor is that all. A similar mutation must have occurred in the professional critic.

It is not easy for us to recapture this state of mind. On the other hand, it helps us to understand Schoenberg's, and of course Webern's, almost exclusive concern with matters of tonal organization. Not that rhythm, dynamics or tone-colour were absent from their preoccupations. Far from it. Colour, to a certain extent, but metre and rhythm in particular (which in Brahms' innovations are still simply concomitants, part and parcel of very personal qualities of style) clearly stand out for the first time in Schoenberg and Webern as factors specifically grasped and used for specific ends. Pitch, nevertheless, is undoubtedly the main concern. Webern's insistence on *Zusammenhang* (coherence, consistency, relatedness) and *Fasslichkeit* (comprehensibility), recurring *leitmotifs* in the lectures, makes it abundantly clear that to him, as indeed to Schoenberg, relatedness depends primarily and overridingly on *tonal* organization. In other words, thematicism is still the sovereign principle; hence, both masters' unwavering allegiance to classical concepts of form-building and, in particular, Webern's predilection for contrapuntal and canonic devices as the most concentrated means for enhancing thematic relatedness.

The passionate resistance to innovation, characteristic of the heroic days, has given way to bland acceptance, tinged at most with gingerly reservations. Daring to face the opprobrium of not being "in the know" – if you are an intelligent person – takes some real integrity. The rank and file critic and rank and file advanced composer alike seem have become "progressive" more by way of conditioning and conforming than as a result of a soul-shaking crisis. Bitter and frustrating as the fight against the recalcitrant critic of old must have been, there can be little doubt which is the more enervating to the creative artist.

Webern has no more than a passing word for the battles fought. But time and again he comes back to the intellectual and affective upheaval which accompanied the decision to discard classical tonality:

> I am speaking to you as one who has lived these things through.
>
> It was a hard struggle; inhibitions of the most terrifying kind had to be overcome; there was an anxious questioning: it that really possible?
>
> As if the light had given out, that's how it struck us."
>
> The style aimed at by Schoenberg and his school is a new interpenetration of the horizontal and the vertical facets, a polyphony that has reached its peaks so far with the Netherlanders and with Bach, and then again with the classics. Always the same endeavour to derive from one main idea the utmost possible. One has got to put it like this, since we are still writing in the forms of the classics. These have not disappeared. What the classics created in the way of highly evolved art forms is still to be found in the new music ... Then let's hold fast to this: we have not gone beyond the forms of the classics. What has come since is simply variation, expansion, reduction – but the forms have stayed – in Schoenberg too.

In his last lecture, Webern says that a twelve-note series is not as a rule (not in general) to be regarded as a *theme*. Indeed, he admits that "thanks to the use of other means for achieving unity, I can also work now without thematicism – that is, much more freely: the series assures me of *Zusammenhang*." The final part of this statement, incidentally, I would be prepared to contradict. However, the point is that with these words tonal organization is once again clearly shown to be conceived as the guarantor not only of *Zusammenhang* but also of the larger-scale notion of *unity* underlying it.

If this be regarded as half the truth, as I think it must, it has also to be stressed that in no way did it preclude Webern the composer from seeing the whole truth and, what is more important, from acting upon it. Indeed, it is mainly through Webern's work that we have been made aware of the high *Zusammenhang*-coefficient inherent in other-than-tonal factors, such as metre (as soon as it ceases to be merely a scanning device), rhythm, span of events, *Gestalt* of eventuation, dynamics (as soon as they cease to be used as subservient to phrasing, and are employed to structural ends instead), and above all motion itself, in its own right, understood specifically in this sense of passage, process, continuity, shift from uniqueness to uniqueness of moment, *corso-ricorso*, and others that would make the list longer still.

It seems to me that the reason why Webern's work has been more seminal than Schoenberg's in these particulars, is that they show in stronger isolation in Webern's music. Though equally present in Schoenberg, they are harder to disentangle from the total integument. The denudation in Webern has the effect of throwing the activity of the new factors into high relief. Thus they appear in a strikingly pure state. Consequently, the whole economy of the work has almost the quality of a demonstration. The miracle – and this is the secret of Webern's alchemy – is how wonderfully this quality blends with the poetic quality of the music.

All the same, the fact that Webern is so neatly analysable should not be underestimated when evaluating his impact on the post-war generation. That Schoenberg's work should have suffered a comparative eclipse as a result, is in the nature of the case. It will only be temporary. No-one would probably have been more amazed at this than Webern himself. What is certain is that nothing could have been more distressing to him than to see his work extolled at the expense of Schoenberg's. Anyone who could have talked of Schoenberg as "dead" would have been received not only with a volley of exclamation marks but also with a memorable rap on the knuckles. If proof is needed, it can be found in the lectures.

24 Twelve-note technique in Stravinsky (1957)[121]

Home is where one starts from. As we grow older
The world becomes stranger, the pattern more complicated
Of dead and living

Old men ought to be explorers

T.S. Eliot, *Four Quartets: East Coker*

That Stravinsky was one day to adopt the method of composition with twelve-note series would have seemed so utterly improbable a generation ago as to be incredible; and yet it has happened. What does it prove? Probably nothing so much as our short-sightedness. The improbable happens every other day; the incredible takes just a little longer. As "contemporaries" we have, perforce, the near-view of contemporary facts and events. Those in which we are one of the terms in a relation, we cannot possibly view from "outside". Strictly speaking, what we grasp is, precisely, the relation; in itself, it is (at least) a third term. It is that which becomes visible only, as we say, in historical perspective.

But we can, of course, compare, The near-view is a grandstand for distinguishing. *Distinguir pour unir.* It is an essential part in the process of understanding. And we can perhaps play it better than posterity: we are, so to speak, better placed. It is the *difference* that sticks out miles for us. What Schoenberg and Stravinsky have *in common* we do not see half so clearly; only distance will bring that out with stronger definition. One day, maybe, the common factors will be seen to outweigh the differential factors so much, that it might well puzzle people then to think that to us, the contemporaries, the work of the two masters offered such a contrast as to suggest almost opposite poles. How could that be? they may well ask. Let us then consign and attest here – if only for the benefit of such a hypothetical enquiry – a view which we know to be partial and short-sighted, because we were too close to the facts: but that is how they appeared to us.

Commenting on the central movements of Stravinsky's *Canticum Sacrum* in his admirable study of the work, Robert Craft says: "Twelve-note series or not, it [the music] is not chromatic."[122] That is exactly the point. There is clearly something of a paradox in this achievement of Stravinsky's, which must intrigue the enquiring mind.

Stravinsky did, of course, use total chromaticism long before he composed with twelve-tone series. Compare, for instance, the *Three Japanese Lyrics* and *Pierrot Lunaire.* Incidentally, I do not think that those who point to these pieces as evidence of an early Schoenbergian influence on Stravinsky are right.

The second piece, with its opening seven-note chord and the "using up" of the twelve notes by the end of the second bar (example 8):

Ex. 8.

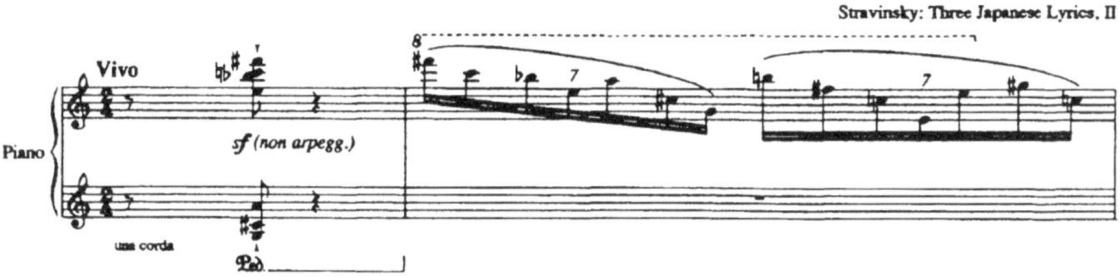

is, for all that, light-years apart from Schoenberg. Stravinsky's seven-note chord is a perfectly straightforward compound of C7 + F# minor. By comparison, a simple triad in *Pierrot Lunaire* is already totally "emancipated". Or take the opening of the third *Japanese Lyric*, with its astonishingly Webernesque two-note motifs (example 9):

Ex. 9.

nonetheless, to the naked, unprejudiced ear, the piece is perfectly tonal. The second is quite as firmly so: as for the first one, that has even got a key-signature!

One remarkable feature of these pieces – whether still clearly heptatonic, though richly inflected (as in the first), or freely dodecaphonic (as in the second and third) is the way in which a steady pole of attraction effectively manages to resist the centrifugal pull characteristic of total chromaticism.

In Stravinsky's coming to terms with – or rather, accepting on his own terms – an idiom which has become established, supra-national *lingua franca*, one is reminded, on a different plane and at a thousand years' distance, of the way Russian chant gradually emerged from the adopted alien Byzantine chant through a similarly tenacious insistence on growing from its own roots and asserting its own nature.

Another remarkable fact that strikes one, when comparing the *Japanese Lyrics* and *Pierrot Lunaire*, is that as early as 1912–13 there should be such firm indications of the divergent paths Stravinsky and Schoenberg were to take later. One realizes that they have never really strayed by the smallest deviation from their respective orbits, even if Stravinsky's is full of twists and turns – rather like Picasso's – which, of course, simply proves that they have had more than one "manner" but not more than one "style", as is sometimes foolishly said.

The first time Schoenberg succeeds in breaking away from the pull of tonality, he characteristically sings "*Ich fühle Luft von anderen Planeten*"[123] – rather as if a barrier had been broken through, a feeling of gravity overcome. For Stravinsky, on the contrary, sound is something almost solid and tangible, something in which he can, as it were, hold fast to *tout ce qui pèse et qui pose*. When he speaks of getting down to work, he speaks, characteristically, of *mêttre la main à la pâte*. The very "breathing" of music consists for him, he says, in the alternate 'drawing together and separation of poles of attraction".

Perhaps most remarkable of all is the fact that the two masters arrive at serial twelve-note music from opposite quarters, having moved from antithetic home-positions by divergent routes. There is a suggestion of inevitability in the result: it brings to mind something almost in the nature of the "curvature of musical space". On the other hand, it goes without saying that one would in any case have expected Stravinsky's twelve-tone technique to be, first and foremost, Stravinsky-an and thus as radically different from Schoenberg's as from the approved modern music particle-scattering manner.

From a technical point of view, the establishment of "poles of attraction" must clearly have been Stravinsky's first concern in the planning of a twelve-tone work. In order to achieve this, he had to take two unorthodox steps which at once created an entirely new situation; first, the restoration of the octave; second, the shifting up a semitone of the natural pivot-point (in the chromatic division of the octave), from the tritone to the perfect fifth. These were far-reaching decisions.

Only the sectarian would quarrel with Stravinsky for restoring the octave in twelve-tone music. Personally, I have always held the octave to be innocent. Its banishment was not strictly fair. Yet it undeniably recommended itself – as things often do in politics – on grounds of expediency. Therefore if and when it ceases to be expedient, there is, I maintain, no reason of principle for continuing to ostracize the octave. In the meantime, of course, the "no octave" rule has become a perfect shibboleth. It can be safely left to the factions.

For Stravinsky's purpose of establishing poles of attraction, the octave would be of little help without the decisive contribution of the fifth. The fifth is the *grounding* interval *par excellence*. The series of *Surge, aquilo* (from the *Canticum*) show how ingeniously Stravinsky has provided for his poles of attraction (Example 10(a)):

Ex. 10(a).

The nodal points of a series (of the double-hexachord variety) are the outer notes of its hexachords, ie 1, 6, and 7, 12. Notice in the present series the chiastic fifth-relations 1–7 and 6–12 across the hexachords, as well as the additional fifths 2–4, 5–8 and 7–9. The structure is positively saturated with quintal feeling.

In this new context it is quite obvious that a piece can no longer be centred on a single tonal point: a fundamental note, a single tonic-dominant axis, or one preponderant, all-resolving home-chord. The very word polarity implies two terms. The truth is that even from Stravinsky's standpoint, the inescapable consequence of Schoenberg's severing of the tonal bonds has been a decisive shift from static to kine-dynamic sound-conception: that is to say, the fundamental, gravid feeling of bass-attraction has given way to a trajectorially thrusting, beyond – itself pointing, 'leading note'-like charge or tension, essentially emancipated from tonal 'gravity'. Naturally to bring a sound-structure back within reach of the tonal pull, the restoration of octave and fifth would not alone be sufficient. It is necessary to establish a true 'polarity'. In *Surge, aquilo* the active poles of attraction are, obviously, the two fifths A flat – E flat and A natural – E natural. There is a constant tug between the two. The arch of the piece is tensed by the opposing attractions. All structural key-points are determined by them. Craft speaks of a "retreat from tonic-dominant tonality" in the present pieces. I agree; but I would argue that in making this retreat, Stravinsky is not scrapping tonality altogether, but, on the contrary, is carrying a modified concept of tonality into twelve-note music.

With regard to serial technique as such, Stravinsky seems to owe more to Webern than to Schoenberg. He favours the linear unfolding of the series into chain-structures, rather than its bending upon itself in order to for ring-structures and establish harmonic fields from within, ie with the series' own intervals (though the opening bar of *Surge, aquilo* provides an instance of the latter procedure). In consequence he usually operates, rather like Webern, with two or more serial orders at a time. They are superposed in the traditional part-writing manner and despite frequent crossings they generally keep strictly to their respective paths. The textural aspect of the whole is therefore predominantly linear.

Structurally, a Stravinsky-an line has not the remotest resemblance to Webern. It is characteristically Stravinsky-an, naturally. Compare, for instance, the initial line of *Surge, aquilo* (example 10(a), above) with the oboe subject of the slow movement of the Symphony of Psalms (example 10(b)) the consanguinity is evident.

Ex. 10(b).

The sole difference is that Stravinsky now writes for the human voice as, in those days, he would only have written for instruments. The length of the phrase, the *ductus*, the preponderance of the *somatic* (seconds) over *pneumatic* (leaps) – to re-employ these telling Byzantine terms – everything is as far removed from Webern as one could think. As for tone-repetition – a factor of crucial importance Stravinsky is positively Italianate where Webern is puritanically non-ornate.

There are two exceptions to the above remark about the various concurrent orders keeping strictly to their own paths. The first (an entirely Stravinsky-an innovation) amounts to a re-emergence of something like the eighteenth century type of *ripieno* part, whose notes in this case pertain (not consistently, but by turns) to any two of the concurrent serial orders. The resulting part has no autonomous standing: Stravinsky uses it as a kind of clasp for the interlocking of the real parts, or else to give stress or relief to particular notes, either for accentual purposes or as an aide to choral intonation (cf. the oboe part, example 11):

Ex. 11.

Stravinsky, Canticum Sacrum, III, 102-4

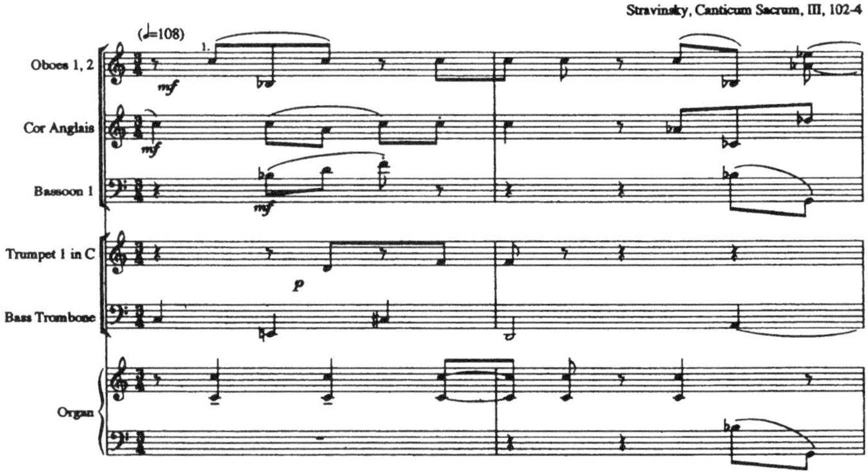

The second exception, again a Stravinsky-an innovation , consists in elements of a given serial order (sometimes up to a full hexachord) occasionally dove-tailing with, or appearing as an inset to, the structure of another order of different pitch or direction (see tenor, example 12(a) and (b) and flute in 12(c)):

Ex. 12(a).

Ex. 12(b).

Ex. 12(c).

The sound-fabric, as already pointed out, is essentially linear. The vertical or harmonic criterion, that is to say, is not strictly serial. The same is, of course, true of Webern's music, where the polyphonic structure is not a function of the serial order but only a result – aleatory to a large extent – of superimposing lines, each one of which unfolds independently the series allocated to it (viz. the String Quartet Op.28). It is a technique that goes back to the sources of medieval polyphony.

Although serially integrated polyphony is less characteristic of Stravinsky's technique, passages of this kind do occur: see, also in *Surge, aquilo*, example 12(b), bars 69-71, and example 13, bars 82 and 85:

Ex. 13.

and especially the opening four bars and the very moving conclusion of Brevis Motus Cantilenae: "*credo, Domine ... adjuva incredulitatem meam*". The last two pages of the *Brevis Motus* reveal a most expressive use of serial technique. Tribute should certainly be paid to the way in which the "unbelief" is symbolized in the last unfolding of the series, five notes of which are caught up in the dissonant chord of the organ, as if in a net, while the double-basses' D, conflicting with the organ's E flat but already confirmed octave-wise by the chord's top-note D, anticipates a "resolution" into a D harmony – harmony which is not simply a major chord, but something far more radiant and tense, embracing as it were the whole "mode" of D major, with its major seventh, its fourth and its fifth, all together above its fundamental. Not the third, you will observe, but only the "perfect" intervals with, in addition, the tensing *leading*-note.

Where Webern and Stravinsky differ again is in the function of the polyphonic parts. Essentially, it is only a question of "range" that defines a Webern bass- or top-line and keeps them in their places. Otherwise a cello and a violin apart, for instance, would be perfectly interchangeable. There is nothing functionally specific about them. With Stravinsky, it is quite another matter: a bass, here is a bass, with its unmistakable Atlas-like stoop; even the descant has a Caryatid erectness, as if supporting an invisible entablature.

From Stravinsky's standpoint there are obvious advantages in a polyphony arising from freely superposed, separable individual lines, as against serially integrated polyphony. On the other hand, he has freedom of choice with regard to the transposition-levels and/or direction of the concurrent serial orders, and on the other hand, considerable elbow-room with regard to the ways in which the superimposed parts can be made to coincide to produce a freely-selected harmony at key points. It is this that specifically assists Stravinsky in controlling his poles of attraction. But it must not be forgotten that he can achieve this control even with parts that are rhythmically committed, as for instance in the fourfold canon of *Ad Virtutes Hortationes*.

For this, the third piece in the *Canticum*, Stravinsky changed his series. It is impossible to discover from the mere printed page why he did so. But we can at least examine the relationship between the series. Craft has pointed out that "the last four notes [of the new series] are the second to fifth notes of the *Surge, aquilo* series in reverse; two of the other intervals are the same notes, and the first and last intervals are minor and major intervals in both".

If we compare the two series in their respective underlying hexachord-pairs, we find that one single operation at the hexachordal home-level is all that is required in order to obtain the second from the first (example 14):

Ex. 14.

One single note changes place: the E flat which was 12 in the first set becomes 2 in the second. Naturally, I am not suggesting that this is how Stravinsky did, in fact, relate his two sets. Of course not. That is how the analytical mind works, not the creative mind. Nonetheless, the objectivity of the connection, as shown between the home-sets, remains a fact. What, in actual working practice, could have sparked off the mutation might have been something rather like the following situation, imagined as presenting itself in the serial chart used by the composer (example 15):

Ex. 15.

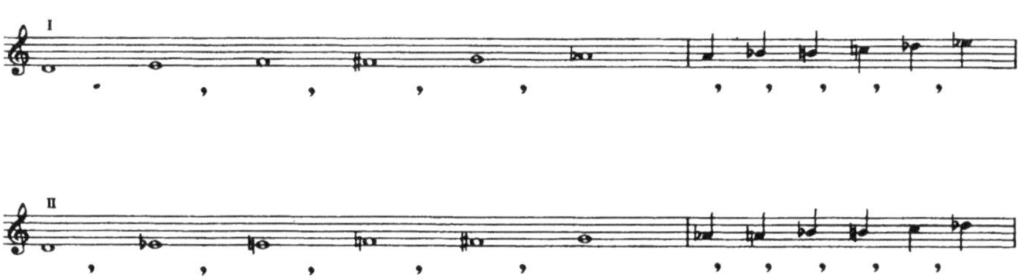

Two contiguous transpositions of the *Surge, aquilo* series show how the *Ad Virtutes* series (indicated by the figures, but reading from back to front) is deducible from its predecessor. It should be noted that both cases show the initial levels at which Stravinsky actually takes the series. Again, I am not suggesting that this is how Stravinsky actually did arrive at the *Ad Virtutes* series, but it is at least a possibility. In any case, example 16 seems to me to throw additional light on the objective relationship between the two series.

Ex. 16(a).

Ex. 16(b).

That Stravinsky's twelve-tone music does not strike us as chromatic may perhaps have more to do, finally, with spiritual climate than with syntax. It is also possibly a question of mood rather than of emotion. Moods are sustained feelings; rather like the weather on a certain day, with that particular look of the sky, that particular quality of light. The mood is, perhaps, in the *sustaining*. Mood and mode would have that in common; the holding on, evenly to that particular temper of time, for a time. For, obviously, when feeling is unstable, restless, veering, the mood has gone. "Undisciplined squads of emotion" are on the march. Chromaticism seems to start from the brooding mood, suggesting the furrowed brow, conflict, suffering. Whereas we seem naturally to connect a certain (far from unfeeling) impassivity, a certain sense of poise and permanence with diatonicism. Diatonicism is the home of the modes.

In the last analysis, the fascination of the Stravinsky-an paradox – non-chromatic twelve-tone music – lies perhaps in the fusion of opposites he achieves. He write twelve-tone music in the *spirit* of diatonicism and diatonic music with a full experience of total chromaticism. No word has been said here of the *music*, but that needs no apology, I think; words only stand in the way.

1 Gerhard with Pedrell, 1921, beneath a portrait of Pedrell as a young man.

2 From left to right: Gerhard, Schoenberg and Webern in Barcelona, Summer 1931.

3 Gerhard in his study in Barcelona, 1934.

4 Roberto Gerhard in Cambridge, c.1947. With the score of "The Duenna" on the piano.

5 Poldi and Roberto Gerhard, c.1952.

6 Gerhard acknowledging the applause after the première of First Symphony, Baden-Baden, 1955 (conductor Hans Rosband).

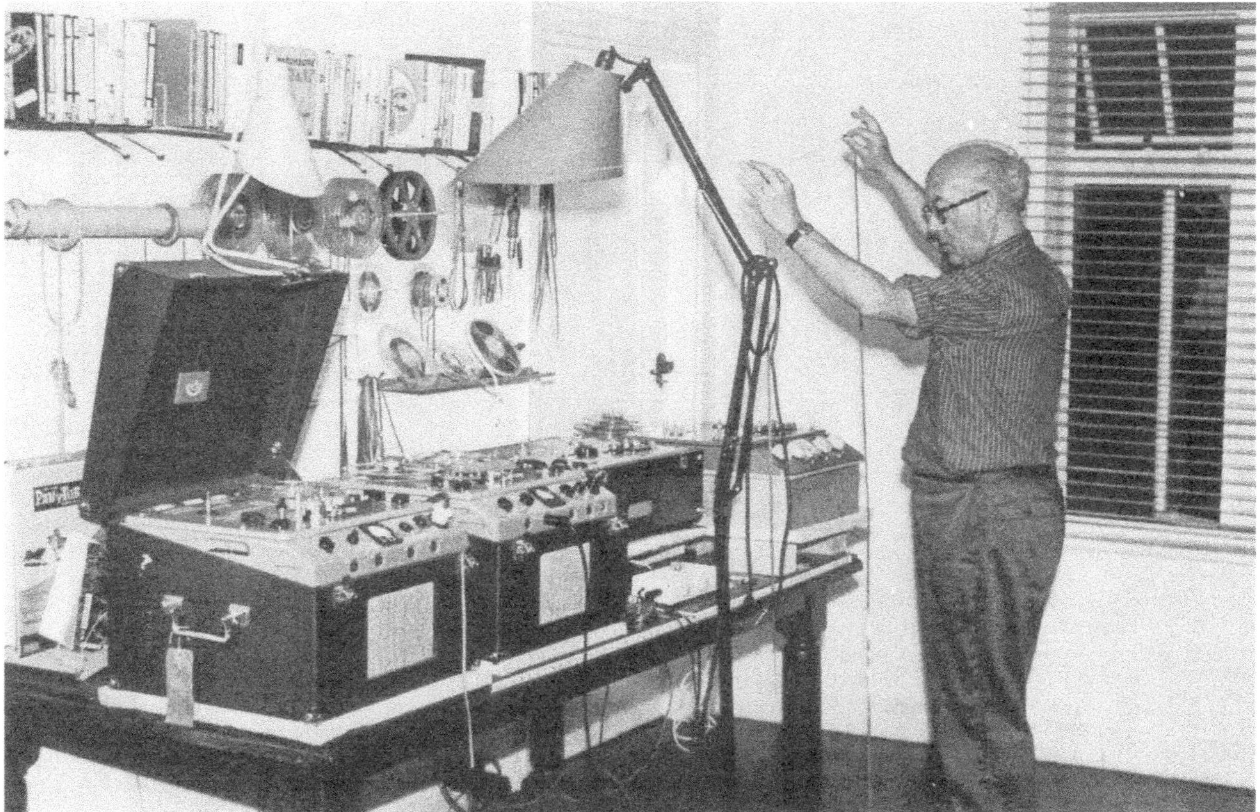

7 Gerhard in his studio at home, c.1955.

8 Roberto Gerhard with Elliott Carter in Dartington, 1956.

9 Gerhard, with Aaron Copland (far right), and their pupils, Ben-Zion Orgad, Jan Bach and Roger Reynolds.

10 Gerhard with Robin Orr after receiving an Honorary Doctorate at Cambridge University, 1968.

25 Functions of the series in twelve-note composition (1960)[124]

The functions of the series in twelve-note composition have become so numerous and diversified in recent compositional practice that they can only be covered to a limited extent here. The two principal dimensions in the world of sound and in musical experience are pitch and time (or duration). The functions of the series apply to both fields. Pitch-organization and temporal organization need, of course, to be co-ordinated: and it's co-ordination of the two and the nature of the problems that arise from this that I want to discuss. In other words, I am chiefly concerned with *process in time*, with how things happen in the temporal dimension, with the way in which music "eventuates". This means that I'm not going to deal in any detail – or more than is necessary for argument's sake – with questions of pitch-structural organization. My discussion will, I have to say, appear a bit obscure to anyone without a thorough grounding in the techniques of Schoenbergian *ars combinatoria*.

It is undeniable, I think, that the more interesting and promising compositional developments that have taken place after Schoenberg and Webern have occurred in the field of temporal organization: and this will be my main focus, that is the bearing of the serial functions on *time*. I speak not, of course, as a detached observer but as a worker in the field with something personal at stake. To do so reduces the scope of my subject, though by the same token, it brings it into even sharper focus.

In a nutshell, I propose to describe mainly what I do myself! I make no apology for this. I think the artist *should* talk in terms of his own work. You are likely to get more out of his peculiarities than from his generalizations. Let's face it, we *are* egotists, after all; and that celebrated definition of an actor as "a guy who, when you ain't talking about him, he ain't proper listening" applies *mutatis mutandis,* to the composer; when he's not talking about himself he's rarely worth listening to.

In Schoenberg's method of composition with twelve notes the basic concept is, as you know, the series. A simple definition of the series is: the arrangement of the twelve notes of our chromatic scale in any one sequential order, out of the number of such arrangements possible. (The total number is, as you know, a factorial of twelve, ie something of the order of 500 million.) How to discriminate in this astronomical mass, how to find criteria for making one's choices among the possible series, is the object of an entirely separate study. We may safely ignore the matter here. Any one sequential order of the twelve notes (where none can, of course, appear twice) qualifies as a series. We adopt one and only one. (Incidentally, Schoenberg regarded it as unmethodical to have two different series operating in the same work, and he was critical of Berg in this respect. Plurality obviously infringes here one of the fundamental methodological principles – one that will, no doubt, be familiar to you under the name of Occam's razor.)[125]

Consider, then, example 17:

Ex. 17.

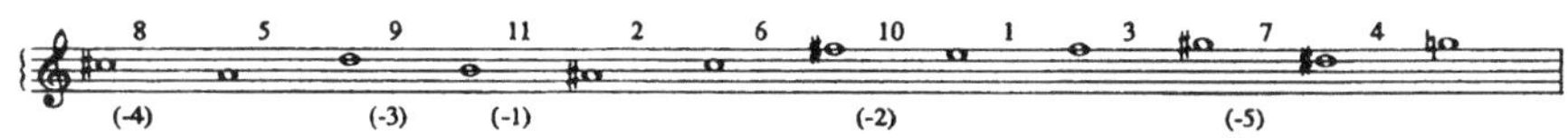

Disregard for the moment the figures and consider the pitch sequence only. Seen in this light, the series is an abstract symbolic structure, it is a code with a fantastically high number of combinatorial possibilities. Operated with the Schoenbergian technique of manipulation with which you are familiar, it becomes the basis or the matrix for a whole composition.

So far we have not yet left the domain of pitch. Our series consists of twelve differently pitched notes, in this precise order of succession, nothing more. There is, above all, no temporal determination. Or more exactly: the series tells us simply the *before* and *after* relation with regard to any note, but not how long, or how brief this (or any) note is to be. In other words, the whole field of temporal relations is left indeterminate in the Schoenbergian construct. Schoenberg and Webern, as you know, didn't go beyond that. Rhythm and form-articulation were handled freely, intuitively. Regulating factors were, so to speak, imported, imposed from without. They did not emanate from the idea of the series. But what is far more important – and, as far as I am aware, has been entirely overlooked in more recent developments – there is another, deeper-seated instance of indeterminacy in the very constitution of the twelve-note series. The Schoenbergian construct lacks also determination with regard to *position* of the notes in the scale of frequencies; in other words, it gives us *relative* not *absolute* pitch. The precise octave-location of the notes is not prescribed. This octave-location is optional by definition. We are at liberty to take any note at any octave transposition we choose, up or down.

The full implications of this condition of indeterminacy do not seem to have been generally grasped – hence my first important point. To make two things, or more, interchangeable *ad lib*, obviously implies that the interchangeable items are regarded as practically identical for the purpose in question, or so near identical as makes no difference. But this is, of course, not quite so in our case. There is no such identity between a note and any of its octave replicas with which we are at liberty to swop it. True, there is the simplest possible ratio between the frequencies of two notes at octaves or double octaves etc but that is not tantamount with identity, far from it. Take, for example, a D natural on the clarinet at different octaves, and compare the notes for sheer physical effect, say, for timbre (which is physically bound up with *absolute* pitch) or for loudness (which is often largely dependent on it) it is perfectly clear that nothing could be further from identity. Physically, acoustically, these notes are, in effect, as dissimilar as could be. And yet, Schoenberg was absolutely right in deciding that a note should be interchangeable with any of its octave replicas *as if* a relation of identity did in fact obtain. This was a momentous decision: one which it takes not a geometer, but an artist, to make. In effect, the Schoenbergian licence makes all the difference in the world; in the first place it alone and by itself establishes the vital *Lebensraum*, the necessary space for manoeuvre without which the method could *not* have been viable. (Incidentally, Josef Mathias Hauer, who clings rigidly to fixed octave-location in his so-called *Tongeschlechter*, seems to have failed to grasp this point, and this is probably what accounts for the sterility of his method.[126]) The latitude, the elbow-room gained through the freedom of octave-transposition is, evidently, the crux of the matter.

Bearing in mind, then, that the two most salient characteristics of the Schoenbergian series are, so to speak, conspicuous by their absence, I mean to say that, for all notes, both the character of *position* and the character of *duration* are lacking, we can perhaps attempt now a closer definition of what the series really stands for. I suggest that in the restricted purely *tonal* aspect, as proposed by Schoenberg, it is essentially an operational code; by virtue of its indeterminacy with regard to *absolute* pitch it virtually throws open the entire auditory range and commands it everywhere, both as far as single pitch-track is concerned as well as with regard to harmonic field. From the serial point of view (as different from that of traditional harmonic tonality), the *harmonic field* could now simply be defined as the possibility of two or more notes appearing jointly and simultaneously, instead of *seriatim*.

It takes only a moment's reflection to realize how intolerably cramped things could become in the harmonic space *without* the latitude of octave-transposition. And *latitude* is, indeed, almost literally the operative word. Take it in its geographic connotation and you'll see that it makes a very good designation for "tonal domain", in the sense of embracing both pitch-track and harmonic field.

Let's now pass from latitude to longitude, as it were, that is to say from pitch to duration. Schoenberg taught us how to order pitch-relations serially. We now want to order durations by the serial principle. In its widest implications this comprises, of course, the complete rhythmical and structural articulation of a piece of music, since both rhythm and structure only exist for us in the time dimension. But for the moment all I am concerned with is to find how the series can assume the function of steering the course of musical events in the field of time. The answer is not obvious. I have been at pains to stress that originally the series was nothing but *tonal* construct and that it possesses no temporal determinant whatever. How then is it going to rule time?

The attempt to co-ordinate pitch and time serially is faced with a number of obvious difficulties. Some composers started with the idea of adopting, together with the twelve-note series, a companion series consisting of twelve different duration values. These would be based on a duodecimal scale of durations. The actual chronometrical value of the basic unit, the rung of the ladder or what you might call the "time-semitones", could vary, of course, according to the general speed-character desired for a piece of music or, simply, for convenience of notation. In other words, your basic unit could be a demisemiquaver, a semiquaver, a quaver or whatever you like. The only requirement is that it should be constant. This duodecimal scale of durations would allow for the co-ordination of pitch and time.

Time-intervals could be measured, like pitch-intervals, in multiples of the basic unit. The duration span of, say, a "time"-second, would be twice as long as your basic unit, your "time"-fifth seven times as long (just as seven is the number of semitones that go into the pitch interval of a fifth) and so on. So far so good. The next step would be to fix the serial order of succession of the twelve different duration values. Many composers seem to have thought that any one order would do, provided that one did stick to it, as Schoenberg had done with the tonal series. I don't think the matter is terribly important, but since there is a simple way of deriving the sequence from the given tone-series, namely quantitatively, ie by multiples of the semitone unit, I personally find it more consistent to do so.

Supposing we had chosen the following sequence:

7, 3, 8, 2, 12, 1, 5, 6, 9, 10, 4, 11

These figures go with a pitch series (example 18):

Ex. 18.

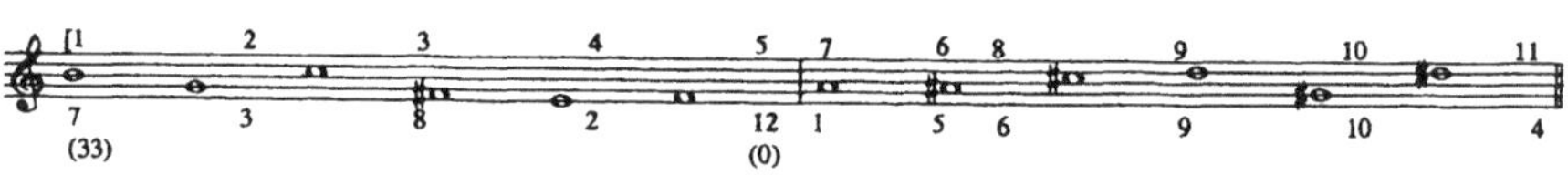

They are magnitudes (undefined as yet) but corresponding to the semitone values of the pitch intervals, as measured from the note E, which is taken both as 0 and, in its octave replica, as twelve; twelve being the number of semitones that go into an octave. Suppose we define now our standard unit of duration as, say, a semiquaver. That would be a relative, not an absolute time-definition (since the latter would require a metronome figure for the standard semiquaver); but that corresponds exactly, so far, to the relative pitch values in the Schoenberg tonal set. With our adopted standard unit equal to a semiquaver we can write our duration series in metrical notation, and this will result in the pattern which you've got on the top stave of example 18. You can also have the equivalent of a retrograde by writing the pattern back to front, as shown on bottom stave of example 18.

Every experienced composer can see at one glance what a scope for rhythmical combination these two patterns afford. They can be broken up into a number of segments of varying size; some of these could be repeated *ad lib*, for iterative rhythmical effect; two or more segments could be superposed, or the two complete patterns, straight and retrograde, could be run together or played, segment-wise, against one another, and so forth. The combinatorial possibilities are far from exhausted in this brief enumeration. Obviously, even with these two patterns alone and without bothering about third and fourth derivations in the form of "mirrors" (which, with a little ingenuity, you could derive from the two right-side-up patterns). the prospects for rhythmical invention are not unpromising. (Incidentally, this idea of shaking an upside-down pattern out of the right-side-up one is not without its *Alice in Wonderland* touch, considering that what is thus being manipulated is, in fact, *time*.)

We now have two constructs, the tonal series and the duration series, ie the series of twelve different notes and the series of twelve different durations. What can be said in favour of this time-set and its co-ordination with the pitch-set is this: it sacrifices theoretical niceties to practical operational advantages. I shall come back to this in a moment. But let's admit for the present that the two sets, fitted together with the purpose of managing pitch and rhythm hand in hand, as one operation, represent a workable proposition.

What are, now, the criticisms? I'll give you two, first Stockhausen's and then my own. To begin with, Stockhausen shows[127] that the duodecimal scale of durations is not what it seems. I spoke of a standard unit for measuring durations, equating it metaphorically with a "time semitone"; consequently, the time-interval of, say, a major second would be worth twice the standard unit, that is, twice as long. But that is not correct, Stockhausen says.

The increase from one "time semitone" to two does not result in a "time second" but in a "time octave"; in effect, twice as much as the ratio 2:1, and that is the ratio of the octave. Consequently, the ratio of a temporal interval of the magnitude of a second is 8:9 or 9:10. The implications of this objection are obvious. It means that the proposed duodecimal time-scale is neither a "chromatic" scale of durations (as the metaphorical notion of a "time-semitone" implied or, indeed, the very model of the twelve-note scale which it tried to reproduce in terms of duration), nor is it a genuine *scale* at all, for the simple reason that the arithmetical progression 1, 2, 3, 4 etc up to 12 is not a scale but the so-called *harmonic* series.

The question Stockhausen asks now is: what is, then, a true chromatic scale of durations, what ought it to look like? He attacks the problem *in toto*, in a generous sweep. Not content with one set of twelve single degrees of length or duration, he considers the complete scale which will cover the entire range of perceptible changes in duration values. To this end he uses the image of a piano, or rather a keyboard, of durations with a span of about seven time-octaves. If the lowest octave did span, say, eight seconds of the clock, then the next higher octave would span four, the next two and so on, with the highest spanning $^1/_{16}$ of a clock second. The twelve degrees within any one octave, the rungs of the ladder, as it were, are not an arithmetic series, an additive one, two, three, four, etc of basic units, but a logarithmic series, where the value of each step or rung – literally, in this case, the "time semitones" – is, as you know....

Unfortunately, our system of notation does not dispose of the variety of symbols that would be required for the adequate expression of such a scale in conventional number values. It is possible, however, to indicate such values quite accurately in terms of metronomical figures. Take, for example, an octave pitched between, say, one clock second and half a second: that means that our scale of durations will start at the metronome figure of 60 and reach to 120 with the upper octave; the actual chromatic scale of durations will thus run at the Metronome figures of 60 – 63.6 – 67.4 – 71.4 – 75.6 and so on, up to 120 for the octave.

While this is theoretically unobjectionable, the measurement of durations by shifting metronome-markings is not much of a practical proposition. Nevertheless, let's waive this consideration for a moment and suppose that, by some means or other (not too difficult, really, with tape, for example), such a scale of durations become practically manageable. What would we do with it? And with this question-mark I am echoing Stockhausen himself at this point, in the course of an argument. *Was fangt man damit an?* he asks. What does one do with such a scale? It is an awkward question, let's face it. Why should it arise at all? Could it be that we have here come up against that type of difficulty which is always liable to creep in when a system – designed on a logical basis – is being imposed from outside, as opposed to an *evolved* system that has been growing from within. One is reminded of Claude Bernard's reply to the question: how does a scientist come to make one of those important discoveries which we call "a stroke of genius"? "Quite simple", he said, "First, he makes the discovery, then he starts thinking hard: how would I have to set about *in order* to make it?" The lesson of this is one that can never be *too* greatly stressed for my liking. It teaches us that understanding is a second stage. First comes origination – *deinde philosophari.*

Stockhausen, is not, of course, at a loss for an answer. The object of his chromatic time-scale is quite clear in his mind: it is the means, and the only means, of achieving direct proportionality between pitch and time. And direct proportionality is, according to him, indispensable for the coordination of the two dimensions serially.

This is where I part company with Stockhausen. I'll give you my reasons in a moment. But let me take up at once the *quid pro quo* we left behind, just in order to stress one point which may help to clarify matters.

The whole argument against the harmonic and in favour of a logarithmic series as the proper basis for a time-scale must be rejected on two counts, I think; first, it is not consistent with writing music for traditional instruments, ie it's not consistent with handling sound produced in the ordinary acoustico-instrumental way, as different from synthetically produced sound, by electronic means (but more of that later); and secondly, it rests on an obvious fallacy which I want to deal with at once. It is true that we perceive pitch relations proportionally: we hear pitch-intervals as proportions and not as differences; but the reverse is true of time-relations. We do not perceive durations proportionally, we do measure them quantitatively. That's as plain as a pike-staff. Before we know what a given duration *is*, or rather, *was*. we must have had it.

In other words, the apprehension of time-relations is Janus-faced, it must look ahead, in order to catch the emergence, the beginning of the time-span in question, and backwards in order to watch for its end. Then, and only then, do we know what it was. There is obviously no other way at all of evaluating durations. We add up duration quantitatively by the ticks of a more or less conscious mental pulse. We either multiply a controllable constant quantum for fairly long time-spans or else we subdivide a longish duration into easily controllable small quanta, guided by the regular tick or pulse of the counting beat.

Compare again the two ways of evaluating pitch and time intervals. With his keyboard of durations Stockhausen presumably means that by depressing a key, the piano would give you, not a note, but a certain duration (by some buzzing, I suppose: of course, with a computing mechanism it could, no doubt, indicate accurate metronomic figures as well). If we depress a second key, just one octave above the first, it will buzz exactly half as long. Let's compare the two buzzings:

bzzz	bz	bzzz	bz	bzzz	bz
1234	12	1234	12	1234	12

– that's easy. But how do I get the respective durations truly right? Quite simply, by mentally counting four ticks to the first and two to the second. It's almost as easy as appreciating the corresponding pitch-interval of the octave (which is also 2:1) except, of course, that I've got to *count* the ticks fairly evenly.

But do please notice this difference: if I play you an octave on an ordinary piano, most of you, I'm sure, will instantly identify my first note: A; ie you don't have to wait a full second and count exactly 440 cycles in order to know that you are in fact hearing central A; and the upper octave will be identified in a flash as a 2:1 proportion, without your having to find out first that it does in fact vibrate at a rate of 880 per second. But what is more, far less simple relations such as, say, 9:10 or 15:16 will be identified with the same ease by the ear and quite as fast; whereas the difference in terms of duration between 9 and 10 or between 15 and 16 is almost undetectable.

In other words, if I play you these six notes (example 18, above), every musician with a good ear will recognize, literally in a flash, and almost as quickly as I can play them, the first half of my pitch series: whereas I'm prepared to accept a wager from anyone who will say that he's able to identify correctly the relative values of the two different beats I'm going to give you, in metronomic figures: 0 54 0 60; I'll tell you, the markings were 54 for the first and 60 for the second; the time-proportion consequently is as 9:10, and that, as you know, is exactly the proportion of as simple a pitch-interval as the major second.

My point is that the idea that you can play about with time-relations just in the same way that you can with pitch-relations and apprehend direct proportionality between the two is a complete fallacy. In the first place, it is entirely beyond the skill of any human performer to string together a series of durations that would reflect, even with a moderate degree of approximation, the interval proportions of a pitch series. And even if it were done by a machine (with time on tape, as it were) you can easily imagine what the result would be: a rhythmic mush, by no means a series of clearly apprehensible proportions. The reason for this is very simple: whereas the ear is fantastically nimble in the domain of pitch, it must be admitted that it is unbelievably primitive and undeveloped in apprehending time.

Pitch is apprehended proportionally almost qualitatively, you might say – since it "speaks" with the immediacy of sensory impressions, almost like seeing blue, red or green; whereas durations, as we've seen, have got to be *lived through* and totted up, quantitatively as we go. The fact is that after seven centuries – to speak only of Western music – we are still exactly where Franco of Cologne left the matter of ordering mensural values. We are quite at home, that is to say, only in the simplest time-relations such as 1:2, 2:3 and 3:4 and that's the end of it. You realize that these are precisely the first relations in the harmonic series.

In other words, we have not yet got to the relation 4:5, corresponding in the harmonic series to the pitch interval of the major third. You will remember how long it took for musicians to accept the third as a fairly consonant interval. Rhythmically, therefore, we are still dealing exclusively with time-octaves, fifths and fourths, in other words, we haven't yet got to apprehend the third in the time-dimension. The relation 4:5 seems indeed to be a limit in the field of durations. I call it the quinary barrier. Whether we shall ever be able to break through is another matter.

* * *

I owe you the promised criticism of our first time-set, as shown in example 18 (above), which I skipped in order to deal with the Stockhausen *quid pro quo*, because I felt that it had logical priority in the course of my argument.

To put it in a nutshell, my criticism of the time-scheme of example 18 is that what it offers is a pattern, not a principle. Look at the Schoenbergian twelve-note series of example 18 and compare the two. We defined example 17 as an abstract symbolic structure. We saw that it is more relevantly characterized by its blanks than by its ostensible attributes; in other words, that the crux of the matter is what I called its condition of *indeterminacy*. This is the condition which makes the Schoenbergian construct a "storehouse of potentiality", so to speak. If that seems too abstract a notion to you, you are welcome to think of it in terms (for instance) of a cage containing a few million cats. The indeterminacy consists of not knowing which one particular cat will come out *and* which way it's going to jump. Whereas with the set of example 18, we *do* know; the cat has jumped just that way; nothing remains indeterminate any longer. It is, in our case, a fully determinate distribution of time quanta; in other words, a rhythmic pattern. It *is* a pattern and cannot be called a series at all, in the sense in which I'm using the notion here. The two are obviously not on a par. Series, in my sense of the notion, represents a code for channelling and steering *process*. Pattern is the outcome of process, one result, this one particular result. I conclude, therefore, that this is not what we are looking for.

Exactly the same criticism applies also to Stockhausen's project; in the last resort it too turns out to be nothing but pattern. I argued previously against a scale of durations based on a logarithmic series, as proposed by him. I now want to point out two rather unexpected consequences which the adoption of his scheme would involve. Example 19 shows the series given by Stockhausen in the essay of his to which my remarks refer:

Ex. 19.

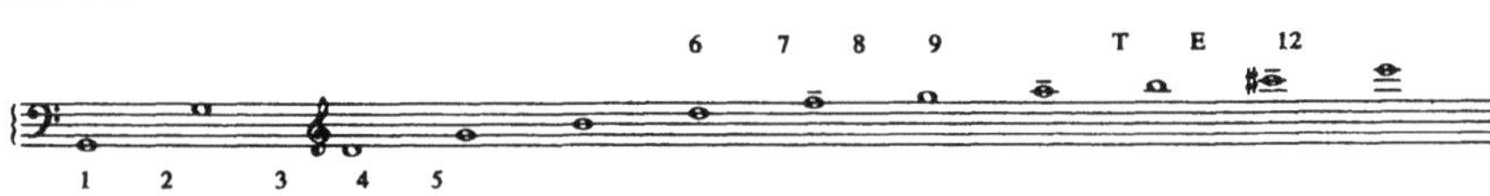

The figures on top of the notes, or below, are my own analysis of the series' interval structure; they indicate the number of semitones for each interval: there are descending and ascending intervals. In my analysis, they are homologized in the ascending scale: so, the descending intervals (which a minus number of semitones in brackets) are counted by inversion as ascending intervals, indicated as a plus number of semitones. Now, if you examine example 19 closely you'll discover that the series contains all the different intervals *but one f*. The exception, the missing interval, is the octave. There are, therefore, only eleven intervals, in fact. (There are, of course, only eleven intervals between twelve notes, just as there are only four intervals between five fingers.) But the question is: are we then offered a system that will be based on a scale of twelve differently pitched notes, but on a scale of only eleven different durations? Will it be, you might say, not dodecatonic, but endecarhythmic?

I'm not quite sure how it is meant. The case is ambiguous in more ways than one. However, it's quite obvious that the very notion of direct proportionality between pitch-set and time-set cannot begin to be entertained except on the basis of some such one-to-one correspondence between pitch intervals and time intervals on the model of the Stockhausen series.

Unfortunately, it is a fact that not *every* twelve-note series would qualify for such a purpose. In effect, not every twelve-note series does contain eleven different intervals. A series which does is called an "all-interval series". How many different serial arrangements can in fact result in all-interval series, I do not know; a mathematician could easily work it out for us, I'm sure. But we *do* know that the all-interval series constitute only *one* class among the various classes of series, each exhibiting its own class-characteristics. Now, direct proportionality being, of necessity, committed to all-interval series, it is clear that it must discard all other types. This means that an astronomical number of series as are perfectly workable in every other respect would be of no use to Stockhausen. For example, most of the series Schoenberg or Webern ever used would have to be rejected on such grounds. Webern, in particular, showed a marked predilection for series with rather little interval variety. The axing that would result from the Stockhausen discrimination would be on a truly formidable scale; a whole subcontinent of the serial world would have to be condemned.

But that is not all. On the premise of direct proportionality, the disappearance of the pitch octave entails, of course, the suppression of the time-octave. What would that practically mean? It would mean abolishing the ratio 2:1 or 1:2. It is, as you know, the first ratio we encounter in the harmonic series 2:1 (or 1:2) and is, in effect, the rock bottom of auditory time-evaluation. With the time-octave, therefore, binary division altogether would vanish from time relations; our division of breve into two minims, four crotchets, eight quavers, sixteen semiquavers etc would become meaningless and would have to be scrapped.

Now this restriction, as you realize, would be even more fantastic than the previous one. It could properly be compared to a pneumo-thorax operation; it would leave music literally breathing with one lung only. I'm not saying that Stockhausen is in fact advocating such restrictions in so many words. That is not the case. Simply, nothing is said about them. Whether the matter is just ignored or possibly overlooked is not clear. What I maintain is that the restrictive results I've pointed out are logically inescapable consequences of the premise of direct proportionality. I contend that it *cannot* lead to meaningful co-ordination of pitch-structural and time-structural organization; on the contrary, it must needs lead to *subordination* of time to pitch. Clearly, by hooking duration intervals directly onto pitch-intervals, pitch is allowed to predetermine duration. That leads straight, once again, to patterns of the type shown in example 18, and misses entirely the point of the Schoenbergian idea of the series.

In my opinion, the thing we've got to match in a time-set is, precisely, the condition of indeterminacy which is the hub of the whole serial idea and by virtue of which the set becomes a storehouse of potentiality for rhythmic invention, instead of remaining just a pattern. The problem, as I see it, is to make integration and interdependence compatible with a positive measure of autonomy in each field. The ear is obviously not *equally* at home in both, therefore the fundamental demand is for a specific treatment in each.

This is one reason why, personally, I'm not at all worried by the contradiction (pointed out by Stockhausen) arising out of the fact that, on the one hand, our method of composition with twelve notes rests on a radically chromatic basis while, on the other hand, the very physical constitution of our sound-material (the sound-spectrum) *and* our spontaneous auditive evaluation of time-relations are both fundamentally harmonic. Another reason is that the contradiction is historically given. This is a state of affairs that is not of our making, we have found it so and, in my opinion, it has simply got to be accepted as a *donné réelle*. Otherwise, Stockhausen himself, in order to be consistent, would have to give up writing for ordinary instruments or the human voice and restrict himself to the possibilities offered by the electronic studio; he doesn't, I'm glad to say. It seems to me that we must be content to make the best of two unequal worlds; that, I'm afraid, is all the consistency we *can* afford.

My approach to the serial co-ordination of pitch and time has one thing in common with the scheme of example 18, namely the idea of framing a time-set in numbers. Take, for example, the numeral series we've got there:

7,3,8,2,12,1, / 5,6,9,10,4,11

But now, instead of assigning these numbers definite duration values (which would immediately tie me down to the one fully determined pattern, as we saw with example 18), I leave the matter open for the moment, and start working from the very opposite end, ie I start at the highest level of generality and then proceed in the direction of more and more defined specifications, so that the final commitment as to definite durations for the actual pitch-track (or rhythmic invention) is a decision left to the actual moment of composition, exactly as happens with the determination of absolute pitch in the Schoenberg series. In general terms, what we expect from a time-set are a number of temporal specifications of various orders.

What is the most general specification of time we can give for a piece of music? The answer is, obviously, the overall length of the piece, the total duration, the real playing-time, as we say. Granted, you may say, but how much use is such a specification to us? Well, banal though the answer may seem, especially in its first part, I would say that (a) when you are composing music in a professional capacity, say, on commission, you'll find that timing (both overall timing and sectional or cue-timing) is given to you in a sheet of specifications you're generally expected to observe pretty accurately, sometimes down to the split second; and (b) that even when you're writing a symphony (where you're supposed to be your own boss and absolute master of your time) the temporal factor – though you may never have thought of it in this connection when studying sonata-form, for example – is the crucial factor, precisely where form is concerned.

It is evident that form – no matter in what medium, and whether we think in terms of shape, or *Gestalt*, *morphe* (to use the apt neologism proposed by the mathematician Hermann Weyl) – must always have a basis of measurement specifications. For us musicians, they are, of course, primarily measurements in time or durations. (Incidentally, I ought perhaps to make it clear that the whole time I'm talking of the *time* of the physicists, ie clock-time or Astronomer Royal time, if you like; I'm not talking now of experiential or virtual time; I'm not concerned with this aspect of time here, and I'm only anxious that the two should not be mixed up.)

It is perhaps not quite so easy in music as it is in the visual arts to grasp to what extent form depends for us too on measurement. Take a beautiful vase, for example, and start fiddling about with the proportion of two main measurements only, say, height and width (altering them as reflecting the vase in a convex of concave mirror would) and you'll see how, by tampering with the proportion, you make the image of the vase pass from an elegant, slender, graceful object into a clumsy, bulgy, paunchy one, or vice versa. Proportion, you see, is the balance of what we call the "vital statistics". What we mean by *shapeliness* clearly depends upon the ratio of the critical measurements. And this is, of course, universally valid, not only in the visual orbit.

The difficulty in music is that most people (including, I'm afraid, a fair proportion of professional musicians) are able mentally to encompass a span of perhaps ten to 15 clock seconds (what psychologists call the "specious present") and rarely much more than that. Listening to music seems to be for many people a manner of creeping along the time track from phrase to phrase, putting out rather shortish feelers that can't really feel a very long way ahead or see round corners and, on the other hand, letting most of the music vanish, almost as fast as it passes, as the landscape vanishes past the carriage window on a train-journey. That is, of course, musical listening of rather poor quality; it does seem to explain, though, why the very idea of musical form, of time-proportions is so foggy and seems so abstract, so insubstantial to listeners with rather short memories.

But it also helps to explain why the idea of musical form is confused in the minds of many composers with simple stereotyped formulas – a-b-a sonata form, rondo form, or what have you – which are really nothing but constructive schemata, conventional lines of assembly or arrangements for purposes of presentation. Looked at in this way, form is but a mould into which you pour something, a carcass which you stuff, not – as it should be – a driving, shaping power which creates its own harmonious or clashing proportions ever anew in the very flow of origination. The whole dichotomy of form-content is unfortunate, I think, and (in music, at least) inevitably misleading. The moment you envisage form as a *thing*, it means that you are really handling formulae, clichés. Even language seems to suggest that "form" is an abstract which we can only see embodied in performance, and that is unique, every time, as we know.

Now, for the driving and shaping power to be able in music to act freely and steer clear-sightedly the most favourable, the most telling course, the mind must be able to encompass much larger spans of time, and these time-spans must be more than cold measurements on paper, they must be felt, weighed, experienced, actually lived through and grasped as one, in their total trajectorial thrust, with an acute awareness of the kinetic and energetic stresses involved, feeling exactly where the line perhaps goes limp, or where it threatens to overshoot the mark.

This is a feeling that can only begin to "speak" when your way of encompassing time is such that you can truly say that you are grasping it in that peculiar state where your past *is* in your present *and* in your future, and where your future *was* always present in your past and (needless to say) *is* influencing the here-and-now, deciding really where, and why and in which way, things do fall into place as we go. How that really works is not always clearly understood, though.

When, for instance, E.M. Forster writes of form apprehension of "the Fifth Symphony as a whole", "where", he writes, "when the orchestra stops, we hear something that has never actually been played ... The opening movement, the *Andante*, and the Scherzo-trio-scherzo-trio-finale that compose the third block, all enter the mind at once and extend one another into a common entity",[128] it seems to me that the distinguished novelist is indulging in wishful thinking. For mortal man to achieve this sort of synoptic apprehension of a symphony he would have to place himself *au point de vue des dieux*, as Valéry would say, and the indispensable first requirement would be that "time must have a stop".

In my opinion, the notion of such instantaneous encompassing of large spans of time as one single act of synoptic vision, as you might call it, is a pure figment. The real thing is much more like television. The mind scans the span, swiftly and continuously and thus achieves the *illusion* of simultaneity. But that's good enough; more would probably be fatal. It's clear that the very idea of things falling into place in the course of a process of growth or development, implies of necessity such a conjugation and reciprocal influencing of the *tenses* as I mentioned before.

The present is what it is, not only in consequence of what happened before, but in function of what I am aspiring to, and this aspirational pull must, of course, have been present from the very beginning, indeed, before the very word – go! ... how else could I possibly have made up my mind on *how* to start?

To come back to the idea of proportion which, as you see, is the key-concept in the matter of form, I want to explain and show you how I use the number-series as a timing device. To this end I must introduce here a new notion which I shall call a "time-aggregate". You know what we mean in dodecatonic parlance by the "hexachord": it is the projection of six notes – in our case the first or the second half of our twelve-note series – into harmonic space; in other words, instead of appearing seriatim, the six notes are there together all at once, in the form of a chord, as shown in example 20:

Ex. 20.

The hexachord can therefore be regarded as an aggregate. Now in this particular case, when the aggregate is made up of differently pitched notes, the sum is a harmonic field of tensions, ie a specific state, irreducible to anything else; whereas if I add up duration quanta what I arrive at is nothing specific or irreducible, but simply a total, a sum, a quantum greater than the addenda. If you add up the first six figures on example 18, the total is 33; the second half of the series total 45. In viewing my time series in harmonic perspective, as it were, the simplest proportion it yields, namely, that obtaining between its two hexachordal aggregates, equals 33:45, which I can reduce dividing by three and express as the proportion 11:15.

Now, in saying that I decide to make this proportion 11:15 my ruling proportion, I begin to describe to you simply the way I work. I wish to stress, once again, that I mustn't be understood as speaking dogmatically on any of this; it's all perfectly empirical. I may perhaps come to feel some day that two main proportions, or even three, might be more convenient than one. So far I'm doing fine with one only. That's why I call it my ruling proportion, and also because it is to be found at all structural levels, from the ground level up; it is really the key to the super-ordination of the span or category of temporal events, in a scale comparable to that of heart-beat – breathing rhythm – rhythm of the action in which I may happen to be engaged – day and night course – lunar month – seasons of the year – the ages of man – his total life, or some such order. Now I start at the highest level, the total span, the duration of a work as a whole.

Suppose I set out to write a piece of the order of, say, half an hour's duration. This overall length is, obviously, as natural as a first specification, as size or scale is for the painter, the sculptor or the architect. That size influences conception, manner, style *and* execution is a truism. I needn't insist on that. To keep matters simple, suppose that my piece should have two main parts, in the proportion 11:15; if I decide to make it minutes, the total length would be 26; if that is near enough my plan of half an hour's piece, I shall go ahead. You can see on my timetable how the proportion will be echoed down, from time-layer to time-layer. For exemplification's sake, it is of course sufficient to show the time-layers and their proportional division just for the first half of the piece, lasting 11 minutes. You can easily calculate the rest if you must.

So far so good for the solitary geometer in the musician's breast. But of course nothing of this could possibly have any meaning if the musician had not been in command from the word go! – indeed, even before that. The geometer has simply devised for me a timetable that could be described as a grid, or rather a number of imbricating grids on different scales which a constant mesh proportion of 11:15 at all scales. But the musician's first specification must needs stem already from the world of live musical imagination. I'm referring to the decision with regard to the choice of my beat in metronome figures. On the face of it, this simply tells me "so and so many ticks per minute". But that, of course, means speed, and speed is part and parcel of musical character. Tempo is an essential specification. Now it's obvious that it can't be made in the abstract, ie you cannot with any shade of plausibility fix on a tempo, on the speed-character of something which is not yet there, moving; how could I, otherwise, with any sense fix on a beat of say 156, which is what we call *Allegro vivace*? There must be some compelling factor in my, as yet, unformulated musical idea, for me to be able to make a decision at all. But as soon as I *have* made it, and chosen, say, the crotchet at 156, my geometer's grid can begin to make musical sense to me. I can further decide, say, on four crotchets per bar and calculate that the first of my pieces, lasting 11 minutes, will have exactly 429 such bars.

Now on the ground-level – where the proportion yields such comfortably manageable time-spans as 13¾ of a bar and 18¾ bars etc – my twelve-note series and my time-series have their first direct encounter. You will recognize my time-series 7, 3, 8, 2, 12 etc in the centre of the table. It does three things in one, here, which I shall point out one after the other.

First, it selects the pitch-level at which my twelve-note series will be employed first, ie number seven decides that my series will start at the level shown in example 1, beginning at B natural. Secondly, number seven also fixes the time-span during which the selected tone-series will be circuiting, after which the next serial number will usher in a different transposition. And third, number seven fixed also both the length of the composed phrase, pattern or structure, and rules its rhythmic articulation.

Now point one implies, a non-stop circuiting of the twelve-note series at varying pitch or transposition levels, the selector of level and operator of change being the number series. In a way this reminds one of modulation in the traditional sense; but it is not used here with a similar intention and anyway, it is continuous like the growth of the piece itself. Points two and three make it, of course, necessary to assign now definite time-value to the serial numbers.

Indeterminacy is thus only given up at the very moment when a creative decision is made, ie when what has been potential becomes actual, is born and for better or worse is uniquely determined. For point two, the value is fixed at eight crotchets or two 4/4 bars. This means that the first selected twelve-note series will be circuiting for 14 common-time bars or the equivalent of 56 crotchets' duration. The adoption of these arbitrary multiples here obeys the necessity of introducing a certain degree of redundancy, not quite in the sense in which the term is used in statistics or in information theory, but simply in the sense that repetition is a *sine qua non* requirement for the very apprehensibility of metre and changes of metre altogether.

For point three, the value of the serial number is fixed at *one quaver*: that means that the music being composed can be articulated rather as 14 consecutive bars of patterns spanning seven quavers' duration each – in which case the patterns will go on shifting across the bar-lines and provide a new accent and constantly changing *rapports* with the basic pulse of the 4/4 bars: or else the pattern can be kept as septuplets within the confines of the bar, in which case, now with seven, one of those extremely tricky relations arise – namely 7:4 – which lie beyond the quinary barrier. The notation of the septuplets at the bottom of the timetable sheet indicates a possible way to guide the performer and make more explicit the precise rapport of the septuplets' quaver to the beat.

Observe also how my ruling proportion cuts across the serial circuit and thus creates a new, unforeseen articulation of its own; for example, the last quarter of a bar of the first time 13¾ span, ruled by number seven, belongs already, as you can see, to the second member of the proportion, which means that the opening twelve-note series spills over and dovetails with the following transposition selected by the number three: this is a state of affairs which closely resembles what the poets call free *enjambement*, when sense runs on, over the line, and onto the next, or vice versa.

I'm afraid I must stop here, because with the next step now I would have to start composing under your very eyes, and I'm not sure that that wouldn't prove rather boring for you and, probably pretty uncomfortable for me. Let me finish by trying to tell you what I *think* I've been telling you. Every word I said referred to matters belonging to the pre-compositional stage. In other words, I've been talking method to you, most of the time. Method is important and it must be admitted that after the discarding of classical tonality at the beginning of this century, the composing of music has been method-starved for quite a time. But it is dreadfully easy to over-compensate, and method can be overdone. The listener, for instance, ought not to take the slightest notice of anything I said here; method does not concern him. Above all, he should not get away with the idea that pitch-set and time-set are a kind of thread of Ariadne for finding one's way in or out of the maze.

Not at all. He's just got to listen. He's got to *live* a piece of music through, and nothing more, be it Beethoven or Schoenberg; the latter demands perhaps at the beginning some readjustment of listening habits and adequate familiarity, but nothing more. Of course, if you are a critic, the case is different and rather special. As for the composer, all these pre-compositional matters are nothing but a scaffolding that is meant to help him erect his sound-edifice. Once the *music* is there, the scaffolding has got to disappear, naturally. But this is not always clearly understood by the composers themselves. It is possible to take a naive pride in all these calculations.

There is little to be said, intelligently, against the use of intelligence in any human pursuit. But it seems peculiarly wrong that an artist should come to believe in a sort of *raison de système*, which imagination knows nothing of, in other words, that the artist should come to hold – as is the case in certain circles nowadays – that method in and by itself can *validate* a work of art. Of course, the young composer of today, placed between the inspired imbecile and the calculating tyros of Darmstadt, is only too likely to plump for the second choice. It's a mistake. It's a mistake to think that he *has* a choice. He has not, because he's got to co-opt both inspired imbecile and tyro and harness the two to the common task, trying to make them work truly – and if possible, smoothly – hand in hand.

VI Music in a Post-war Context

26 England, spring 1945[129]

"It is a blessing", a friend once told me, "that as a rule you musicians should be inarticulate". I need hardly add that my outspoken friend was himself a literary man. The answer, which of course did not then occur to me, might have been: "Well, what of it? If we take it that the only thing worth bothering about is the *ineffable*", though I doubt whether my friend could have agreed. He went on:

> Look at all the nonsense your best people have uttered as soon as they generalize upon characteristics, and, above all, upon the merits of their own or other nations' music. From Rousseau, if you accept him as a composer, to Debussy's *Monsieur Croche Anti-dilettante*, one could make a staggering anthology, and that is leaving contemporaries in peace.

True enough. Clearly, we must needs take the literary man at his word, but who would dream of taking a musician at his? The English: that unmusical nation *par excellence*, is a notion still deeply rooted in Continental minds. English music since Delius, leading the world in "quality and quantity", is a more recent view, propounded by no mean authority on this side of the Channel. The extremes, I suppose, compensate and cancel each other. Still, one often wishes to exclaim with Swift: "I have hated all nations, professions and communities, and all my love is for individuals."[130]

Individuals, indeed, and small groups of individuals at that, are my only course of direct experience of the topic on which I propose to dwell, and I would be most chary of generalizing; the nation is not my concern. Take, for example, amateur music-making.

I live in an English university town. I have often taken part myself in amateur music-making. I have even sung in a choir. Now choral singing is perhaps a thing by itself, about midway between the professional and the amateur: highly professional, I should say, from the point of view of the man in front, training and conducting us, but wholly and delightfully *dilettante* to at least most of us in front of him. Choral singing here is outstanding, and I know what whenever I return to the glare and reedy quality of Spanish boys' and female contralto voices, these English voices will haunt me like the memories of the soft Northern skies or the enthralling loveliness of the Northern spring, rain or no rain. But let me come to real, full-blooded amateurs. I have met college dons, mostly scientists, who play the bassoon, or specialize in Bach and investigate some of his toughest puzzle-canons, and even two or three who go in for contemporary music, the whole thing taken up with tremendous zest, like Ingres with his violin. I have met scores of undergraduates from all the faculties, not only music students (they, of course, could not be regarded as amateurs) who are uncommonly good at some instrument or other. From solo items up to full orchestral performances you may hear capable, sometimes very good, renderings of the most familiar as well as some very out of the way things which one would never come across in the professional's repertoire.

Now, what surprises me is the strongly conservative taste shown in the overwhelming majority of programmes. I think it would be fair to say that Delius or Debussy are about as far as the majority will go. On the other hand, one cannot help noticing (alas! not without joy) the truly great regard this brilliant young generation have for their own representative contemporary composers, from Vaughan Williams to Benjamin Britten. Notwithstanding this, contemporary British works hardly appear in the common run of programmes.

Now this strikes me as very odd. One would have thought a milieu like the one I am trying to describe the ideal one for discussing, trying-out and really coming to grips with whatever is challenging to the listener's habits in contemporary music. The disturbing fact, to my mind, is that such an elite exerts an influence which has always been vastly responsible for finally bridging the gulf between whatever bold innovations an age has brought forth in artistic matters and that slow-moving majority which always resents and long resists them. Either I am much deceived or something does not seem to work in this case. Or else, one would have to ask: is there some truth, after all, in the saying that the Englishman regards art as of little consequence, or at best as a recreation, as Sir Osbert Sitwell has put it?

Before leaving the subject, I should like to view it from the opposite end. I have never visited a mining district or a manufacturing town in this country. But I have listened to many records and broadcasts of brass bands formed by colliery workers and others employed in various industries. Some of the performances I remember were superb. The quality of sound, power of modulation, nimbleness of attack, the elegance of *cantabile* phrasing were all, to my mind, of the highest order. I soon became a brass band fan; but I find it hard to keep it up. The trouble, as far as I am concerned, is again with the nature of the programmes, though in a somewhat different way. Obviously, very little but arrangements of pieces originally written for quite different media are available for brass bands. Arrangement is a word which easily causes a frown – quite wrongly, very often. All the same, it is true that in the long run one cannot live on a staple diet of arrangements only.

I happen to know that some of the foremost living British composers have occasionally written original pieces for brass band; but I do feel that the matter is worth far more than a polite gesture. This working-class brass band movement constitutes an asset to British musical life not generally estimated at its proper value and significance. Here is a challenge, as well as an opportunity, which it would seem shortsighted to ignore. I am under no illusion as to the probability of this working-class elite taking to the new and unfamiliar, and more readily than the educated elite, though this might possibly prove quite different from expectation. Within the frame of reference of the working-class mind, the shock of a merely unfamiliar musical idiom might conceivably lose a great deal of its sting.

I cannot help anticipating it as something of a test case whether or not contemporary music should prove able adequately to provide for this new elite of music amateurs, especially in view of the much broader issue which seems here involved. No contemporary artist who is aware of our peculiar situation in modern society can have failed to realize with increasing acuteness how strangely lacking in comprehensiveness, the notion *le style c'est l'homme,* has come to be. Surely, a shrewd notion of the "other man", the man one talks to, or what has been called the artist's "sense of his audience" has always powerfully helped to determine style. It seems a pity to lose any opportunity of checking and putting this link to the test.

27 Concrete music and electronic sound composition (1959)[131]

Electronic sound-generation and magnetic tape-recording have provided the composer with a new medium, whose main feature is that it enables him to work directly in actual sound, as directly as a painter, for instance, works in paint. That is to say, instead of writing the music down on paper, as a collection of conventional signs (known as a score) that have to be translated into actual sound by instrumental or vocal interpreters before they can reach the listener, the composer produces the finished sound composition, fashioned by him in every detail, exactly in the form in which it will reach the listener. There are, of course, two sides to this by-passing of the human interpreter. According to one's own esteem of the interpreter in general and to one's experiences with particular interpreters' idiosyncrasies, the fact has been variously greeted with relief or with regret. But that's another story.

So far two main varieties have developed in the new medium: electronic music and *musique concrète*. All I shall attempt to do here is to characterize briefly the two schools of thought in order to compare methods and results and then present some specimens on my own experiments in this field of sound composition.

I speak, however, as a composer who, in his main work, is committed to the traditional media of instrumental and vocal sound, which is live, that is preferably non-recorded and, at any rate, non-manipulated, unprocessed. In other words, I approach the electronic medium strictly as a sideline, more or less in the way a painter, for example, takes to ceramics or mobiles.

Obviously, the handling of the new material requires different tools and techniques, and the change begins of course at the beginning in the very mode of conceiving and originating. The upshot of it all is a number of far-reaching morphological changes in the manner of organizing sound and it seems to me that these changes are bound to affect methods of composition in the traditional field of instrumental music as well, and that's why I personally take an interest in the experimental use of the new tools and techniques.

Both electronic composers and practitioners of *musique concrète* are fond of telling us not only that our traditional kind of music is coming to an end, but that it has been vegetating anyway at a comparatively low evolutionary level from the beginning of time, hemmed in as it has always been by the limitations of the primitive materials we are still using today: cat-gut and horse-hair, perforated bones or pipes, stretched animal hides, bits of wire, wood or metal and all that. ... They admit, of course, that even so, traditional music has produced a number of handsome pieces of work in different cultures throughout the ages.

But that does not detract from the fact – as they put it – that our kind of music has always dealt with sound in a somewhat rough and ready manner, and necessarily so, since it had to take sound from the primitive sources I have mentioned. Now at least (they point out) composers have gained access to the intrinsic structure of sound, thanks to a technological advance which is bringing about changes that rank in importance with what geneticists call a "mutation".

I don't agree with all of this; I don't believe that traditional music (or real music, as I'd better call it) is coming to an end, at least not until our society begins to disintegrate in much more radical ways than it seems to be doing at the present moment. But we can readily admit that the electronic composer, since he starts from scratch, that is from sine-tone, can in effect indulge in spectrum composition; indeed he has no choice but to do so.

Now, by comparison, it is clear that the traditional musician takes sound, as it were, fully-fashioned from the start, its tonal structure fully determined already in its acoustic source of human voice, trumpet, violin, or whatever it happens to be. The claim made by electronic composers that they have direct access to the intrinsic structure of sound boils down to this: they can now produce an entirely new range of colours. Granted; but the first thing to say in this respect, it seems to me, is that colour (in music) is never at the heart of the matter. Indeed, we know that whenever music uses "colour" for *effect*, for its own sake, whenever a composer deserves to be called a "colourist", he is in reality escaping at a tangent from the crucial issues and engaging in a side-show instead. One of the crucial issues is the structure of *music*; the intrinsic structure of *sound* is not.

Furthermore, the initial claims put forward by the electronic composers as to the unlimited range of new colours to be obtained from spectrum composition were in fact erroneous. Their own acousticians have been quite definite about this. I dare say most of us had already noticed for some time that, whether German, Italian, Dutch or Belgian, electronic music sounds curiously alike in its timbral aspect. If the possibilities were really unlimited, one couldn't help feeling that these composers were strangely coincident and repetitive in the use they made of them. Now this is not to deny that they have in fact produced quite an array of novel sound-colours, never heard before (if I may go on mixing my metaphors). But surely, novelty is a relative criterion. The point is: what are these new colours like; what are they worth? The answer is that they are extremely characteristic and certainly telling: no less attractive than the vivid material used in fashionable luminous socks!

I think it must be said in fairness that electronic music at its best is interesting not so much on account of its colouristic novelty but for more substantial musical reasons. In relation to the morphological changes I've mentioned before, it seems to me that, in comparison with the more advanced stages of composition in the traditional medium, we are aware of both gain and loss.

To take as an example, Luciano Berio's *Mutazioni*[132], leaving aside the colour factor – which, I think you'll agree, shows novelty, but a novelty that seems to pall fairly quickly on the ear – the striking characteristic of this piece is, I would say, a structural impoverishment rather than again. Considering the awe-inspiring complexity involved in the planning and execution of the piece, the elementary structure of the finished product stands in stark contrast with the means which went into the making of it. The fact is somehow glossed over and in part successfully hidden by the novelty of its patterning technique. The incidence of sound-impact, single or in clusters, its popping up all over the auditory space all the time in a quicksilvery *perpetuum mobile* seems to succeed in filling it up evenly, and with a satisfactory illusion of broad surface-plane effect.

Of course, in itself this patterning technique is not absolutely new: Bach, for instance, excelled in it; think of the astonishing quasi-polyphonic *trompe l'oreille* effect of his figurative patterning in the pieces for unaccompanied violin or cello. A cheating of the ear it is, nonetheless, and Berio is not quite as successful in hiding the fact that his piece is but a single-part composition in one solitary strand. Berio misses the polyphonic depth, the structural richness of the interlocking simultaneous pseudo-strands which Bach achieves.

To put it in a way that slightly over-simplifies but does not distort the actual state of affairs, Berio's piece could be compared to a pianist – admittedly a purely hypothetical one – playing with one finger (sometimes with several, just for clusters of notes) – all over the keyboard, at very great speed and always hitting the right keys. The flatness of the resulting structure is a loss, I would say. It reminds me of a humorous saying of Lorca, who once described the poetry of a fellow-poet he did not admire much, as so thin, so improbably thin, that there was really only one side to it: if you went round to look at it from the back, the whole thing had vanished. However, this anecdote is not quite fair on Berio, for whose work I have a sincere regard – and I have no doubt that he would disagree with my assessment of the piece. I am aware that the absence of illusionistic depth which I have pointed out is in fact deliberate. Simplification, often extreme simplification, is a necessity in the artist's act of inspiration. A revolution may come from concentration on one single point; it more often than not does come from the laying bare and stripping down even of essentials. The Spanish saying *cortar por lo sano* – to cut where the tissue is still healthy – holds good in creative work no less than in surgery.

To take another example, Stockhausen's *Gesang de Jünglinge (Song of the Young Men)*,[133] the most important criticism I have to make – and it would apply to Berio as well – is one which affects a matter of crucial importance in music: that which is involved is *time* itself. The way time is felt in electronic music differs entirely from the way time is experienced in traditional music.

Something is lost in the build-up of electronic music in the time-dimension, namely, the sense of temporal trajectory. The course of time appears flattened-out, as it were. It has become a lifeless quantity, a pure chronometrical extension. The almost biologically rhythmical sense of growth and trajectorial thrust has gone. The sense of temporal passage is no longer the rhythmical experience *par excellence* out of which music shapes the total form, as well as the ups and downs, the breathing of the form. Instead, the form has become, in electronic music, an artificially animated sequence of stills, as in films.

On the other hand, my criticism of the Berio piece does not apply to Stockhausen. On the contrary, the many-stranded texture is here a constantly evident feature. The strands of pure electronic sound and those of vocal origin blend and interact in a way which is more satisfactory, because it is more adequate to the technical resources brought into play. The main thing to be noted in Stockhausen's piece is precisely this introduction of a non-synthetic element taken from a natural acoustic source, namely boys' voices. It indicates, I think, an intelligent departure from the straitlaced orthodoxy of the beginnings of electronic music, when any contribution from natural acoustic sources was firmly rejected as impure.

Paradoxically, it is precisely the presence of this electronically impure (because non-synthetic) element that infuses its characteristic radiance to this music, the sense of lyricism which seems almost alien to the nature of electronic music.

The fact remains, nevertheless, that to this effect of radiance and lyricism the pure electronic sound contributes nothing at all. Let's face it: sine-tone has a rigid, cold, dead-signal quality. It is utterly unsuited to convey anything warm, tender, vivid, alive in human experience. The flashing and blinking of scattered sound, shooting up, exploding in clusters, or streaming in cascades of sonic fireworks seems to be somehow the natural mode of being of electronic music. When on rare occasions a phrase of *cantilena* character emerges, it jars terribly; suddenly the lifelessness, the *castrato* quality of synthetic sounds stands starkly revealed. It's useless denying that this is indeed a serious flaw in the material. On the other hand, it must be granted that this radical imperfection of synthetic sound is scarcely apparent and does not bother one at all when the composer exploits it for its specific structural potentialities, when for instance, sonic vents develop at a high pitch of activity and take on, as they are apt to, almost the character of audible semiograms. Stockhausen's piece shows a considerable mastery of the medium, even if the teething troubles are not yet over. The slide effect, for instance, whether you do it on the harp or on the ring-modulator, is a cheap device, I think.

The basic materials of *musique concrète* – and that's where it differs from synthetic electronic music – are all or nearly all of acoustic origin, that is to say, their prime source is not the frequency oscillator but the microphone. This makes of course for a very different picture. The microphone captures the living spark of the natural acoustic source; sound is thus taken fully-fashioned with its intrinsic harmonic structure, its attack, its main characteristics of body and decay and also with the noise-content inseparable from it, all complete. Personally, I feel that this, as it were, naturally animated material is preferable to the synthetic electronic sound, built up from sine-tone with its lifeless signal quality.

The basic unit with *musique concrète* is no longer a pure frequency of a disembodied cluster of pure sine-tone, but a living cell, often with an already complex organization of its own. This cell is what Pierre Schaeffer (the originator of *musique concrète*) has called, perhaps rather unfortunately, an *objet sonore*. But the term is no doubt characteristic of the whole French attitude to the matter. In principle, anything that comes from an acoustic source is possible material for *musique concrète*. This, of course, throws the gates wide open – too wide, perhaps – to material of all sorts, musical and not so musical. The French themselves, for instance, are not above using pots and pans for their *exercices aux casseroles* as they describe them.

On the other hand, the analysis or breaking-down of this material, even of just noise, is apt sometimes to reveal a pattern-content which had not been evident in the original. The simplest means of analysis available to every owner of a tape-recorder is the slowing down of tape-speed by one or various jumps down the octaves. It is like listening with a magnifying-glass. In the new scale, the identity of the original sound may no longer be easily recognizable. It may have undergone a true metamorphosis. And that's precisely what the composer is after. It must be admitted, though, that the result of sound-manipulation is, nearly always, an impoverishment; some of the vitality of the original sound is forfeited through loss of top or bass. This is the reason why, personally, I am chary of subjecting true musical sound to any great amount of manipulation. Noise, on the other hand, is over-rich, chaotically rich, as you know. It can only benefit from impoverishment. Less, then, becomes more, which is one of the basic tenets of the creative artist's economics.

As a sample of *musique concrète* we might consider the *Symphonie pour un homme seul* by Pierre Schaeffer and Pierre Henri.[134] There is, in fact, no very striking metamorphosis of basic materials in it. The identity of the so-called *objets sonores* remains pretty obvious throughout. Their line-up, too, is more in the nature of a loose sequence than of an imaginative sound-montage.

If the result of sound-montage (which is here, of course, the crucial operation) is not a new and compelling overall structure in which the component parts as if under a magic spell are made to play new roles – musical roles, I mean, to which their original identity could never have given us any clue – then sound-montage remains something of a game; something like a jigsaw puzzle with pieces upside-down or the wrong way round, bumping into one another and thus emphasizing their isolation, rather than giving them a common purpose which would lift them onto a plane of poetic imagery.

While the main ambition of the electronic composers and the practitioners of *musique concrète* is to compose works of art in their own right, fully self-sufficient, personally, I am mainly interested in this field, in applied works, that is, I mean, incidental or strictly functional contributions which sound composition can bring to works of radio and television, for the stage and screen. The belief that sound-montage is more readily adaptable to such techniques than music written to traditional instruments is growing into something of a conviction with me. And for reasons which are fairly obvious. As once composers were deeply conditioned by training and by all our techniques to think and to work in terms of completely self-sufficient musical organization, now it is difficult to see how music can be self-sufficient and incidental at the same moment – at least to our way of thinking.

Few theatre-directors nowadays seem to favour Mendelssohn's score for *A Midsummer Night's Dream* or Beethoven's Overture for *Coriolanus*. They are not our idea of incidental music in a subsidiary and strictly functional role. What I call bright music, in such a functional role, calls for a far-reaching structural simplification, for something like the style of newspaper headlines with their powerful allusions, something abbreviated and direct as poster technique.

Introduction to *Lament for the Death of a Bullfighter* (1960)[135]

The setting of this beautiful poem by my countryman Federico García Lorca[136] was suggested to me by the BBC. I was free to choose my own terms for the setting. There was one condition, naturally, which was that it should be an English version of the poem. This I accepted with pleasure, since A.L. Lloyd's translation seemed to me extremely successful.

I decided to have the poem recited, not sung, and to frame it and support it with a composition in electronic sound. So, we first recorded the poem on its own, recited by the actor, Stephen Murray. This tape-recording I then took home and played through over and over again, mapping out its overall time-structure pattern: I mean by this the length of lines, value of breathing pauses when delivered, changes in speed of speech and levels of vocal loudness and so on.

Once I'd arrived at a kind of blueprint of all these data, I had, by the same token, a kind of negative for the framework of a sound composition that would fit the speech, satisfying one important condition, namely that sound would never endanger the audibility of speech by covering it, but that the two would dovetail, avoiding a head-on clash of word and sound at all the semantically critical moments.

I have been using the electronic medium for some time. My materials here consisted of pure electronic sound and of sounds from other sources recorded with a microphone. This raw material was then processed in many ways in order to metamorphose it, as it were, and make it flexible enough to be used as a strand or thread in the total sound-fabric. That fabric is made up of many threads: in other words, of many tape-loops run together, sometimes as many as ten. The poem is divided into four cantos and each of them was treated somewhat differently and uniformly both in sound-colour and patterning. The opening sounds, dominating also the first canto, for example, are all derived from the piano and subjected to a certain amount of tape-manipulation in order to achieve the effect of tearing, rending sound – an effect I find expressive, in aural terms, of the wounding of the famous bullfighter Ignacio Sanchez Mejias, who lost his life on that fatal afternoon in the arena.

28 Sound observed (1965)[137]

Music is sometimes compared with architecture – rather irrelevantly, I think. Architecture as "frozen music" or music as "architecture in flux" are a little far-fetched as metaphors, revealing nothing. The two arts have in fact hardly anything in common, apart from generalities such as number, proportion, scale or size which we share, of course, with all the other arts. Music and architecture differ most significantly, it seems to me, even where they have apparently some common ground.

Take the notion of symmetry, for instance, which we musicians have obviously borrowed from the arts of space. As a constructive idea, symmetry has undoubtedly played a major role in all music. The classical forms are firmly grounded in it. Nevertheless, the idea is a borrowed one; it isn't a genuine temporal concept at all. In music's world of time, symmetry has the status of a naturalized citizen of foreign origin. The indigenous, time-born concept is that of periodicity. Needless to say, every musician worth his salt has always handled symmetry, in the specific temporal sense of periodicity, as a means of controlling overall balance. But balance in musical form is a far cry from balance in architecture. The parallel is purely verbal.

Yet it must be admitted that composers have allowed symmetry, the alien, space-born citizen to dominate the time-world which adopted the stranger. And in allowing this we have shown a certain mental laziness, an easy acceptance of ready-made formulae, rather than a true concern with intrinsically temporal concepts. In the experience of musical time, all inter-relations involve transcience, and all realization involves implication. Nothing could be farther removed from the inter-relation of symmetry in space.

The growth of musical form in time could be compared with a system whose behaviour differs according to its past, according to what happened before. Nothing could be more inapplicable to static, frozen form in space. In short, it is obvious that the citizen of foreign extraction called symmetry has for too long imposed on us its static focus, while the natural one with us musicians is a moving focus. It is time we came to realize that when we speak of erecting sound-architectures, we are in fact doing something for which the art of building with stone, bricks or ferro-concrete offers no counterpart at all.

There is one important fact, however, in respect of which composer and architect find themselves in exactly the same predicament. The composer and architect are the only two artists whose work is carried out entirely in the abstract and at a considerable remove from the concrete materials in terms of which their work is conceived. So while the painter, the sculptor, or the poet work directly with the stuff of which their work is made, composer and architect do nothing but paper-work, consisting in a set of instructions which tell someone else how to realize the work using specified materials. Consequently, whereas the painter's, the sculptor's or the poet's work leaves the hands of its maker in exactly the form he made it and in exactly this form meets the public for whom it is destined, composer and architect need a host of skilled helpers or performers. They alone can translate the projected work into concrete reality. In other words we have to rely on interpretation. There is a gap, therefore, between the original creative process and the indispensable re-creative process, and we are seldom in full control of this. I have no idea of what the hazards are where the architect is concerned, but I have a pretty clear idea of what they are for the composer.

It isn't surprising, then, that composers should have seized eagerly upon a new medium which abolishes the middle-man and allows them to work in as direct a contact with sound as the painter works with paint. I am referring to sound-composition directly realized by the composer on magnetic tape, by means of a tape-recorder. This raises a number of important issues, with some of which I want to deal now.

If we begin with the image of the traditional composer working with pencil on paper, in silence and, preferably, in sound-proof isolation, the situation is clear. He writes down sounds as he ideally imagines them, ie musical ideas that take shape in his mind are encoded with the help of a system of graphic symbols which the performing musician is able to decode and translate into live sound. A nice point arises here: what does the composer actually hear in his head? How accurate is the mental prefiguration of what he writes down? What will it sound like in performance? I am not suggesting that these are the kind of questions to fire point-blank at a composer: he might be put out and think you impertinent. There are also composers who make no secret of the fact that things sound sometimes much better than they had imagined, sometimes not nearly so good. It would certainly be a mistake to suppose that what the composer hears in his head is anything like a realistically accurate replica of sound as heard with one's physical ears. You couldn't compare it, say, to the projection of a sound-film onto the screen of the composer's mental ear, it's not at all like that.

In my own experience, the outstanding characteristic of mental audition is its striking economy. It could best be compared to a drastically abbreviated shorthand, to something as economically diagrammatic as the print, not the sound, of the sound-track of a film, ie comparatively little in it is spelt out in detail and a great amount is packed with implication. The reading of a train of signals as given in mental audition has something in common, too, with the reading of a difficult hand-writing. The eye scans the writing in a flash. The grasping of its meaning is a function of the scanning, not of the spelling. It is well known that even quite illegible words, or blanks and omissions, can be restored as a function of context.

Clearly, context is the focus. And that is true of mental audition as well. Another way of putting it is that *wholes* are grasped as entities, and much faster than it would take the mind to tot up the sum of their parts. In drawing the sums, we can of course go wrong. Errors can occur in mental audition – they even occur in physical audition – and such errors go some way towards explaining occasional miscalculations on the part of the composer. Alternatively, they also serve to explain the freakishness of responses with which the listener's physical ear sometimes surprises the composer. Moreover, communication theorists point out that a certain loss of information is inevitably incurred, in transit from sender to receiver. This is a fundamental fact in all communication. It would be unrealistic to ignore it in music.

The composer is well aware of this phenomenon of dissipation which occurs between ideal conception and practical realization – which, incidentally, helps to explain why a sketch can sometimes be far more alive than the elaborate final product. As for the amount of dissipation that occurs in listening to a live performance, no score-reading listener can be unaware of the magnitude of the loss. The number and importance of the data that may fail to register consciously can sometimes be baffling indeed. On the other hand, this may be partly the explanation why repeated hearings of even familiar music may give the listener the impression of a fresh, novel experience every time.

It's common knowledge, too, that a composer may be consistently successful in imagining sound, and yet far less dependable in analysing sound when he actually hears it. Orchestral players have a fund of anecdotes, true or spurious as the case may be, about even distinguished composers who fail to spot wrong notes in performance. A dull-witted orchestral player may well have a sharper ear than the finest composer. This may seem odd. One would have thought that someone who can be superbly accurate in mentally devising complex sound patterns, with his inner ear alone for a guide, would be bound to detect the slightest discrepancy between what he so clearly heard in his head and what he hears with his physical ear in performance. But this is not invariably the case. What does it prove? It looks possibly as if an over-development of mental audition in the composer could sometimes result in an imbalance between his outer and his inner ear. The two seem liable to get out of step on occasions.

The composer may indeed develop an aural squint, so to speak, which ought perhaps to be regarded as professional hazard, resulting from the sheer amount of paper-work he has got to do, compared with the infrequent opportunities afforded to him for checking imagined sound against its physical counterpart in realized, live sound. While the inner ear seems to be an innate gift that can certainly be developed, but perhaps not acquired by someone who lacks it, there is ample evidence to show that the outer ear is wonderfully apt to learn, if given a chance. And the best change lies here – as with many other matters – in *observation.*

What I mean by "sound observed" is not simply careful listening. Strictly speaking, it is not even listening to *music*, since observation would be the wrong attitude in that case, the sheer physics of sound being subordinate to the more important activity of aesthetic apprehension of the piece listened to. Neither is it listening to a playback of a tape-recorded piece, since what we get in this case is only a second-hand reproduction, a kind of photograph of the original, or, indeed – to use a James Joyce pun – a fadograph of the live performance. The sound I am speaking of as being under observation is the sound which the composer himself produces from scratch, by electronic means, for use in composition on tape. This is an entirely new case. No longer has it anything to do with reproduction. On the contrary, this sound is the original stuff of which a piece will be made. Putting sound together in this way, literally *com*posing, composing directly with sound on tape becomes the equivalent of the painter putting paint on canvas in the process of making an original work.

The dictionary definition of "sound" as "that which strikes the ear, that which may be heard" does not take us very far, but at least it brings up immediately that other word "noise". The use of the word "noise" in a quasi-positive sense – as when we say: "a lovely noise", meaning a pleasing sound – has always struck me as one of the engaging oddities of English. It seems to me to indicate an instinctive refusal, as it were, to draw too pedantic a line between "sound" and "noise". And this is absolutely right, I think. Sound and noise must not be taken as opposites in the sense, say, of order and confusion. This would be quite unrealistic. In the first place, the very definition of sound as "that which may be heard" logically includes noise. Secondly, sound and noise are always inextricably mixed together. There is a definite noise-content in the purest sound that a violin can produce, and it is indispensable, it is part and parcel of its character. If we could eliminate it, the sound would become emasculated. For instance, the lifeless, quasi-synthetic quality of so-called pure tone – known as "sine", or "sinusoidal tone" – is as much due to its lack of noise-content as to the absence of overtones. But I shall not be concerned with acoustics here. All I want to suggest is the acceptance of a more liberal definition of the word "sound" which, to begin with, must not exclude notes or be taken as its opposite. In addition, the meaning of "sound", as I take it here, should be understood to cover both pitched and indeterminately pitched sound.

When regularly pitched sound is the main factor in a piece, we say that the piece is based on a tonal system, constituted of a select number of fixed and constant frequency values. Western and non-European art and folk-music variously illustrate such tonal systems. When a composition is built entirely, or predominantly, of data whose pitch is not fixed or constant, we are in the presence of something different and entirely new, for which there is no historical precedent, since the use of this type of sound became only possible through electronic sound-generating and recording.

Now I have compared the composer writing a musical score with the architect drawing up plans for a building and stressed the abstract nature of both these activities. The comparison is, of course, no more watertight than such comparisons usually are and, in the present case, for obvious reasons. Whereas the composer is concerned with what, fashionably, would now be called a "happening", ie with prescribing the course of a chain of aural events, accurately timed, down to split seconds, the architect is solely concerned with prescribing what to put where, in space. Time, which is of the essence of the operation to the composer, is only marginally – perhaps economically – relevant to the architect. So, in reality, more than an architect, the composer resembles a general directing a battle by remote control, from a distant chateau or dug-out. The chain of events, their linking and timing are of course paramount. Yet whereas the general is at least currently in touch with the front line and is kept informed of how the battle is going, the composer at his desk is merely directing a phantom battle, a battle that is not being fought here and now, but will only be fought in earnest some day in the future, when the orchestra actually plays his work.

This, I think, is a better illustration of the difference between composing with pencil on paper and composing with actual sound on tape. The composer at the tape-machine is like a commander in the field. He is in the very thick of events, taking quick decisions in anticipation of events or in reaction to them as they arise.

This is a tremendously exhilarating situation. Direct action with sound stimulates aural alertness to an unsuspected degree. And – what is more important – it also stimulates thought as applied to strategy and tactics in new ways. Incidentally, it has in addition the inestimable advantage over military strategy, that one is at liberty to discard – by washing out – those bits of the battle where one found oneself on the losing side. One can then fight the episode all over again, with the added knowledge gained from analysing the stretch where things went wrong in the first encounter and finding out why. Just like Picasso does in a film showing him in the act of painting. At a certain moment he starts making rather a mess of things. "*Ça va mal* ..." – it's not going well at all, in fact, it's going very badly, he mutters. Then suddenly he begins to obliterate, boldly paints over and retrieves the situation. Obviously, this is a thing the composer on paper cannot do, or can only do after the event, after having heard his work played; ie he must sustain the defeat first and then risk again similar hazards when correcting a miscalculation, since the correction will have to be done again in the abstract.

It is, I think, a common experience with composers who work in the electronic medium that the immediate aural perception of what one is doing promotes a highly discriminating, almost hyper-sensitized sound-awareness. After a full day's work by the tape-recorder, one suddenly discovers that one's ears have become amazingly attuned to all manner of sound, indoors and out-of-doors, to which, one realizes, one had been completely deaf before. It is as if, suddenly, one had once more acquired primitive man's ears. Primitive man must have been endowed with an acutely discriminating apprehension of his surrounding sound-world, simply as a matter of survival.

Equally, as a matter of survival, modern man, living in industrial surroundings, has been forced, on the contrary, to make himself deaf to an increasingly vast amount of sounds, thereby reducing the world of sound observed to a narrow code of signals that carry useful information. Discrimination within this shrunken band-width of semantically valuable signals is, no doubt, extremely refined in civilized man. Nonetheless, it has had to be paid for with an all-round impoverishment of sound-perception, which the contemporary composer has come to feel as a definite loss.

A clear indication of this attitude can be seen, I believe, in the increasingly abundant use composers make nowadays of sound of indeterminate or of non-constant pitch. Already a generation ago, Sir James Jeans asked: "How long will composers keep on being satisfied with a tonal system that offers strictly no more than twelve semitones within the octave?"[138] This is, of course, another story. But I have no doubt in my mind that both the use of non-conventional sound in today's instrumental music and, more particularly, the exploration of the domain of electronic sound, are symptoms of an increasing uneasiness with regard to the limitations of our traditional pitch-system. However, I am not saying that I also agree with Edgard Varèse, who declares that our traditional musical instruments, as well as the pitch system on which they are based, have become obsolete. I, for one, do not wish to see them abolished. I don't believe in decrees of abolition in matters of art, but rather in gradual, if incessant modification of that which is already established, by that which is new and through reciprocal interaction or both.

To describe that heightened sensitivity, that sense of re-discovery of a lost sound-world which one gains from working in the electronic medium, it might be said that it amounts almost to the lifting of the sound-blockade which the urban and industrial environment has forced upon modern man. The ear registers and quasi-mentally amplifies the slightest departure from absolute silence. Anything that sounds is listened to. The ear is deaf to no vibrations impinging upon it.

No more waste of sound. The most trivial sequence, seemingly, of sonic phenomena may reveal unsuspected patterns, unfamiliar, sometimes delightful modes of sound-behaviour. The ear focuses sharply on those phenomena and observes them from every possible angle: for pitch, either orderly interval-movement or random pitch-drift; for texture or grain of the signal; for timbral characteristics; amplitude; single or multiple strains of sound; background; shape of the whole train of signals in time, both in the sense of rhythmical configuration and in that of overall trajectory ... and so forth.

The experience stimulates with unusual intensity the listening to sound for its own sake, divested of all extraneous associations. True, there are people who complain that electronic sound always reminds them of something else.

The trouble, they say, is that one simply cannot shut out associations – usually of a prosaic or even of a downright ludicrous sort. To me, this seems to indicate shortcomings in the listener, rather than in the stuff listened to. It reveals, I think, a failure of the auditive imagination, in the same way that some listeners' habit of spinning private yarns while listening to familiar music, reveals a failure of the musical imagination.

Besides, people who can't help being reminded of the kitchen sink, or worse, by electronic sound forget that our associations – voluntary or not – are entirely the product of our own minds. We can choose to entertain them or to dismiss them. He who chooses to entertain the more sordid ones deserves the impressions he gets. Except, of course, that the whole thing is also a piece of self-deception and evasion: because trying to equate a sound with something else of which it reminds you is simply an attempt to foist a false identity upon that sound, instead of trying to grasp its acoustically objective one. Yet I admit that in my own way of listening, associations play indeed an important role. But – and this is another aspect of the experience I am trying to describe – sound does not remind me of something else, it reminds me only of *other* sounds.

Comparing sounds actually heard with associated images of sound stored in the memory has the effect of bringing out in sharp outline the distinctive characteristics of the sound observed by focusing attention on similarities and dissimilarities between the two. With some practice, one begins – unconsciously at first – to classify sounds by groups and into families that have common characteristics.

This opens up a fascinating subject – something like a genealogy of sound – with which, however, I do not feel qualified to deal, since I am no acoustician. I have to rely on my naked ear alone, and it would therefore be presumptuous for me to put forward here what are mere subjective impressions as if they were tested and accepted facts.

Nevertheless, with this proviso, I will admit that I have come more and more to believe that the overall sonic domain is perhaps not as vast and diverse as one is at first inclined to assume. Rather, it seems a finite and bounded domain and, as such, in more aspects than that of frequency alone. I suspect that when acousticians take these matters up, it will probably be found that the number of existing distinctive families of sound is not inordinately large. What makes me think that this might indeed be so, is the fact that the sound of a given family can be modified, by suitable operations, and made to resemble less and less the original sound from which it developed. Gradually, it will adopt a novel character, but the degree of novelty that can thus be obtained is not unlimited. After a certain amount of change, there comes a moment when the sound simply begins to show characters of another, different, but already well-known family. In other words, it would seem that it is possible to develop new varieties, but no new families.

The number of basic sound-families seems to be comparatively small. Most of them are probably already represented in the modern orchestra. If a section of tuning-forks were added – standing for spectrum-less sine-tone – the representation might be considered to be fairly complete.

Two examples from my own *Collages*[139] might show what I mean by the modifications and metamorphosis of sound. One consists of two drum-rolls – for side-drum and tenor-drum respectively – each starting very softly and getting louder by degrees, ending abruptly at their loudest. The second example was obtained from the original microphone-takes of the two drum-rolls. The change in the character of the sound is so extraordinary that I doubt if anyone who had not been told would still guess, let alone recognize the source of the sound. The original drum-rolls could, of course, immediately be identified as produced by instruments of the family of membranophones, but the jet-like sound of the second example could no longer be taken as belonging to that family. Rather does it exhibit characteristics which are distinctively what is known as "white noise". Now, whether or not an acoustician would accept that amount of change, startling though it is, as proving my theory of change of family through sound-mutation had perhaps better be left an open question. Although I remain convinced that by still more radical processes, which can affect the very micro-structure of sound, the theory of change of family *could* be validated.

I should explain that nothing as radical as that was responsible for the metamorphosis of the drum-rolls. What happened is this: the original recordings of the two rolls were variously speeded up by factors from four to six, pitch up, in a retrograde form. The back-to-front playing reversed, of course, the dynamics; this is why the new sounds start with a sharp attack and decline fast, instead of increasing slowly towards the strong accent, as at the end of the original rolls. But I should also explain that the second example is already an instance – if a primitive one – of sound-composition. Instead of the two single original drum-rolls, many different replicas of the speeded up and reversed version. By spacing the entries variously in playing them together, a pattern of several strands was obtained which has a rhythmic and dynamic interest apart from the novelty of the colour. To my mind the main attraction of the pattern lies in the startling increase of sound-energy and especially in the varying incidence of the jet-like outbursts. This is interesting and it leads me to the crucial point about sound-composition on tape.

The kind of sound-behaviour illustrated here is something beyond the scope of our present orchestral instruments. The operative word is *behaviour*, it will be noticed, not colour; colour is never of decisive importance. Instead of "behaviour" I might have used the term *sound-activity*.

The electronic medium, in effect, makes possible new modes of action with sound which have greater freedom of tonal movement, of configuration and of textural weaving than those which our traditional instruments permit. This is not to say that the electronic medium is, therefore, a more perfect one than the orchestral medium. All I am saying is that it is different. It is still practically unexplored. Its potential can only be guessed. And because this potential exists, composers will explore it just as a still unclimbed mountain peak will be attempted *because it is there.* The statement is not meant to be flippant. As Whitehead pointed out: "The entertainment of unrealized possibility is a major factor in human mentality."[140] Exploration of the world and the lifting of unexperienced reality onto the domain of experience is the essential motif. Activity, needless to say, is of the first importance in the arts of time. What is happening, and the way things happen, are the very lifeline of composition with sound. The actual sound-elements in themselves are less important. As with the pictorial collage they may even be insignificant scraps. What is important is the total animated form, the time skyline they built up through active continuity.

But the new has its own laws which must be discovered and obeyed. This lawfulness is violated when the new is used to produce "oddish" replicas of the old. Such seems to me to be the case with the work which Milton Babbitt has produced with a synthesizer at Columbia University. Babbitt's tonal configuration hardly goes beyond what could conceivably be played by hand on a Hammond organ with still more stops. Nothing that instruments or the orchestra can do as well or better can be justified in the electronic medium. To be justified, both the sound-stuff and the way it is organized must be original growths of the medium.

29 *The Plague* (1964)[141]

"It is as reasonable to represent one kind of imprisonment by another, as it is to represent anything that really exists by that which exists not."[142] With this quotation from Defoe, which Camus sets as a motto for *The Plague*,[143] he makes it clear that he intends us to read it as a parable, a *conte philosophique*. Yet at the same time the book can be read as a straightforward story, as the factual account of an imaginary outbreak of plague supposed to have afflicted the town of Oran sometime in the 1940s. It is not only possible, it is perhaps inescapable to read it thus. And this is, I suggest, how it should be read. This is how I have composed it.

Camus's artistry as a story-teller is employed wholly to this end, to make the tale ring true. The factual, almost clinically detached narrative aims at complete make-believe. This has been my own aim, too. I conceived the role of the musical setting as an attempt at aiding and abetting in this task of making the listener believe in the reality of the fictional events recounted.

Nevertheless, *The Plague* is a fable, and as in all fables, the animals stand for man. This is not a tale of rats but of men. It is a tale of our time. It could not be one of final victory but one of endless defeat. At the end of the chronicle, when the chronicler searches his heart for the reasons which impelled him to compile it, he can only find very modest ones. He resolved to compile it "so that he should not be one of those who hold their peace, but should bear witness in favour of these plague-stricken people; so that some memorial of the injustice and outrage done to them might endure."[144]

What he had to record could only be "the record of what had to be done, and what assuredly would have to be done again in the never-ending fight against terror and its relentless onslaughts by all who, while unable to be saints but refusing to bow down to pestilences, strive their utmost to be healers."[145] The plague, then, is a symbol. We can no longer think of pestilence as a natural calamity – it is a savage killing of men by men. And it behoves us to remember that "the plague bacillus never dies or disappears for good; that it can lie dormant for years and bide its time; and that perhaps the day may come when, for the bane and enlightening of men it will rouse up its rats again and send them forth to die in a happy city."[146]

Camus's novel took my imagination by storm when I first read it some years ago and I immediately decided to use it as the subject of a composition, if I could think of extracting a libretto from the book and find a musical form to fit it. The script proved the longer and more arduous task, in fact. It began to take shape as I realized that the various characters in the novel were merely distinct facets of the story-teller himself. This made it possible for me to begin to imagine a musical form that would involve no more than two characters: the central one of the plague-stricken people (chorus) and that of the narrator (speaker). Vocal soloists, I felt very strongly, would have been quite out of place, as would any substantial interludes that might have prompted the composer to "take the stage". The neutral tone of Camus's narrative made this unthinkable.

The part of the narrator, I decided, should be spoken throughout in a manner that would reflect as faithfully as possible the detached unemotional style in which the story is told in the book. Speech backed by music – melodrama, to give it its proper name – is unfashionable nowadays. Nevertheless, I am convinced that melodrama is a perfectly legitimate device when the intrinsic character of a text demands it. Only it should not be used "melodramatically": that, for me, is the whole point. It almost inevitably turns in that direction when the text is a highly formalized one, more concerned with diction than with information.

Speech of this kind arrogates to itself a quasi-musical function which in truth it cannot fulfil. On the other hand, only speech which is stripped of all rhetoric and carries vital dramatic information only can make no such claim, since it strikes the imagination with a directness and urgency that leave no room for merely formal effects. Once the proper function of such a text is recognized as the unfolding of the dramatic thread on a conceptual plane, it is evidently best left to take care of itself in its fulfilment of this function.

The speaker's voice can be regarded as one more thread in the weaving of the sound-fabric, one that possesses two salient characteristics. First, the intonation of indeterminate pitch: that is, its inflexions are those of a spontaneous utterance, emotionally and logically motivated. Secondly, its rhythmical structure is metrically indeterminate, freely flowing.

The coupling of the two systems, one determinate in pitch and metre, the other indeterminate in both spheres, is no longer considered impracticable. (Incidentally, the future of electronic music and the opening up of a wider musical domain lie probably in the fusion which will follow from the breaking down of the conceptual barriers which separate these two systems. With the composition of *Collages,* I gained some experience in this field which I was able to put to a novel use in *The Plague.*)

The speaker's voice is not just one isolated indeterminate element in the whole organization of the work, but one among many others. The chorus, for instance, is often used in this way (whispering, speaking and shouting, besides singing) and so are such instrumental groups as lend themselves to indeterminate treatment, notably the stringed instruments, the strings of the piano and, of course, the percussion. Since there are large areas, both vocal and instrumental, where the two modes of sound-production overlap, the transition from one to the other, the mingling as well as the clashing of the two, becomes possible.

In order to serve as a text for a musical setting which would not exceed the permissible duration of a long concert work, the story had necessarily to be condensed to bare essentials. I took from Camus's novel the following nine episodes, which constitute, I think, a fair epitome of the main course of events:

1. Oran
2. The outbreak
3. Impact on the population
4. The Health Committee
5. The closing of the town gates
6. The death of the girl
7. The burials
8. The boy's agony
9. Abrupt ending of the sickness

Epilogue.

The choice of text dictated also the musical form of the work, which consists of a steady alternation of spoken narrative and choral pieces, both framed and moulded by the orchestra in an overall design. Stylistically, my aim has been to identify myself, as closely, and as completely as possible, with the particular style of the book as a chronicle. Camus alludes to contemporary realities, symbolized in the fictional events, as a poet would: metaphorically. In a similar way, a musical image that may have started, say, in an objective or even descriptive vein, is sometimes given a metaphorical turn that makes allusion to the reality behind the symbol, as – to quote a simple example – when the climax of the rat-invasion turns into a sound-image that may well recall an air-raid warning. The music's technique of allusion is constantly employed to this end, sometimes by gradual metamorphosis, sometimes by a violent clash of images.

It is only rarely that music, with its intrinsic lack of semantic definition, allows us to guess at the motives which may have prompted the composer's work, and the evidence is seldom more than circumstantial or anecdotal. The musical medium itself is often thought of as "timeless", in the sense of being ineffably remote from any concrete, time-bound concern, as though the composer lived, thought and worked outside historical time altogether. It came, therefore, as a welcome relief to me to have been able, just for once, to break out of this "timelessness", and to give expression to a passionately felt concern with one of the most oppressive tragedies of our time.

30 Introduction to Symphony No.2 (1959)[147]

It is no easy matter for me to say something about my new symphony. For one thing, I am writing this only a month after it was completed, so I've not had much time to get really acquainted with it. I always feel a work becomes a little distant the moment it is finished. What strikes me most in retrospect is a certain air of unfamiliarity the work seems to take on all of a sudden. I know that the heart of the matter is never disclosed to me while I am at work and I think this is as it should be: but it makes it a little difficult to talk about a new piece.

I could, of course, write at length and in detail about the formal problems I've set myself in the symphony and about the serial controls to which I've subjected the elements of tone and time. But it seems to me that to have a composition explained in this way by the composer is about as helpful as having a battle explained by the Chief of Staff – very good, if you happen to be a strategist; if not, not.

What I can try to do, first, is to tell the listener at least what *not* to listen for. There are, for example, no first and second subjects in my Symphony, for it isn't planned thematically. The music, that is to say, does not evolve from melodically more or less self-contained subjects. The very concept of "part-writing" has been discarded here in favour of a new mode of organization. A musical idea is no longer presented as a principal "part" on a privileged instrumental plane, or in terms of mainly melodic delineation, developing in thread-like continuity horizontally, as it were, and supported by other tonal layers of a subsidiary character, all polyphonically or harmonically related.

Instead, the musical idea arises and develops as a sound-structure spreading out over the undivided – or rather, non-stratified – auditory space. The resulting sound-image may thus be composed of any number of elements, located at any point of time and pitch, which have to be integrated into the whole which they constitute. Listening is therefore concerned with the grasping of structure, with togetherness, in the literal sense of the word "symphonic". Consequently, the ear needs to be deflected from its ingrained habit of listening mainly to melodic contours, tunes or themes, and coaxed towards the centre of the proceedings, so that it may grasp the unfolding of the complete structural shape.

The Symphony is in one continuous movement subdivided in two main parts. The first part is preceded by a brief introduction, *poco sostenuto*. This sets out the basic time and tone elements in the form of an almost static sequence, in which these root-ingredients are simply spelt out or indexed, as it were. The main *Allegro assai* follows then immediately.

The second part is subdivided into three sections. The first one, *Lento*, opens with a passage for percussion alone, consisting of up to twelve simultaneous percussion parts, each in a different metre.[148] The instruments used are Chinese and Korean blocks ranging, at roughly equal intervals, from the tiniest wood-block, for the highest sound, to the largest Korean block for the lowest. The resulting percussion pattern comes and goes, five times in all, alternating or in counterpoint with the rest of the orchestra. Each time the overall rhythmical configuration varies according to the number of percussion parts involved and according, also, to the order of their respective entries.

This interplay between percussion and orchestra articulates primarily a dramatic idea. But it is also inspired by the wish to make the percussion department serve in a truly structural capacity, instead of keeping it restricted to its traditional use for emphasis for purely colouristic effects The end of the *Lento* section leads straight into an *Allegretto* section which is characterized by a marked relaxation of tension. Here everything is light, gentle, almost playful, somewhat chamber-like in texture. The last section, the Finale of the Symphony, *Molto vivace*, reverses course midway and is then mirrored backwards, in the manner of a palindrome. It is introduced by pianissimo rolls on three cymbals of different sizes and the bell-like sound of the tiny antique cymbal. At the end of the Symphony these sounds are reached in reverse order, and after the bell-like note, the vibration of the suspended cymbals is allowed to die down in silence.

31 "Is modern music growing old?" (1960)[149]

The late Edward J. Dent, in a small book entitled *Terpander*,[150] concludes his enquiry into the future of music – not the same thing as the music of the future – with the following quotation from Dr. Burney:

> It is difficult to refrain from numbering Plato, together with Aristotle, Aristoxenus and Plutarch ... among the musical grumblers and *croakers* of antiquity. They all equally lament the loss of good music, without considering that every age had probably done the same, whether right or wrong, from the beginning of the world: always throwing musical perfection into times past, remote from their own, as a thing never to be known but by tradition. The Golden Age had not [got] its name from those who lived in it.[151]

Dr Burney certainly puts musical grumblers and croakers in excellent company. Of course, there are always grumblers and croakers. There are degrees of distinction even in grumbling – one of the fundamental human attitudes, shared by great men and smaller fry alike. The success of the "angry young men" of the 1950s seems to prove, once again, how much satisfaction, direct or vicarious, we derive from the exercise.

It's an odd thing how much people seem to enjoy being displeased. As a rule, we take it as characteristic of advancing age. One comes to suspect, though, that the yearning for the good old days is in reality something more like the perverse satisfaction we take in being just bad-tempered, rather than a true nostalgic recollection of a Golden Age or a genuine, deep-rooted conviction that everything was in fact so much better when we were young. It also serves to camouflage, to hide as much from ourselves as from younger people, the fact that we hate being made uncomfortable, being nonplussed by something new and unfamiliar. As we grow older, we settle into acquired habits and routines and resent having them disturbed when our power of adaptation to change begins to decline. It's natural, too, that the riddle of the future should intrigue us less, when there is only a little more future in store for us, than when there is still a good deal left. It is a fact, however, that, whether old or young, we all advance into the future facing backwards – *reculons,* as Valéry has said – facing backwards and sightless, as it were. No wonder, then, that one should often stumble over obstacles and that so many things should only begin to be more clearly understood after the event. Hindsight seems to be our natural mode of vision. More than that, it seems necessary for us to let go of things, to cease being actively concerned with them before they can begin to be seen anything like *sub specie aeternitatis*. It is a truism to say that no contemporary concern of ours can possibly be seen in that light.

Now we are all agreed that critical appraisal of contemporary works of art is an arduous and hazardous business. Responsible criticism, I suppose, must aim at something as close as possible to finality. It's in the nature of criticism. It is probably impossible, and yet every self-respecting critic seems to feel compelled at least to try. At its best, contemporary criticism can sometimes achieve that rare balance between principle and perception which is the only way that leads to true insight. The adjudicator who can truly achieve that balance and maintain it poised and ever self-correcting is a rare bird indeed. Such a critical mind is as rare as a truly original creative mind. The most common critical pitfall, the real booby-trap, in which the critic is most often caught, is that under pretence of examining a work objectively, in reality he may let himself be lured into giving us a piece of his mind. Rather than ascertain what *is* he will let himself be tempted into telling us how things *should be*. If this is done from a position of theoretical strength, fortified with aesthetico-philosophical, psycho-acoustical or musico-sociological argument the assault can be very impressive for the dispassionate observer. During the last few years, new music has often been taken to task in this fashion, and mostly left for dead or expiring on the battleground. Let me review some of these fatal encounters.

One of the most resounding attacks came from Theodor Adorno, a German writer on music of wide international reputation, and a teacher of philosophy and music-sociology at Frankfurt University. During the Second World War he spent some years in the United States and was associated with the group of scientists connected with Max Horkheimer at the Institute of Social Research. He has published a number of books on philosophical and musical subjects, among others *Philosophy of Modern Music*,[152] a provocative tract published in 1949. I would like to quote here from a more recent work entitled *Dissonanzen*.[153] One chapter in this book has a caption reading: "Modern Music is Growing Old".[154] The author detects signs of premature ageing in new music. To him, the signs are that even where it is still "subversive", as he puts it, it is no longer "menacing"; that it has lost its bloom because it has lost that "aura of apprehension" that surrounded its finest moments, 30 or so years ago; in short it is growing old because "it has become afraid of being afraid". The following passage fairly sums up his attitude:

> Certain pages of *The Rite of Spring* or of Alban Berg were so outrageous and shocking when they were heard for the first time, because they truly expressed the state of anxiety and bewilderment and the sense of insecurity which are so characteristic of our time. As long as modern music was vital, it would repudiate the fallacy that, once the first surprise was over, it would be found to be quite as beautiful as traditional music. As long as modern music obeyed its natural impulses it would spurn a certificate of good conduct. That it should now be possible for us to give it such a certificate, and for modern music to accept it, that is the final knock-out blow.

In order to put things in the right perspective, it's perhaps as well to add that over many decades, surprising though it may sound, Adorno has been one of the staunchest supporters of everything advanced in contemporary music. It is not, therefore, as if we were listening to one of the typical jeremiads of the disgruntled critic for whom things have gone "too far" or, at any rate, far enough to call a temporary halt.

I think that this would rather apply to Virgil Thomson's attack on new music in the magazine *Encounter*,[155] which aroused dismay among even the mildly liberal English critics. The view *he* takes of the present crisis could best be described, I think, in the historic phrase "desperate but not serious". The case with Adorno is very different. His attack on the so-called *avant-garde* does not come from the rear, as usual, but from a forward position. Let us look at his main charges one by one.

> It would appear that modern music today is in danger of being mixed up with those so-called cultural activities and manifestations whose object is to attenuate or camouflage *Angst* of any kind, whereas the very nature of this music and, indeed, the reason for its existence, obliges it to refuse any such compromise and to express and give form to the disquiet which marks our epoch.

To clarify what he means, Adorno chooses an illustration from recent literary history. Referring to *The Last Days of Mankind* by the Austrian writer Karl Kraus, published after the First World War, he writes:

> The frontispiece of the book showed the execution of the deputy Battisti, convicted of espionage, with a horrible photograph of the grinning executioner. In a recent edition of the work this frontispiece was omitted. The alteration, although exterior to the work itself, nevertheless considerably changed its impact and significance. In a less obvious way, this is what is happening in the music of our time: it uses almost the same palette as thirty years ago but the element of anxiety – *angst* – so characteristic of its finest moments, has been repressed. The anxiety motif has now grown to such proportions that its direct transposition into the language of art is no longer bearable; afraid of being afraid, modern music is allowing itself to grow old.[156]

The key word is *Angst.* The sentiment and both the illustrations and the vocabulary chosen to express it are so obviously and so irreducibly subjective, that they hardly need be discussed. What the Germans call *Lebensgefühl* – a given existential feeling – is not a matter for argument. But it is worth pointing out that in giving us a piece of his mind, and wrapping it up with subjective existential feeling, Adorno also provides some strong dogmatic thought, in regard to what he defines as the "very nature of new music" and even "the reason for its existence", which are somewhat large claims.

Is there really anything, however, to the pretended anxiety-content as the truly authentic characteristic of the finest works of 30 years ago? Is it true that one could unerringly pick out the handful of works in that category by the "aura of apprehension" that surrounds them?

And if so, is it true that these works are the finest because, in expressing the state of anxiety, bewilderment and insecurity of modern man, they are the authentic spiritual products of our time; and finally, is it then a fallacy to expect that modern music, after the first shock of surprise is over, could ever be felt to be in any sense beautiful, quite as beautiful as traditional music?

Let us go back 30 years. Can anyone imagine that, guided by the alleged "aura of apprehension", one would be bound to pick out works like, say, Schoenberg's Serenade Op.24, the Suite Op.29, or indeed his comic opera, *Von Heute auf Morgen*, all works belonging to that period, any more than Webern's String Trio, his Symphony or Quartet Op.22, or Stravinsky's Octet, to name just a handful of works from that time. I suggest that someone going about with a sort of Geiger-counter that would register degrees of anxiety-content would be bound to miss each and every one of these.

Incidentally, there is one score written exactly 30 years ago which, I'm afraid, we would have to concede to Adorno – Schoenberg's *Music for a Film Scene*. As the subtitles of its three menacing movements indicate, the composer had attempted to illustrate "Menacing Danger", "Angst" and "Catastrophe"; in other words, the genuine Adorno climate, complete. The irony of the case is that this work cannot be said to be one of Schoenberg's most memorable achievements.

I can't help thinking that when Adorno refers to the finest works of 30 years ago he is not being careful enough about dates. What he really has in mind are probably the representative works of 40 or 50 years ago, say Schoenberg's Five Pieces for Orchestra (1908), *Erwartung* (1909), Webern's Six Pieces Op.6 (1910) and the Five Pieces for small orchestra (1913), Berg's Three Pieces for Orchestra (1914) or Stravinsky's *The Rite of Spring* (1913). These works do have a certain climate in common. Vague and subjective though the feeling is, one would even concede that this might possibly be described as something like an "aura of apprehension". That they did shock audiences in their time and were felt to be, in Adorno's words, "menacing" and "subversive", we know from contemporary reports. But I very much doubt that audiences today would choose to describe their experience of these works in just those terms.

But what about works like Schoenberg's *Pierrot Lunaire* (1912) or Stravinsky's *Les Noces* (1917) and *Histoire du Soldat* (1918)? Assessed on the basis of the Adorno anxiety-index these works would have to be classed not only as utterly unrepresentative of the temper of the age, but even as spurious, by the Adorno standard of a work's aesthetic raison d'être which is supposed to be the necessity to "express and give form to the disquiet that marks out epochs". They are in fact as far as could be from doing that.

Summing up, Adorno exclaims: "What works today could be considered authentic unless they reflect intense fear? And who, short of being a Schoenberg or a Picasso, feels genuinely strong enough to undertake such works?" The answer seems obvious: to remain unaware of the fact that both Schoenberg and Picasso have also been able to express what we understand by *joie de vivre*, one must be afflicted with a rather large blind spot.

As to whether or not the works I've mentioned can truly be felt to be beautiful when sufficiently familiar, the question seems to me a purely rhetorical one. Beautiful and ugly are little more than expletives used in disputation. Clearly, any work, no matter what its style and expression, that can hold our attention deeply in listening to it, and can be listened to, time and again, without going stale or cloying on repetition, has something to it that baffles analysis, something maybe akin to life itself, something that will suggest to different listeners a host of attributes, none of which fully catches the elusive quality of a complex and absorbing artistic experience.

If some such experience has been denied Adorno, if, as he maintains, it is a fallacy to expect that the best music of our time could ever come to be felt, to be beautiful, then one is hard put to understand how anyone holding such a view could have been bothered at all with contemporary music as a major interest for 30 or 40 years of his life.

But I'm forgetting here Adorno the music-sociologist. In his *Philosophy of New Music* he surveys the music of the first half of the century in the work of five major composers: Bartók, Berg, Schoenberg, Stravinsky and Webern. The reader of his book has the impression that he is watching the critic sailing over the five major provinces of our musical continent on a low cloud, as it were, casting dark shadows on the ground and he, the critic, wrapped in eschatological mourning, as Krenek used to say. Yet from his aerial perspective, not unlike modern archaeological photography, he makes astonishingly revealing observations. Each new one is greeted with the excitement of discovery, but this soon passes and, in the end, a fine mist of blight seems spread over the whole territory, covering flats and elevations alike. One leaves the book with the feeling that here is a truly knowledgeable man of uncommon perspicacity, but for whom *tout comprendre*, turns alas, into *tout mépriser* – to understand everything leads, not to pardon, but to condemn everything.

Adorno might protest that excitement and enthusiasm as a critical state of mind are a doubtful proposition. The question is whether a conspicuous lack of enthusiasm is not even more blinding. As Dr Johnson has put it, "it is a good service that one does another when he tells him his manner of being pleased". This service Adorno could never render, for the simple reason that he never *is* pleased. More than that, it would be wrong, he tells us, to expect any pleasure, not only from contemporary music but from any music whatever, nowadays.

In *Dissonanzen* he has gone so far as to say: "... anyone who still hankers after the beautiful passages in Schubert or the appetizingly wholesome fare in Handel's *Concerti Grossi* ranks as a sort of butterfly-collector among the so-called custodians of cultural values."[157] According to him, anyone who fails to realize that responsible art today tends to become a critique of our contemporary situation, is living in the past, not in this present world of ours. In other words, all art now would aspire to the condition of *knowledge*, no longer to the condition of ***music,*** as of yore. Accordingly, all that is vital in modern art makes it its business "... to drive home relentlessly all that contemporary man desperately tries to forget." Surely one might have expected that someone who is deadly serious about critique and enlightenment would have chosen a semantically less ambiguous means of communicating than music or the arts. Besides Adorno himself does not seem to be so terribly serious about this mission since, according to him: "... it has by now become by no means certain that matters appertaining to aesthetics can still be taken seriously", which makes the artist's proposed new assignment of critique and enlightenment pretty stultifying.

Adorno quotes a contemporary German philosopher, Theodor Hecker, who has written that, in this bewildered and spiritually disoriented world of ours, "human beings will no longer have the *right* to express or describe their own condition". This crippling, catastrophic view reminds one also of Thomas Mann's protagonist in *Dr Faustus* – incidentally, a modern composer and one to whom the novelist has cavalierly attributed the invention of the twelve-note technique. This fictive composer, too, is troubled with the doubt as to "whether the work of art as such still stands in any legitimate relation to the problematic conditions and lack of harmony in our social situation; whether all appearance, even the most beautiful, or rather precisely, *the more beautiful*, has not become today a fraud and a lie". The same sentiment is echoed by yet another expatriate from the Hitler Reich during World War II, the Austrian writer Robert Musil. One cannot help wondering whether such a nihilist attitude, whether such an act of symbolic self-mutilation as that performed by the artist who would deny himself "the right to express or describe his own condition" may not have been prompted by the treacherous solicitations of guilt and an overwhelming desire for self-punishment. To have seen from a safe distance cataclysmic retribution inflicted on one's own nation may be far worse than having to take one's personal share in the ordeal. The roots of it all, however, may well go deeper than that.

One can imagine that it must make a Hegelian's blood boil to realize that Hegel's dismal vaticination "... that art is ... and will remain for us a thing of the past ...", is still unfulfilled 130 or so years after it was made! The contemporary confusion might easily lead pessimists to believe that the fulfilment of the prophecy is now within sight and that all there is for them to do is to hammer it in, to make us come to our senses and persuade us to give up for good.

To my mind, the contemporary confusion in the field of music and the arts is rather what one would expect from a social body deep in ferment and teeming with creative energy. It would seem a poor show if an epoch does not manage to develop its "contemporary" ideas fully in all directions, to the utmost limits of contradiction. Even by linguistic implication, contradictions evidently belong together. If truly fierce contradictory terms are not achieved, the case betokens a half-hearted spirit of adventure in an epoch. Whatever may be said against ours, half-heartedness is the last thing of which one could accuse it. Like the French general, we move in all directions at once, and in each to the fullness of our bent. No wonder then, if to a non-committed observer or, even more, to the general public, the state of affairs we are in seems frankly chaotic. One may certainly pity and sympathize with the poor newspaper critic who, having lost his bearings, is nonetheless supposed to pass snap judgments of value. But music-sociology might profitably give itself time to understand and not want to jump to conclusions.

There is no denying that there is plenty in contemporary music that is highly problematic. But the suggestion that we have reached an age of senility and a state of stagnation is fantastic. The boot is on the other foot. The very ways of using and organizing sound have changed almost out of recognition since 1945. There is no denying that the composing of music has long been method-starved and that, consequently, the formidable proliferation of ideas on "method" is just what one would expect in an epoch rich in creative sap.

No doubt method has made deep inroads upon what has traditionally been regarded as the preserve of "inspiration". But surely a healthy body of instincts is one that can absorb and react positively to the inoculation of even a stiff dose of systematic or theoretical concepts. After all, it's not inconceivable that it might prove possible to harness rationality, at its highest pitch of discipline, to the task – not indeed of *doing* the work of imagination, but to *work for* imagination in a selfless, truly altruistic manner. Imaginative logic and controlled intuition may seem a contradictory pair. I do not regard them as contradictory, in the sense of cancelling one another. On the contrary, opposites need one another, not only for definition, not only for complementarity, but in order to *be*. Their reciprocal need of one another is rooted in the very nature of totality.

A good deal of the confusion in the contemporary scene comes from the ambiguity in what we mean by the social significance of art in general and of music in particular, in other words, when we try to define the creative artist's social function and status. The approach to this problem suffers from the ingrained cultural superstitions which still cloud the much debated issue: Art and the People. Some time ago Sir Herbert Read quoted Paul Klee's famous cry, "*Uns tragt kein Volk*!" (the people are not with us).[158] There is something pathetically naive, almost childlike, in those sad words. The artist feels unloved, forsaken. And yet, the irony of it all!

Would anyone deny that the phase that comprised people like Cézanne, Picasso, Kandinsky, Mondrian and Klee, or in music, Debussy, Schoenberg, Stravinsky and Webern will rank as one of the outstandingly original creative periods in the history of the modern world? The idea that the work of these men could have had a popular support seems preposterous. What, then, was Paul Klee crying out for? What is the meaning of the term "the people" in our mechanized society? For whose support was Klee longing? Surely it could not have been those amongst the masses catered to by mass-produced entertainment? True, the German word for people, *Volk,* has romantic overtones and emotional reverberations to which nothing, it seems to me, corresponds in the English word. Is it possible that Klee was hankering after the sense of security, the warm feeling of belonging to a large human community, rather than after the sense of respectability, not to say the glamour, which the romantic artist still enjoyed in nineteenth-century bourgeois society?

It's obvious that the re-grouping and re-shaping consequent upon every major upheaval and change in the social fabric, compels art, too, inescapably, to change place and find a new niche in the overall social framework. The place of the artist in tribal society or in the Homeric world, in classical Greece or in mediaeval Christendom, in the Renaissance or in bourgeois nineteenth-century society differs from our place and standing in contemporary society by all the factors that have made our world different from that of those ages. Evidently, our social status has declined tremendously from that quasi-priestly dignity of the creative artist in ancient cultures, or even from the exalted position of the nineteenth-century artist with his divo-nimbus.

But it does by no means follow that we, today, are left with no status at all, floating in a sort of social void, if that were possible. There is no such thing. Social nature abhors the void no less than physical nature does. We simply have had to climb down and are now perching on a lower rung of the social ladder. Obviously, the scientist's standing today is far higher than ours. We have simply got to accept this for a fact, but we have no cause to feel jealous or suspicious of the scientist. The so-called pure scientist is, on the contrary, a close relative, almost a twin brother. It's rather the technocrat and the cultural managerial boss who are to be dreaded.

Our world tends to make specialists of us all. It's essential to be aware of this and of the importance of escaping from one's specialization and coming up for air from time to time. A specialist commands a limited audience. The range of communication widens or narrows down with the particular degree of specialization. At worst, the specialist is intelligible to other specialists in the same field. There, undoubtedly, lies the danger for the artist. The broad humanistic approach has been in retreat in the arts for some time. The spirit of specialization fosters inbreeding: the painter painting for painters, the poet writing for literati, the composer composing for experimental music festivals. Read was voicing qualms about this state of affairs in the contemporary plastic arts. His views seem to coincide with those of Adorno. He, too, believes that the renewal that took place after the breakthrough in the first decade of the century has come to an end after the efflorescence in the Twenties. This is a narrow view with which I disagree. If anything is clear, it is, possibly, that nothing has come to an end.

The movement that started early in the century is still in full swing, growing and branching out all the time, and in more directions and at a higher speed than may seem comfortable for clear survey and critical appraisal. But that's the critics' baby. And if they hate it and wish they could throw it out with the bathwater, one can understand their plight. The truth is that in this still growing process there has been no break to this day, and certainly no significant reversal of direction, apart from the periodic backwash normal to every forward trend. Hindemith's naturalism and Stravinsky's *pastiche* or neo-classicist *velleities* have been chiefly responsible in our time for these periodic recoils.

If, on the other hand, what the critics mean is that the leading composers of our day are lesser men than the master who achieved the breakthrough and opened the way for us, then I have no quarrel with this opinion – *ai posteri l'ardua sentenza*. My point is that the last thing of which music today can be accused is of having grown old or derivative. On the contrary: not only has the spirit of exploration not abated one whit, but in the handling of tone and time it has led to new modes of musical thinking which, though having roots in the work of the pioneers, had not in reality been foreseen by them. What is more, we are witnessing nowadays a vigorous effect of stimulation of the older generation by the younger generation. Stravinsky is a case in point. All this is not exactly indicative of a generation of effete and decrepit hangers-on. It rather seems to me that if a new generation has got to be on its own, *fare da se*, in order to legitimate itself as a living link in the chain, then music today is doing so abundantly.

Finally, coming back to the question of our so-called social function, it seems to me that contemporary music, minority concern though it still is at present, addresses and can reach that particular Cinderella class in our present-day class-system – the educated and the self-educated middle-class man and woman (mostly in a lower income-bracket than the mass-entertained working class) who are gifted with more intellectual alertness and spirit of exploration than means or opportunities to exercise and satisfy them.

I know that for this Cinderella class in England, for example, a decline in the output of the BBC Third Programme can become a matter of serious deprivation. They are people who bring to listening, viewing or reading a mental equipment and a response that are uniquely the product of our time. In teaching and training them thus to listen, view and read, contemporary art has played a great part. I think that a contemporary artist who has had a part in creating such an élite, can be proud of it. This élite, rather than *das Volk*, or the millions Beethoven longed to embrace, constitute the potential audience of today's music. I feel that to have established such a relationship is social integration enough for us, in fact, it's all we need or can bear. For the slogan about integrating art and society, a rather vague notion though it has always been, has nevertheless an unmistakeably ominous ring. While the case of Thomas Mann's and Adorno's self-mutilated artist must be counted among the sad individual casualties in the battle, there can be little doubt that in the business of integrating art and society, integration from above would always be at the artist's cost. And we may be sure that the mutilation the artist would suffer at the hands of the culture-commissar would be likely to be pretty drastic.

But to end on less gruesome note, I would like to quote from a great American poet, Wallace Stevens:

> What is [the poet's] function? Certainly it is not to lead people out of the confusion in which they find themselves. Nor is it, I think, to comfort them while they follow their leads to and fro. I think that his function is to make *his* imagination become the light in the mind of others. His role, in short, is to help people to live their lives. Time and again it has been said that he may not address himself to an élite. I think he may. There is no poet whom we prize, living today, that does not address himself to an élite. The poet will continue to do this – to address himself to an élite, even in a classless society, unless, perhaps this exposes him to prison or exile.[159]

32 Art and anarchy (1961)[160]

Hegel's dismal prophecy that, in a scientific age, art would become and remain forever a thing of the past, has haunted the imagination of historians, critics and sociologists ever since it was made. Powerfully amplified, with a good deal of distortion and rattling of loudspeakers, it recurs in Oswald Spengler's *Decline of the West*. The reverberations of that spectacular intellectual upheaval have by no means completely died down yet. In Edgar Wind's brilliant Reith Lectures, the ripples are still distinctly perceptible and the source of the commotion is not difficult to trace. He rejects Hegel's prophecy.[161] He accepts nonetheless the analysis of the situation which, according to the German philosopher, was bound to lead to a drastic shift of the arts in the human interest. And whereas Spengler could express the hope that men of the new generation might be moved by his book "to take up engineering instead of poetry, join the Navy rather than arts school, become politicians rather than philosophers", Wind is willing to examine "what we ourselves, as recipients of art, might do, or refrain from doing, to render our participation in art more vital".[162] Clearly, with the catastrophic obsession, the oracular pretensions have gone too. Only the general diagnosis is confirmed, the malady persists, but the patient is not given up.

It is Wind's contention that art has become dehumanized because of the artist's indulgence in a shallow mimicry of "scientific procedures".[163] What are we to understand under the blanket phrase "scientific procedures"? It looks suspiciously like the new bogey-man. I suggest that we try to exorcize it. We may still be left with an unmanageably large-scale topic such as "scientific method", but this offers at least some common ground between art and science. The notion that inspiration is all the artist needs – a notion Wind himself is at some pains to dissipate – assumes, perhaps a little too readily, that we all are in the secret of what inspiration is and of how it works with the artists, which is doubtful. Granted that the creative artist needs method too – and it would be foolish to deny it – it stands to reason that he should have a good method rather than a poor one. The scientist will simply be incapacitated by poor method; the artist, I am afraid, will not; he may always muddle through with some measure of success. But if he is not satisfied with muddling through, and that is his own business, I see no reason why he should not try to learn, if he can, from specialists who depend on high standards of method for sheer efficiency.

In the saying that the whole man and nothing but the whole man is good enough for producing a good work of art, surely the implication is: all the innate gifts in their true proportions. In other words, more method than the artist's intellect can handle or less than his temperament needs: there is trouble either way. It is an artificial antithesis that would keep art and science rigorously incommunicado. In every age, the dominant ideas have had a way of fertilizing more than one field of speciality; and it is a fact of common experience that ideas, wherever they may grow, never benefit from confinement.

Gide's words about *peinture decérébrée* and the *acte gratuite* sound incredibly futile. Incidentally, what an odd choice of words: *decérébrée* for intellectualized, and "gratuitous" as a degrading epithet: after all, the root of the word is "grace". The true meaning of the so-called "gratuitous act" is perfectly understood by scientists and artists alike. The hunch, the intimation, the divination – or, if you prefer, the dropping of one's logical stitches – goes often with the very flash of insight that can lead to the sudden discovery. The point is that the discovery comes first. The rest is methodical sweat and toil concerned with how to set about making that sudden glimpse work. Every artist knows from experience that he can be method-starved as well as inspiration-starved. There is a good deal he can do about method: about inspiration, nothing. Therefore, experiment must go on, in the studio no less than in the laboratory. Needless to say, what counts is the outcome. Experimental art *as* the outcome is a contradiction in terms. It simply means bad art.

If, by "dehumanized" art, what is meant is abstract art, it is difficult to see why we should put it beyond the pale. Surely it is too simple to think of all art-experience, indiscriminately, as a "tremendous mode of excitement". The opposite, a "serene mode of excitement", is equally conceivable, in spite of the apparent verbal contradiction. I think that no one, to whom this notion remains unintelligible, can ever have listened with true involvement to, say, Bach's *Art of Fugue* or even to the *Goldberg Variations*. Such works offer a range of imaginative experience perhaps greater than that of works the pleasurable response to which depends largely on more intense emotional reverberations.

To regard the far reaches of the mind as "dehumanized" because they cease to thrill us in the ordinary emotional sense of the word seems impossibly narrow-visioned. The view that art which probes into those reaches could be "out of touch with the central energies of life"[164] seems more typical of *l'homme moyen sensuel* than of the average spiritual man. If we ask what may be wrong with us today as recipients of art, we should first know who it is that asks the question, what is his "attitude", as we say; whether he is an art historian or connoisseur with the scholarly approach. Wind has raised pertinently the question of the will, since it is the will, or rather the gradations between willing and surrender of the will, that basically define the attitudes.[165] The scholarly attitude obviously puts the will at a premium. Indeed, the refined abstract techniques of expertise, so vividly described in the Reith

Lectures amount by definition to a deliberate, if temporary methodical refusal to surrender the will. I am not questioning the benefits accruing to the study of art from the temporary methodical disengagement that reduces the scholar's artistic perception to an "emotionally untainted sense of form". The doubt arising here concerns the possibility that this professional bent might conceivably produce a permanent crease: in other words, that it might eventually prove difficult for the scholar to find his way back to a full-blooded response, to an attitude of communion with the work of art. Let me put it boldly: when Wind diagnoses an alarming attenuation of our responses to the work of art today, is he really speaking for all of us, or is he giving us an illuminating piece of personal introspection? Is he not, in fact, describing the predicament of a specialist no longer able to escape from his specialism?

We should not under-rate the perils of deadening closure that can follow achievement and block the passage towards new thought and fresh insight. The very success of the models of the world which mathematics can set up today, to cite an example, is causing uneasiness in the minds of some mathematicians. Whitehead has warned us that "the sense of penetration tends to be lost in the certainty of completed knowledge".[166]

In the sombre picture Wind has painted for us, facts and interpretation fit easily enough when we try to look at things from his viewpoint. The distribution of light and shade is pretty consistently what one would have expected from the bias and perspective of the observer. If we discount these, the picture changes considerably, and the general validity of Wind's observations remains questionable.

If we ask how far his observations are true of the common reader, the common viewer, the common listener, the only possible answer is that neither I nor Wind can know what they are. Our evidence of other people's feelings, reactions and motivations is indirect and notoriously ambiguous for the most part.

What is Wind's evidence that art in our time has ceased to be a fundamental human need? The short answer must be: degeneration or, in his own words, "a growing atrophy of the receptive organs" due to our excessive consumption of art. "Diffusion", he says, "brings a loss of density".[167] The Spanish saying that he who embraces too much cannot hug tightly seems to sum up Wind's idea. I am fond of proverbial wisdom, but I cannot overlook the fact that atrophy of an organ is more commonly associated with lack of function than with excess, and that loss of density through diffusion – a plain enough observation in the physical world – is far from self-evident in the sphere of cultural diffusion.

But, analogies apart, let us consider Wind's definition of what we lose in our too large and bland embrace of art today. "The sacred fear is no longer with us", he says.[168] That is the loss. The demon of the imagination Plato tried to exorcize can no longer scare us. Frankly, I think that Plato was more consistent than Wind. One cannot logically allow for causes of anxiety in

Utopia, by definition a perfect state of affairs. But we are late-comers in civilization: what sense does it make to wish, as Wind seems to, that we were more primitive than we really are? Besides, the dread of the artist' imagination that haunted Plato is overshadowed by today's more substantial fears. We have learned to dread the scientist's imagination more than the artist's. The demons we have to cope with are of a different calibre. Certainly, the obsession with fear in our time is understandable, and in relation to that obsession we can readily agree that science has driven the arts into a marginal position in the imaginative life of man.

This is so obvious, it would not be worth stating were it not for the new twist it has been given by the more hysterical among the commentators, who are already clamouring that any contemporary work of art that does not reflect "existential terror" is merely inconsequential, humanly irrelevant doodling. I cannot imagine Wind agreeing with the music-sociologist Theodor Adorno in this view. *Art engagé*, of which Adorno's is as bad a form as any, is a notion that Wind dismisses, and, I think, rightly.[169] The creative artist accepts no task-master. His activity is an activity of the mind, of the whole mind, which is something more comprehensive than any one single manifestation in which it may express itself. To quote the American poet, Wallace Stevens:

> The mind has added no artifice to human nature. It is a violence within that protects us from a violence without. It is the imagination pressing back against the pressure of reality. It seems, in the last analysis, to have something to do with our self-preservation; and that, no doubt, is why the expression of it ... helps us to live our lives.[170]

The life that art helps us to live is the life of the imagination. How other people live the life of the imagination we can only conjecture; we can feel it sympathetically, but we cannot know it with any degrees of certainty. Yet if we can observe that what contemporary art has to offer is absorbed by our generation with an "eagerness and with a degree of intelligence which leaves older generations speechless",[171] as Wind observes; if the new and unfamiliar no longer produce the tantrums that, as he says, it used to produce in the past, then it is hard to see why this should be taken, as Wind takes it, for an alarming surrender to art "on almost any terms".

On his own evidence, the terms are eagerness, intelligence and emotional balance: terms on which we must surely wish to entertain, in Stevens' words, the "supreme fictions" which give life whatever savour it has. It is the imagination *without* intelligence which begets the demons that frightened Goethe and Plato. Their reservations refer to a type of imagination which might be called "romantic" in the pejorative sense of the word. "The romantic", to quote Stevens once more, "is to the imagination what sentimentality is to feeling. It is a failure of the imagination precisely as sentimentality is a failure of feeling."[172]

Thus conceived, the imagination is one of the central energies of life.

Indeed, what – except such a power – could sustain creative effort? What – except such a power – could save man from the dulled vision, the blunted ear, the cold heart, from the film of familiarity which slowly clouds all his perceptions? Renewal by transformation is the law of life; there is something biologically arrested in mere reproduction.

Inevitably, the emergence of novelty entails disruption. Whitehead maintained that "the essence of life is to be found in the foundations of established order".[173] He thought that life is doomed to degenerate "when enclosed in the shackles of mere conformation", that "a power of incorporating vague and disorderly elements of experience is essential for the advance into novelty" since "the essence of great experience is penetration into the unknown, the un-experienced", so that "details hitherto un-discriminated or dismissed as casual irrelevances are lifted into co-ordinated experience".[174] He required philosophy "to explain the rise of types of order" and "the transition from type to type".[175] He required it to understand that "the interweaving of change and permanence" is a primary fact of experience. That the history of art, or at any rate the history of Western art, conclusively testifies to the uninterrupted pursuit of such objectives cannot be denied. If there is one aspect of the present situation about which there can be no doubt, it is the immense vitality with which this pursuit presses on in our time. The good and the bad are mixed, as always, in unequal proportions; but to be despondent because life will produce monstrosities as well as healthy strains would seem a far more serious symptom of mental sickness than the very abnormalities we deplore.

Let it be granted that even the best of contemporary art is still a minority interest. Art addresses itself to an élite, but to a lesser or larger extent it always has done and will always have to. Yet one of the effects of the diffusion of art, which Wind deplores, has been to make the experience of art accessible to sectors of the community which were previously debarred from that experience. I cannot see how our techniques of mass-communication could have failed to have this effect.

The question is, can it be said to be entirely healthy? Probably not. The influx of new audiences for the arts is historically unprecedented. The increase in numbers brings with it an increased proportion of sheer snobbishness and shallow dilettantism, but it also includes new contingents of fresh intelligence and sensibility. Our real audience can easily be sifted from the noisy crowd by one characteristic: a sense of commitment which for me is identical with true participation. Audiences tend to specialize, but by and large it can be said that the arts today, all the arts, draw on this one committed audience.

This is itself one of the most remarkable creations of modern art. We have taught and trained this audience to read, to view, to listen *differently*. To have achieved this, to have helped the élite to live today the life of the imagination, is social relevance and social integration enough. It is all the integration of art and society we want. And it certainly is all the integration I personally care for.

33 The Muse and music today (1962)[176]

"For ten years, paint bamboo. Then, become bamboo. Finally, paint it without thinking of bamboo." Admirable. Of course, it's important to remember, with aphorisms, as with medicine, one should shake well before use. The good sense of the first recommendation by the Chinese sage is obvious; that of the second, a bit difficult to gauge; that of the third, unquestionable. However, one could perfectly imagine that among the possible consequences of observing scrupulously the mandarin's rule, is routine work, pure and simple. Naturally, there is routine in every technique and one has to admit that routine today is too greatly devalued a concept: the English philosopher A.N. Whitehead observed that it is an indispensable factor in the economy of existence.[177] But technique has aspirations above this indispensable routine level. The question really is where does it reach: where does technique finish and inspiration begin? In so "immaterial" a medium as music, there is no clear dividing line.

It isn't possible, without being arbitrary, to separate the "way" technique operates, from the "medium" within which it operates. Thus, one could correctly say that in fugue, for instance, the fugue is technique and technique is the fugue. It's evident, however, that we don't gain anything in practice, by erasing the profiles of useful words and that when we say technique or inspiration, we know perfectly what we are referring to.

True, we distinguish in order to unite. But when the Chinese sage concludes that "an infallible technique hands the artist over to inspiration", decidedly, he ends by barking up the wrong tree. No. An infallible technique would be a technique with no risk. Therefore, the artist of infallible technique would be a passport more for the Academy than for the Temple of the Muses.

It's also true, on the other hand, that a powerful inspiration is capable of undermining, opening fissures in the most solid technique and still, maybe, of ruining an entire system. The history of music is, amongst other things, a chronicle of "disaster" stories of this nature, which only are such – note well – for those who not merely maintain a live tradition but transform it.

The reader will notice that I have been talking without circumlocution about "inspiration" – nowadays something completely taboo. It is a taboo I'm happy to challenge. Why indeed all this caution, not only in music, but in all contemporary art, when we use the word "inspiration"? It's easy to try to wriggle free of this question, as if it were a rope with which to hang oneself: though, incidentally, I'm not saying there's a lack of gallows in the entire panorama of contemporary art, nor a lack of bodies hanging from them. In my opinion, it is a problem with deep roots, one worth meditating upon carefully.

In *avant-garde* circles – using the word in its militant and therefore exclusive sense – it is maintained with rare unanimity that "contemporary" music begins with Anton Webern. It would be wrong to take the assertion as simply denoting a diffuse, current fashion, or as a vague declaration of faith. On the contrary, it's a *credo* rigorously based in doctrine.

Webern, when he died in 1945, virtually unknown to the general public, was constitutionally so incapable of doubting the intrinsic value of his music, as not to doubt the decisive influence it was destined to have over the post-war generation. It's comparable in many aspects with the work of Paul Klee in painting, specifically in what Klee called *Andacht zum Kleinen* – a poetic reverence for the world of the minute, significantly coinciding with the awakening in contemporary science of an interest in the microstructure of the universe.

What the international *avant-garde* deliberately ignores today is, firstly, that Webern could glimpse the remote horizons of his contemporaries' vision, for he was lifted up on the shoulders of a giant. The desire to separate Webern's work from that of his master Schoenberg is childish and arbitrary. Secondly, the fact is overlooked that if Webern concerned himself with innovation, he despised theorizing. His intentions are consequently a matter for conjecture: everyone can interpret them as he wishes. Up to now these interpretations have been so varied, oscillating between opposing extremes, that his work seems to have represented for the post-war musical world a genuine intersection of misunderstandings.

Less important is that, with the natural enthusiasm of posthumous discovery, Webern's stature has been exaggerated: time will rectify that. Without doubt he has secured himself a niche in the history of music as maybe the greatest of *Kleinmeister*, of similar rank to that of the English "minor poet". But the attempt to downgrade Schoenberg's work in comparison with that of his disciple has been absurd. Webern himself would have been scandalized. Undeniably, however, his influence came to eclipse that of Schoenberg in the horizons of post-war musical youth: although for many reasons understandable, this in my opinion represents a transitory state of things.

However, to see clearly how the transformations that characterize the most recent music have been produced, one has to admit that they all originate, either directly or accidentally, from Webern's innovations. One of the most important was the personal twist he gave to the serialist technique originated by Schoenberg. In his hands, the only object of that technique was to facilitate the methodical control of only one of the "variables" of the phenomenon of sound: the "tonal" variable, that is, pitch, as much in succession as simultaneous. Historically, this came to rectify the anarchical egalitarianism in the use of the twelve notes of our chromatic scale, which was produced by the relaxation of the principle of tonal hierarchical relations linked in heptatonic scales and in the triadic harmony of classical music. At bottom, Schoenbergian serialism is essentially a distributive method, despite the very different purpose for which it was conceived.

I think that the importance of "automatism" in serial distribution has seldom been remarked upon, though its function in the other arts is nowadays perfectly well understood. In Schoenberg, the distributive automatism gives serial technique an extraordinary degree of flexibility, thanks to the composer's favourite procedure of segmenting the series in various ways – in adjoining segments, in groups of separated notes, or adjoining and separated, but "seriatim" – and using those segments as threads for the layout of the polyphony. In parenthesis, it is interesting to note that in biology, passing from multi-cellular organization (in "one-piece" organisms) to that of organisms like the *anelidae*, which adopt the principle of segmentation, is considered as a decisive ascending step in the evolutionary scale.

From a certain point onwards, Webern rejected specifically the segmentation procedure, which guarantees the flexibility of the Schoenbergian method, in favour of the exclusive use of entire undivided series. The biologist would probably consider this as a step backwards. In musical practice, this variation, apparently of little account, had unsuspected consequences. At first the concept of the series is in Webern, hypostatized. What was essentially pragmatic, in Schoenberg, merely a norm of craftsmanship, *modus facendi*, acquires in Webern the category of "law", of *nomos*, and soon after, in his successors, of fanatical shibboleth.

Meanwhile, Webern cannot operate with a single series any more: for he needs to use so many doubles or replicas of it as voices or parts in a polyphonic texture. Once again, his attitude, if not regressive, is at least conservative and retarding, since it consolidates a principle of stratification applied to horizontal layers or part-writing: the latter, in Schoenberg, had already begun to give way to a unified concept of the musical space needed to overcome the dichotomy between the horizontal and the vertical.

For the reader who doesn't know about music, it would be almost impossible to imagine what Webern's procedure involves in practice, but the reader-musician will quickly see how and why the adoption of the undivided series limits the melodic invention, at a horizontal level, to the intervals predetermined by the series: while at a vertical level, the superimposition of concurrent series reduces the control of the overall harmonic progress, transforming it into an essentially fortuitous result of the varying progress of the voices in the polyphony.

In this brief incursion into technical territory, my sole concern is to become detached from the paradoxical arrival of – and common ground between – two antithetical principles, one determinist, the other – in Webern's work – fortuitous, contingent, aleatory. However contradictory this phenomenon, we cannot forget that a contradiction, always fatal in logic, is not necessarily so when conceived by an artist.

On the other hand, one should admit that every strict system necessarily involves some kind of predetermination, no less in what it prescribes than in what it proscribes, and that the contingent factor arises with every freely chosen activity. The connection between the appearance of an aleatory factor in harmony and the abandonment, in contemporary science, of the natural law in favour of a probabilistic conception of the universe, can also not be denied.

Meanwhile, the determinist difficulty in Webern remains obvious after the manner of Unamuno's dictum (as I recall it): "If you always wanted that which is, it would always be what you want." In effect, the conflict between the artist's will and the obligatory basis of the series disappears at the point at which Webern renounces willingly the multiplicity of melodic intervals, choosing series that only include a few. What this severe limitation illustrates with unsurpassable clarity is the radical change that occurs, in Webern's work, in the function of the interval. Once completely understood, this change ensures that the structural prevails over the lyrico-rhapsodic in contemporary music. It includes as its premise a non-thematic style, corresponding to the abstract, non-figurative style in painting. Naturally, this was already implicitly contained in Schoenberg's technique, though Schoenberg remained loyal, in all his work, to the pan-thematicist ideal that looks towards the opposite extreme; proof, indeed, that opposite extremes can make contact. And Schoenberg was not the first great inventor from whom all the future significance of an idea, going beyond its immediate objectives, was concealed.

Considered from a purely methodological standpoint, there is no doubt that in Webern tonal organization achieves a rigour, clarity and elegance foreign to that of Schoenberg. The predominance of his interest in the tectonic aspect of tonal organization and his predilection for schemes of exact symmetry, produced in Webern's music configurations that are like crystalline structures, an intellectual beauty unsurpassed even in the more daring contrapuntal music of J.S. Bach himself.

Writing essentially more geometric than that of Webern presupposes a rigorously quantitative, indeed commensurable element. As such, this makes Webern's operations like the logical demonstration of a theorem. The analysis of a composition reveals his plans, its achievements objectively provable. If there has been an error or a lapse in the performance, it's possible to point it out. It might seem from this that we have reached the antithesis of what we understand by intuitive or inspired. So far as Webern is concerned, such an opinion would be erroneous. What is marvellous in his music is, precisely, the secret alchemy (unanalysable, of course) by which the reflective and the inspired are trans-substantiated into a live work of art.

However, it is also true that the quantitative analysable aspect of his music is the starting-point for all the advanced tendencies appearing in music during the last ten years or so. The quantitative factor has proliferated with unbelievable self-indulgence, invading regions not explored by Webern himself. The apothegm, "I am commensurable, therefore I am" expresses and sums up the orientation of the first wave of post-Webernian activity.

The sonorous phenomenon has, actually, more than one variable factor – the term used today is "parameter" – which is capable of quantification and measurement. Tonal and temporal factors, which are perfectly quantifiable, have been in force since music began. Now we have proceeded to the quantification of volume or intensity of sound – much less common previously (except in electronic music) – and of timbre (or vocal and instrumental colour), an acoustic phenomenon not yet fully understood. But this has not prevented people from adopting *ad hoc* methods of measurement that would permit the application of the serial method to all the parameters, ie integral serialization.

As we have seen, Schoenberg and Webern, in their different ways, applied serial methods to the tonal parameter, that is exclusively to the relationships between pitches. In the temporal dimension, that is from the standpoint of rhythmical configuration, Schoenberg has, in an entirely intuitive way, emulated the classic composers. In Webern's own work there is still no trace of a "temporal series", although it is evident that note-values, durations, already have for him a new, unmistakeably structural meaning. However, for the following generation of composers, the instruction is – integral serialization: the determinist principle ends up affecting all the parameters of the composition.

It is a curious phenomenon that might interest the sociologist: for the post-war generation distinguishes itself straightaway by its frankly anti-lyrical attitude and enthusiasm for discipline. The ardour which it brings to systematic planning transforms profoundly the entire musical economy giving it all the features of a *guided* economy.

Unless we go into excessive technical detail, it's impossible to emphasize the formidable difficulties, paradoxes and contradictions that global planning causes in practice. The difficulties are insuperable. Possibly the only acceptable work that has been produced under these conditions has been the first book of Pierre Boulez's *Structures*, although this work only represents a limited application of integral serialization. Where the ambition is fulfilled unreservedly, as in the works of some Germans and Belgians of the second rank, the result is unutterably dull. Unavoidably, having been elevated to supreme rank and sole command, the quantitative has abolished the imponderable, transforming the enterprise of composing into an intricate, but at bottom, simplistic task of accountancy and logistics.

With music having reached, at this point, a cul-de-sac, suddenly there opens up one of those rare perspectives on the world of paradox, that can only be glimpsed from the vortices of extreme situations. The image of a pendulum swinging suddenly in the opposite direction is inadequate. The transition from the determinist principle to the aleatory principle of the following stage is more than a change of front: we witness one of those irridescent transformations where extremes do more than just touch, they melt, are subtly intermingled. In truth, all this has gradually produced the antecedents of a new stage.

One of the most significant characteristics of the previous one – an unavoidable consequence of the quantifiable principle – was an attitude of growing indifference towards the intrinsic qualities of the interval – its expressive character and physiognomy. The specific potential of tension (melodic and harmonic) between two notes is reduced when within the widest statistical conception of the field of power (control). Thanks to the phenomenon of rarefaction that this induces, the tense linear, almost crystalline, structures of Webern's music give way to a concept of homogeneous plasticity of sonorous matter, upon which the composer operates, in terms of "densities" rather than counterpoint. One need hardly say in passing, that with this transformation of structural values, the function of serial method itself is diverted from the centre of operations towards the periphery; from being the prime parameter of composition, serialism is reduced to a role of distant monitor of the global processes determining the overall progress of the composition.

It is at this superior level that the aleatory principle at last enters open territory. In Karlheinz Stockhausen's *Klavierstuck XI*, for instance, the composer allows the performer to decide at will the entire course of the piece. The printed score which the pianist sees is like a railway network map, where all the lines connect and through which one can circulate without restrictions, determining the itinerary *en route* and changing at will. The essential details of the "instructions for use" and, in particular, how one decides one has reached a destination are now beside the point.

The description given here is sufficient to indicate what the system has in common with Meccano. A series of isolated pieces (musical phrases) is supplied that can be joined in different ways and then added together in all kinds of formats. The final model is therefore, clearly, an invention of the person who builds it: likewise, the form that Stockhausen's piece presents is that given by the pianist wishing to perform it. And since, according to the given instructions, the pianist's itinerary must proceed at random, departing from visual impressions of the printed page, it is clear that the result will each time be a piece with a different form, a new construction, within the limits of probability for the case.

Leaving all critical considerations aside, it's important to see clearly how the phenomenon of "indifference", appearing initially in relation to the interval, multiplies from category to category, reaching at last the point where it affects the entire form. It ends up with the composer pretending not to know about his personal, untransferable sense of responsibility in this respect, or if you like, rejecting the traditional concept of the work of art as a unique and intangible final product. It would be pointless to pretend that Stockhausen could in fact have foreseen the result of all the possible permutations and thus maintain supreme control over all the possible formal transformations of a potentially polymorphic piece. Even reducing the number of phrases to a modest dozen, it is the case that the factorial of twelve exceeds one hundred million, and this would be less important – "patience and shuffling", as Durandarte (in *Don Quixote)* said – compared to the prodigy of ingenuousness that would be needed in order to ensure that all the undesirable permutations remained automatically excluded.

Thus, all of them being equally desirable, it follows that none is, or can be, in optimum degree, and given this – and it is given – it's evident that the factor of "indifference" affecting everything from material to form, ends up by insinuating its way into the very attitude of the artist towards the work of art.

To compare this attitude with that of a painter like Jackson Pollock is inaccurate, since his fortuitous procedures within painting are pure incidents of the technical process which do not suppress the overt and definitive identity of the finished product. In the "indeterminate" music of John Cage, however, the aleatory process is, by definition, illimitable and thus, rejects the concept of the immutable identity of the work. In this sense, one could then compare Cage's work with the most recent painting of the New York School – called "collage explosion" by a sympathetic critic – which tries to suppress the solution of continuity between the work of art, as immutable form, and life, as "continuum" and incessant change.

Now, despite how far these extreme manifestations have taken us, there could not be a greater proof of incomprehension than to stop here and conclude that contemporary art is bankrupt. To do so would be to ignore what an original adventure it has been.

Ortega y Gasset, to whom we owe so many sagacious observations about contemporary art (along with others, we must confess, that are fallacious) insists, in his *Meditations of a Quixote*, on the heroic sense that "the eternal resistance to the habitual and customary"[178] has in the artist. He does not think there exists a deeper kind of originality than this, his "practical", active, originality in which every movement he makes has needed first to defeat custom and invent a new form of gesture ... "a constant tearing of that part of oneself submitted to habit, prisoner of matter". Certainly, the new cannot be produced without tearings, erosions, and even moments of delirium. One shouldn't forget either that Don Quixote doesn't remain definitively defeated but that he recovers.

Every adventure of the spirit involves a culminating moment in which one decides between the life or death of determination. Nowadays, it's very significant what the aforesaid excess of "indifference" has in common with the mental attitude called *accidia*. There is a suspicion of disinterest, of lack of "tone" in both senses of the word – physiological and philological – in the statistico-quantitative conception of a sonorous phenomenon. Luciano Berio, in *Incontri Musicali*,[179] speaks concretely about "the enhancement of the sensation of a series of pitches (or notes) and of intervals, so as to favour a sensation of sonorous quality and register, considering these last ones as the active and determinant elements of the formal structure". The note, the interval, therefore, are worthless, they remain underrated. This goes deeper than any of the purely stylistic changes that the history of music registers. Before form, it's the turn of sonorous materials themselves.

It seems as if for the first time the word "atonal" might be just about to acquire meaning. For, on the other hand, it's clear that asking that the intrinsic qualities of the material be the "determinant of the form" is not a new requirement. Every art that has not been essentially decorative, has always complied with it. What happens now is different. Remember what engineers call "metal fatigue": a kind of exhaustion in the bosom of the material itself, a wear-and-tear of its essential properties. For there is no doubt that up to now the "pitch focus" of note and interval have been considered, in all the cultures we know of, as indications of the "semantic" dimension *par excellence* of music. In rhythm, the semantic dimension is much more ambiguous.

But at this point, we are concerned with asking for the cause or causes for this devaluation of the tonal. An obvious one is the phenomenon of auditive tolerance which is produced as the ear gets used to dissonances (tensions) of greater dynamic potential. There is a point beyond which the economists' law of diminishing returns starts to operate: this is, the auditive tolerance that the same process of dynamic intensification has induced begins to lessen. The dissonance, as far as dynamism is concerned, produces less. Hearing desensitizes itself in the tonal domain. Finally, tolerance becomes "indifference".

Understandably, on reaching this point, the composer begins to get interested in other than traditional sonorous materials derived from the instruments currently in use. I refer, of course, to electronic music. But this would constitute another essay. However, the reference is inevitable, since what happens today in the field of electronic music is closely linked to the course that things take in the field of instrumental music.

Edgard Varèse has incidentally declared that instrumental music has already entered a stage of obsolescence, and is destined to disappear, to be replaced by electronic music. In fact, everything that can be observed today in practice indicates the opposite. Let us leave aside what is inconsistent in Varèse in putting this principle into effect, by limiting himself to the almost exclusive use of instrumentally-derived sounds that are simply altered electronically – the procedure he adopts to produce his organized sound in *Déserts.*

An important aspect of electronic music is that not only does it facilitate but it obliges the composer to deal with the analysis of the micro-structure of the sonorous phenomenon. The analytical tendency, as we have seen, is a characteristic relevant to electronic music, and in certain aspects, foreshadows it. This analytical phrase might be defined as one of *de*-composition, although in fact, as we have pointed out previously, tonality and rhythm are really inseparable in any concrete sonorous phenomenon and the same applies to the other parameters. However, from the viewpoint of the composer, the dissociation, the systematic isolation of parameters has been undertaken consciously. Each one has been thought about separately, so as to control better its particular contribution.

Now, in practice, this intervention within the anatomy of music forces us to cut the complete integument that secures the cohesion of the musical organism. Undoubtedly the cohesive function is a pre-eminent feature of the melodic aspect. We have also noticed the semantic superiority that secured it always has absolute primacy; rhythm, its rival and consort, only achieves predominance in primitive music.

Strictly speaking, in art music, a matriarchal regime has prevailed for a long time. Melody, mother of music, has maintained her offspring under firm subservience throughout all evolutionary vicissitudes. Only those branches through which pure melodic sap runs, were able to grow and develop their latent potential (polyphony, counterpoint, thematic strands, variations etc).

With regard to the rest, their virtues remained alive for a long time before beginning to flourish. Thus, for instance, the values of intensity or volume, accents and modulations of amplitude have remained almost entirely subordinated to melodico-expressive conventions; the values of articulation or sound-attack – comparable to the function of consonants in Phonetics – have been used more as colours than as structural factors; quality and types of texture, scale of eventuation or variability of musical events; continuity-discontinuity; control of auditory ambit and of densities of simultaneity; all these more or less intuitive variables that the composer has traditionally managed, have been retained, restrained, incipient, incidental, inside a musical economy essentially dictated by melodic *vis* or strength.

Now, as the melodic springs slacken off, the necessary conditions are created for the emancipation of those non-tonal values. Not only do they now proliferate strongly, quickly reaching the point where they subvert the established order, but they end up, so to speak, by kicking out the mother of music, in other words, transforming her into *ancilla musicae*, reducing to the condition of *serva* she who previously was *padrona*. This explains the absence of melody in new music, the disappearance of the self-sufficient ballad which the music-lover can hum at will on leaving the concert-hall.

Music has passed from the concept of "line" to that of "field". The "musical" exists not only in a privileged strand, but in groups of parameters, their assemblages, the way in which they are put together and interwoven at several levels. One can understand therefore that the listener who keeps on looking for it only in the melodic strands must necessarily feel deceived. The old auditory habit is a bit like narrow focus vision, of scarce, empty, peripheral sensitivity.

Obviously, there's good and bad new music, if you allows such simplification. It would be stupid to try to define what the goodness of the good consists in: the completely achieved work preserves – and it is probably inevitable that it preserves – the quality of enigma. Of course, one has to reject as utopian the idea of an infallible technique. But to compose in a risky way doesn't mean that one closes one's eyes to the risks that one is going to run: on the contrary, it is to foresee and calculate them. This attitude is diametrically opposed to the indifference of aleatory tendencies in new music.

It's important to see clearly what kind of risks are run by music which has toppled melody from the throne. One might ask: in this case, where does the composer get his "ideas" from? Well, exactly, from the "composing". Do not forget that it is more difficult in music than in any of the other arts to say where inspiration ends and technique begins. Replacing melodically inspired ideas, with their enigmatic, subliminal nature, with concrete ideas regarding the organization of "musical material", one tends without doubt to make the "poetic" sense literal; the stress falls now on the "making" more than on the "made thing".

Evidently, there can be loss and gain, and the needle of balance oscillates here in a vital dimension; the huge and elusive problem of "communication" is at stake and it cannot be solved with recipes and theories, but by grace, and that naturally cannot be ignored with impunity.

Unquestionably, on the other hand, the intellectual phenomenon that appears today in all the contemporary arts, is a genuine indication of the *Zeitgeist*. We can't go backwards. To dream now that the artist can return to the condition of "divinely inspired idiot" would be like asking that we returned from the spirit of scientific exploration back to magic. The paradox in art is that there is no alternative: it's necessary to adopt both at once.

Finally, we can probably say that it's doubtful whether we have passed from the first stage in the Chinese sage's "curriculum", that we are still painting bamboo. It is possible. But maybe it's also possible to guess what the second stage might mean. In his admirable essay *Uber das Marionettentheater*, Kleist[180] talks about the paradox of the conscious, of its perturbing effect on the artist's creative activity, of the way that as the conscious clouds over, grace increases in brilliance and power.

In Kleist's *Ringfernige Welt* (organic world), as in Vico's circular universe, where not only do "minima" coincide with "maxima" and "maxima" with "maxima" – "*wenn die Erkenntnis gleichsam durch ein Unendliches geganen ist, die Grazie wider ein*" (Grace itself returns when knowledge has, as it were, gone through an inactivity).

One of the speakers in Kleist's dialogue asks: "Is it necessary, then, to eat again of the tree of knowledge in order to return to a state of innocence?"

"Of course", he said, "but that's the final chapter in the history of the world."[181]

34 An inaugural lecture (1961)[182]

Let me speak personally: in a piece of mine, every incident must be heard as part of an unfolding process, as one wave in the stream, where no image can or should be complete in itself. A truism, but one that is often forgotten by the composer who holds with "thematic" relationships. Something you can whistle on your way home from the concert has, undeniably, a high degree of self-sufficiency.

However, let us start with general ideas which shall house both generality as ideas and particularity in that they are very particularly my own particular views.

An idea that will start an artist working can be pretty indefinite. An artist does not approve an idea by its definition. On the contrary, too much definition will tell him that the idea is already grown and, to some extent, spent. That's why a *brilliant* idea is so often a trap. We'd better beware of brilliant ideas. A fruitful idea reveals itself in the mind by a certain urgency of the desire to realize it, by a kind of dim but compelling feeling for its potential. Like a seed, or any living organism, it has parts that will decay in the growing process, while other parts will sprout. The decaying makes for fuel: it isn't necessarily total waste.

On the contrary, it is the elements that fail and fall by the wayside that generate fresh energy. It is, above all, the deliberate discardings, like pruning, that provide new drive. This is the real meaning of self-denial, of restricting and depriving oneself of muchness, of much of a muchness. Part of the growing things will produce suckers. It is not only these that need to be cut – that's elementary – it's the cutting of healthy shoots which will prove most invigorating. Every amputation is a provocation; every casualty calls *forth* new life.

In its first adumbration an *idea* is perhaps something like a call to adventure. It suffices that it should provide the notion of a target, of direction of aim, and, most of all, that feeling of urgency, of intense desire to realize its felt potentiality. Yet that feeling too is often misunderstood. It is to be distrusted when it is too definite. It isn't a powerful feeling, or an emotion keenly felt that the artist translates into a work. One may often start work with some such strong definite feeling. I generally experience that when such is the case, my original feeling tends to dissipate more and more as the work proceeds, to make way for an entirely different feeling that is actually generated by the progress of the work itself. I think this is the genuine stuff.

By comparison, the affective stimulant which one may have naively thought to want to try to express, becomes something as irrelevant to the artist as the disturbing news one has read in the morning paper. There is no *self-expression* in the sense that the work comes from one's feelings. It's the other way around, one's feelings come from the work in process of growth. They are still one's own feelings, of course, but they are the feelings one didn't know about, the ones the composition unveils and reveals. They are more deeply rooted than anything you may have brought from the outside before starting to work.

Also, there is much misunderstanding as to the role of feeling during the process of working. It fluctuates according to how one is doing, how successful one is being. Personally, I find that when the going is too good, the day when you seem to have green fingers and everything you touch sprouts luxuriously, I tend to give up and pause. It is a feeling not so much of surfeit, of "embarrassment of riches", as a genuine lowering of one's sense of orientation. When everything happens to turn out equally well, there seems to be no reason to turn one way rather than another. This situation is probably the trap of the prolific, successful composer. Even a very good one will probably not produce his best in this condition. A mild state of anxiety, stemming from an authentic amount of difficulty encountered and real struggle to master it seems to be of the essence of the operation, for optimum results.

In other words, it is the succession of intervening crises – certainly, as much as that of successful phases – that keeps one going. It is the chain of decisions taken in full action, the rectification of course, that give one the feeling of actually shaping it. If one could make a graph of the working process, of the ups and downs, and connect the various points of crises in one continuous line, this line would represent to the artist himself – though not necessarily to anyone else – the true shape of his creative experience. Just as the like connecting of the points of surprise, the points where one has been deflected from, even jolted out of one's train of settled expectation and made aware of turning-points and changes of direction would represent the time shape of the listener's experience of a musical work. However, in the first graph, one would surely discover that the moments of crisis are peaks, crests of the waves not troughs, and that the points when all is going well are at best high plateaux, but as often as not, just shallows.

It may seem contradictory, but it is truly senseless to feel depressed when the going is tough. On the contrary, this is the moment of truth, these are one's opportunities. One had much better be on one's guard when the going is good. The more it kicks the more alive the thing is. That tinge of sadness which seems invariably to accompany the sense of achievement – which made Goethe exclaim "Stay thou moment a little longer" – is surely the affective resonance of that awareness. Valéry's phrase, "*la faiblesse des apogées*" has the same overtones. The automatic pilot in flight is convenient for an uneventful course.

In an eventful course, the flight captain has to take over the controls and rely on his wits, and the good functioning of his reflexes. Inflexible adherence to pre-assigned stipulation may spell disaster.

What, then, is the real function of pre-compositional planning or, more generally, of pre-determination?

Stressing the obvious, the prefix in both *pre*-compositional and *pre*-determination indicates with sufficient clarity that what we refer to is anterior and external to the actual moments of work. In other words, with pre-compositional pre-determination, we are still in the domain of possibility or potentiality.

This is an abstract domain where we deal with generalities. We build in it a frame of our own devising, consisting of the co-ordinates necessary to the actual compositional handling of all the variables of the auditory phenomena. The frame is an embodiment of method and method is a *modus operandi.* That is to me the manner of working, not the actual thing produced by the working. To put it another way: method imposes common relationships on all that happens in the work, but cannot impose *what* that relationships shall be. With a slight terminological variation, one of Wittgenstein's propositions can be made to read "to the method belongs everything which belongs to the act of projecting but not *what* is actually projected; ie the possibility of what is projected but not this itself". For our purposes the main thing to retain from this definition of method is that it provides the indispensable safeguards for spontaneity. It divides and connects the two domains of order and freedom, order begins for the artist paradoxically the domain of volition, freedom that of surrender of the will.

Valéry cautions us that as an artist: "One must want, but not want too much." In Wittgenstein's terms we could say that any encroachment of the act of pre-compositional projecting into the compositional field of actually projected and shaped things is an act of trespassing in the sense of Valéry's warning.

The spontaneous – by definition the non-willed – must be allowed elbow room. Its living space must remain inviolate. This living-space of the spontaneous is, of course, the artist's true battleground. The contestants are logical thought and intuitive thought. The battle goes on incessantly. We must prevent the *encroachments* of logical thought (in the sense of invasion and occupation) but we cannot and should not try to prevent its *incursions* into the domains of the spontaneous, the "raids on the inarticulate". It's this strife which marks creative activity or the true adventure of the mind. Since the battle must go on – rest not being our business – combatants should be fairly evenly matched. Paradoxically, the artist's victory lies in averting a checkmate. In other words: more method than the artist's intellect can handle or less than his temperament needs, there is trouble either way, one partner will suffer defeat and the game come to an end. As for the partial reverses and partial successes, the points gained and the points lost during the game: they are actually the highlights and give the whole adventure the excitement and fascination it can have.

Talking of points gained and lost: the most disconcerting thing that can happen to the intellect is to bump against a contradiction. The intellect is simply flummoxed by contradictions. Whereupon, intuition has a chance to pull a fast one perhaps and hit the target. Contradictions and deadlocks are far from being a calamity in practical thought; they are only so in formal logic. Yes, even scientists know that a clashing discursive blunder has often generated a flash of genuine insight.

Or, again, it may be imagination that flags and a counter-attack of disciplined thought may bowl it out of court and with luck, perhaps, put it into a new orbit. Which is precisely what happens at major turning points in the evolution of the arts. There is no end to the variations that this interplay between reason and intuition can bring about.

There is obviously nothing one can say about the spontaneous before the event, and little one can say after it for that matter. All belongs here to the domain of chance, the aleatory of inspiration. The artist himself can only know or try to find out *a posteriori* what has been happening. He cannot know much about it while it is happening. A psychological principle of indeterminacy – in the proper meaning of the word – obtains here. Observation tends to affect the process observed. Yet the domain of chance and chance operation exerts a powerful attraction in the arts today. It is important to try and define one's ideas about the nature of aleatory processes.

Method, on the other hand, as something conscious, deliberate and based on discursive thought, lends itself readily to theorizing. We can say a lot about method – very little about inspiration. It is a methodological point to proceed from the simple to the complex, to start with the definition of one's terms and their application to the clearly observable. This is the way the scientist proceeds, and since he is a specialist in *method,* one must needs follow his lead when we deal with method.

The creative artist, on the other hand, need not, and hardly ever does, start with clear ideas but rather with adumbrations of a vague, yet stimulating notion of possibility and variety. "Everything important is well hidden" (Valéry). Seeds must be sunk into the soil in order to germinate. Light must not reach them directly but in the dark, at a remove, so to speak. The assumption in much art teaching is that we must needs start with method and concentrate on method almost exclusively. This is dangerous, because it is the opposite of the creative attitude.

Passing from being methodical to becoming creative calls for a complete reversal of orientation. A young artist who would believe that he can get – even from another creative artist – a set of devices which he could put to work directly as he gets them from the horse's mouth would be in for a lot of trouble. To be quite frank about method, we may roughly call it a more or less precise and refined know-how. It is better to have grasped it clearly, but as soon as it has been understood, it must be forgotten.

In other words, one can teach and learn the ropes, but we do so ultimately for the benefit of the unconscious mind. It is the liminal or subliminal man whom we want to learn the ropes. But we have no direct communication with him. We can only semaphore in his direction from an upper level. He picks and chooses entirely to his own liking. And this is as it should be. A certain amount of insistence and perseverance in the exercise of sending information to him gives subliminal man a good chance to put ways and means to his own recondite tests before assimilating or rejecting and, then, employing probably anything that really suits him.

With this in mind, let's consider what we propose to him about matters of method. Reason proposes, subliminal man disposes, but of course, *the whole man composes*, and nothing but the whole man will do for that.

Musical organization is largely based nowadays on principles of serialization. Some of you may have come to feel that serialization is on the way out. This is possibly so. I for one am not prepared to defend any *status quo*.

If serialization is on the way out today, it is nonetheless evident that classical serial technique, as in Schoenberg and Webern, has been the nursery where new ideas grow. It is doubtful whether a young composer may safely ignore classical serial techniques. As with tradition, one does not escape its influence by ignoring it, one only suffers it in a more obscure and probably warped or maimed fashion.

Serialization and thematicism are antithetic. Non-thematicism is in music what the non-representation, the non-figurative is in the visual arts (I do not say the word "abstract", this would need amplification), or is indeed in the other arts, poetry, novel-writing, or play-writing today. Obviously, in thematic music, the thematic thread and network of relations was as much the main organizing agent as representation or figuration was in painting, story-telling in the novel, or plot in the play. Their formative agency once cancelled, it became necessary to introduce new devices to act as organizers. This is exactly what serial devices are, organizers and nothing else. It is important to understand – and many critics and composers do not – that like enzymes or catalysts these organizers do not *add* anything *material* of their own to the stuff organized: they just set the pace and steer a process. You cannot detect in them anything but their *effects* (they are not things but modes of operation).

It might be asked: what was the necessity for throwing overboard good old thematicism, storytelling in writing or plot-engineering in plays?

The answer is that from time to time a generation becomes thoroughly impatient not only with the style of the previous generation – every generation tends to reject the style of its immediate predecessors – but with the very subject-matter which was a favourite with them. We discover that we are no longer interested, we simply do not like it any more. The imaginative stimulation has gone out of the stuff. This change of subject-matter is the crucial moment in art-evolution – it happens at crises or turning-points.

It is the new subject-matter that demands and forges the new tools and new techniques. Style is always the function of subject matter.

There are always complex social factors underlying the emergence of radical novelty in the arts. They cannot be traced in a hurry and the study of them must be left to specialists. But we can pick out a few. I shall briefly mention two.

First and foremost as a contributing cause in the design of the subject-matter, there has been a definite shift in the attitude of the artist in relation to his own work. The artist no longer wishes to put himself at the centre of the work, but rather firmly and deliberately off-centre, so to speak. To say he tends towards objectivity is not good enough: he never ceases to be both objective and subjective. The shift is more subtle and has wider implications: it affects not only the artist himself and his work, but most importantly, it affects also the attitude of his audience. The audience must adapt to the change.

It isn't easy to change an attitude that has become second nature since the days of the humanistic movement and the Renaissance. An image that comes to mind to illustrate what I mean is that of a portrait whose eyes look straight at you and do not leave you for a moment whether you move to the left or to the right of the picture. Essentially, the same happens whatever the subject: a perspective is inbuilt within the composition, it corresponds not only to the artist's vision, he occupies this centre of vision like the spider at the centre of its web; but it is also the main avenue, the royal road, from outside, into the work. You have only to adopt this perspective to be in line with the artist's vision.

The artist who stands off-centre gives you no such clues. It isn't that he wishes to break lines of communication. All he wants is for you to make your own effort. "Charity", the Chinese sage said, "consists of letting alone". Communication is what you make of it.

The imaginative reading of the work is an integrative effort of your own. We want the audience to be engaged at a true recreative level, we do not want to spoon-feed it. As I said before, although serialism issued in reality from thematicism, and for some time was thought to further thematicism's ends – as it does, in fact, in most of Schoenberg's work and, to a lesser extent, also in Webern's – the truth is that it was calculated to supersede it. We are only at the beginning of a new road, but it can already be seen that, a little further along, there are branchings off in very different directions.

Taken at its most extreme, the off-centre attitude of the artist and the introduction of a set of organizers that take over from thematicism the formative steering of compositional process – this can lead to the wish, on the part of the composer, to stand right outside the work, not merely off-centre. To let the organizers do the work entirely of their own accord, as it were.

Total serialization has already led very nearly to such a state of affairs, but not quite. It is, of course, possible. All you need is such an amount of predetermination as will cover all the variables and an efficient programming technique that will take care automatically of all their possible combinations: in other words, you could watch the work composing itself as a self-piloting, truly cybernetic process. The operation could be a colossal impersonal game of chance, with no choice: or rather all your choices would have been made in the programming itself, that is to say, in the abstract.

Nothing like that has been achieved yet: and who would wish to try, since computers could do it more efficiently and much faster than composer?! It all may sound like idle speculation but it brings up a variety of notions worth considering, such as predetermination, automation, or self-steering, chance or choice. Serialism has relevant connections with each one of these notions. Yet none of them stands for something which is radically unprecedented in music. It is only the use of the name that is new and is apt to blur our familiarity with the entities for which the words stand.

Take *predetermination*, for instance. Some degree of predetermination is obviously of the very essence of any musical system. The most important features of scales – in Western and Eastern music alike – are the inherent, in-built form-determinants that characterize modes, ragas, Arab *magms*, Byzantine *echoi*, etc. They prescribe: 1) note-catalogue (the notes available); 2) ambitus; 3) centre-note; 4) fixed and subsidiary dominants; 5) leading tones; 6) fixed subdivisions of scale for order of exposition (eg upper pentachord before lower tetrachord): and also (in Eastern music and, to some extent still, in Gregorian chant) actual typical motives and note-progressions. There is nothing unprecedented, there, in the notion of predetermination, as inherent in a pre-compositional system.

The novelty in modern techniques is not that they derive form-determinants from a pre-compositional system (scale, series, or set) but simply that they derive more form-determinants from the system, that is not only in the melodic dimension, but also for the harmonic, for the rhythmic, to some extent, even for the dynamic and possibly for the timbral structure of a piece of music. Predetermination is clearly pushed *ad absurdum* if it should reach the stage of automation. It would then represent not an incursion of method into the domain of the spontaneous but a whole-scale invasion and occupation of the subliminal man's living space and his total subjugation.

To understand the true purpose and positive value of pre-determination it must be understood as a dialectic. It brings into play two opposite biases, a catalytic and a stabilizing one. It introduces both organizers and resistors.

Organizers trigger off trains of suggestions of structural or combinatorial possibilities derived from the systems, form-determinants. Resistors preclude absolute combinatoria free play: they exclude all the possibilities that lie outside the frame of the system. It is easy to persuade oneself of the usefulness of organizers. It isn't so easy to persuade oneself of the value of resistors. To my mind they are the crux of the matter. The most powerful inbuilt resistor in Schoenberg's twelve-note series is represented by the fact that not every note is available at every moment. The order of succession imposed by the system can only be felt as an irksome restriction by a composer who is trying to work against the grain or the bias of the system.

If you try to work a folk-tune-like melody, or possibly even a theme, in the traditional sense, you might find the resistors very inconvenient indeed. But you would have missed their point: the challenge they offer to the imagination, the powerful stimulus the composer gets from finding himself with his back to the wall, with no other recourse than to grapple with purely musicianly problems.

This is what I call the non-egocentric, the off-centre position.

It need not be feared that his humanity will desert him: any attempt to exclude it brings it back at the gallop, as Voltaire points out. What *is* thus effectively excluded is his own repertoire of facile and unconscious clichés. It must also be realized, though, that organizers tend, in the long run, to lose their catalytic power and resistors their inhibiting force. We do wear resistors out and produce new clichés. We breed them inevitably. Both organizers and resistors are best observed in an early phase of a stylistic epoch. As long as the intellectual sap flows vigorously and reflexes respond, they stand out as starkly functional, even aggressively so. Approaching stylistic maturity, intellectual and instinctive motives tend to merge and become more and more indistinguishable. In a late stylistic period, the organizers have become mere routine. The purely instinctive begins to luxuriate. The intellectual sap declines and habit, conditioning, "learned behaviour" sets in. The pruning becomes necessary to start a new cycle of growth.

This is the reason why, for instructional purposes, it seems best to me to study new modes of organization at an early stylistic phase. There will be no conclusion, of course. Which reminds me of a William James saying: "There is no conclusion. What *has* concluded that we might *conclude* in regard to it? There are no fortunes to be told and no advice to be given. Farewell."

Farewell.

Notes

Gerhard's own footnotes are here marked *

1. Two articles, both entitled *Com escolteu musica?* – here combined as one – first published in *Mirador*, 64 (24 April 1930), 5 and 63 (1 May 1930), 5, respectively.
2. First published in Rollo H. Myers (ed.), *Twentieth Century Music* (London 1960), 52-61.
3. First broadcast on BBC Radio on 13 August 1957.
4. Victor Zuckerkandl, *Sound and Symbol: Music and the External World* (New York 1956). Zuckerkandl (b.1896, Vienna, d.1965 Locarno, Switzerland) worked as a music critic in Berlin (1927–33), then taught in Vienna before moving to the USA just before the Second World War. Subsequently, he taught at the New School for Social Research, New York (1946–48), before joining St John's College in 1948. He retired to Ascona in 1964, lecturing at the Jung Institute and at Eranos Conferences in Zurich.
5. Ibid., 74.
6. Ibid., 144: Zuckerkandl actually wrote: "... music is *not* a phenomenon of the inner world, nor is it a phenomenon projected from the inner to the outer world; it is a phenomenon of the outer world."
7. Ibid., 173–4.
8. Ibid., 20.
9. Ibid., 21: this is a paraphrase not a quotation. The original read: "There is not tone in music without a specific dynamic quality."
10. *Ibid.*, 115; the quotation is from Henri Bergson, *Matière et memoire* (Presses Universitaires de France, 1896. See English translation by N. M. Paul and W. S. Palmer (Zone Books, New York, 1988), 202.
11. Zuckerkandl, *op. cit.*, 138.
12. Ibid., *op. cit.*, 138.
13. Ibid., *op. cit.*, 347–8. This is a paraphrase.
14. *Op. cit.*, 154. N. I. Lobachewski's definition of time is quoted from J. Alexander Gunn: *The Problem of Time*, 24, n.3.
15. Ibid., 202.
16. Ibid., 202.
17. Ibid., 173–4.
18. First published in *The Score* no.16 (June 1956), 7–18. The first four paragraphs, beginning with the same story as opened *England, Spring 1945* (see pp.177–9 above) and further ruminations thereon, are omitted here. The article originated as a talk given at Bedford College for Women, London, in early 1956.
19. Hermann Weyl, *Philosophy of Mathematics and Natural Sciences* (Princeton 1949), 116.
20. This appears to derive from a passage in Simone Weil, *Cahiers* (Paris 1953), I, 226–7.
21. The poor old fiddler in Grillparzer's *Der arme Spielmann* (1848) succeeds in

attaining inner peace and harmony in his self-imposed isolation from an indifferent, vulgar and materialistic society.

22. First published as "La musica a la cort d'Alfons el Magnanim", in *Mirador*, 364 (6 February 1936) 8; see also n. 38 below. Alfonso the Maganimous (1416–1458), King of Naples, Sicily, Sardinia and Aragon, was the earliest Spanish monarch to become a generous patron of the arts.
23. The records regarding Johannes Cornago (fl.1466) are sparse. He is referred to in one document as a Franciscan residing in Rome on an annual pension of 300 ducats granted to him by Alfonso. After the monarch's death, Cornago became chief almoner of Don Ferrante, Alfonso's successor to the Neapolitan crown, in which office he dispensed royal charity. After his sojourn in Italy, Cornago seems to have returned to his native land: his name crops up in a list of Ferdinand V's court chapel singers during 1475.
24. Based on a draft for a broadcast talk given on BBC Radio in the 1940s.
25. Antonio Eximeno y Pugades, *Dobbio ... sopra Il Saggio Fondamentale pratico di contrappunto* (Rome 1775); cf. however, Robert Stevenson, in his article on Eximeno in *New Grove* (1980), vol. 6, 323: "Late 19th-century Spaniards rightly considered Eximeno a national hero in his polemical and theoretical battles ... but they erred in attributing to him the remark that 'a nation's music should be based on its folksong'. He was an iconoclast ... [and plagiarist ... who] equated good taste with his own."
26. Valls, 1918–22; 2nd edition, 1936; reprinted by Casa Editorial Boileau, Barcelona, 1958.
27. "Sessio Robert Gerhard" in *Revista Musical Catalana*, 313 (January 1930), 8–10.
28. "Sessio Robert Gerhard" in *Revista Musical Catalana*, 313 (20 & 27 February 1930), 110–13.
29. The background to the whole of this debate is outlined in Père Artis, "La polemica Robert Gerhard-Lluis Millet", in *Revista Musical Catalana,* 23, 1986, 28–29.
30. First published in *Mirador*, 53 (30 January 1930), 7.
31. Paul Valéry, *Variété* IV (Paris 1938), *Remerciement à L'Academie Française* (Text of a lecture given on 23 June 1927), 15.
32. First published in *Mirador*, 54 (6 February 1930), 5.
33. Gerhard plays here on the Catalan equivalent of *schlagworte – mots de cop/cop de mots* (literally, "hit-names" or "name-hits").
34. First performed at the Opernhaus, Frankfurt, 1 February 1930.
35. First published as "Fuga: al Mestre Millet" in *Mirador*, 56 (20 February 1930), 5.
36. Valls, Gerhard's birthplace, means "valley" in Catalan.
37. First published as "Fuga (acabament): al Mestre Millet" in *Mirador*, 57 (27 February 1930), 5.
38. Like Gerhard, the Catalan priest and musicologist Higini Anglès (1888–1969) numbered Pedrell amongst his teachers. In his youth he collected more than 3000 folksongs in the Pyrenees and other parts of Catalonia, but devoted the greater part of his career to the study and publication of art-music. In 1931, he founded the Publicaciones del Departmento de Musica de la Biblioteca de Catalunya. Included in this series was the early fourteenth-century Las Huelgas Manuscript, one of the principal sources of medieval polyphonic music, still at its place of origin, the Monasterio de Las Huelgas, a convent for Cistercian nuns founded in about 1180 on the outskirts of Burgos by the warrior-king Alfonso VIII. The manuscript includes nearly 200 compositions, of which over half are polyphonic.

It was published in facsimile and transcription, with detailed commentary by Anglès (Barcelona: Institut d'Estudis Catalans, 1931) and reprinted after his death in 1977. [See also: Robert Stevenson, *Spanish Music in the Age of Columbus* (The Hague, 1960), 35–39.]

Here, however, Gerhard is probably referring to the *Llibre Vermell de Montserrat*, a thirteenth-century manuscript found at the monastery of Montserrat; this manuscript contains several two- and three-part canons – hence the reference to the Concertino. (I am indebted to Julian White for this observation.)

Anglès also collaborated with Gerhard in 1933 on editions of Six Quintets for strings with organ or harpsichord obligato by the Catalan composer Antonio Soler (1729–1783).

39. Willem Werker, *Studien über die Symmetrie in Bau der Fugen und die motivische Zusammengehorigkeit der Praeludien und Fugen des Wöltempierten Klaviers von J. S. Bach* (Leipzig 1923).
40. *L'homme armé* was a fifteenth-century melody, widely used as a *cantus firmus* in polyphonic Masses from the second half of the fifteenth century through to the first part of the seventeenth century; the composers of these Masses include Busnois, Caron, Ockeghem, Obrecht, Tinctoris, Josquin, Brumel, La Rue, Morales, Palestrina and Carissimi. There are also several polyphonic chanson settings.
41. First published in *Mirador*, 63 (10 April 1930), 5.
42. First published in *Mirador*, 64 (17 April 1930), 5.
43. First published as "Musica Aplicada" in *Mirador*, 124 (18 June 1931), 5.
44. *Der Jasager (The Yes-Sayer)* was first performed in a live broadcast on Berlin Radio on 23 June 1930; its stage premiere took place at the Zentralinstitut für Erziehung und Untterricht, Berlin, conducted by Kurt Drabek. The orchestral players were students from the Staats-Akademie fur Kirchen-und Schulmusik and from other Berlin schools. A revised version, benefiting from Brecht's presence and advice at rehearsals, was prepared by students at the Karl-Marx School in Berlin-Neukolln during the autumn of 1930.
45. First published in *Quaderns de poesia*, no. 2 (July 1935), 18–22.
46. Valéry quotes Berlioz's introduction at the start of "Note et Digression" in *Variété* (Paris, 1924); his essay on Leonardo follows.
47. First published in *Mirador*, 101 (8 January 1931), 5.
48. *Die Massnahme, 'Lehrstuck'* (with text by Brecht), for tenor, three speakers, male chorus, mixed chorus and small orchestra was first performed on 13 December 1930, at the Berlin Philharmonic Hall, with Karl Rankl conducting.
49. Gerhard is most likely referring to the first of Eisler's two early Piano Sonatas (from 1923 and 1924 respectively) which won him the Vienna Arts Prize and was published (on Schoenberg's recommendation) by Universal Edition.
50. Eisler's 4 Piano Pieces Op.3 (1923) and 8 Piano Pieces Op.8 (1925).
51. *Palmström:* Studies on twelve-note rows, for sprechstimme, flute, clarinet, violin/viola and cello are settings of five texts by Christian Morgenstern and date from 1924. They were written at Schoenberg's request for a programme that included *Pierrot Lunaire.*
52. Eisler provided music for the following Piscator productions: *Heimweh* (1926); *Der Kaufmann von Berlin* (1929); *Tai Yang Erwacht* (1931); see John Willett, *The Theatre of Erwin Piscator* (London 1978).
53. First published in *Mirador*, 105 (5 February 1931), 5.
54. First published in *Mirador*, 106 (12 February 1931), 5.
55. First published in *Mirador*, 118 (7 May 1931), 5.

56. *Lo Straniero* was first produced at the Rome Opera, 29 April 1930.
57. Pizzetti wrote the incidental music for D'Annunzio's play *La Pisanella*, produced at the Chatelet Theatre, Paris, 11 June 1913; his orchestral suite was first performed in Rome in 1917.
58. Composed 1915–21, it was first produced at La Scala, Milan on 16 December 1922.
59. First published in *Mirador*, 120 (21 May 1931), 5.
60. Baltasa Samper (1888–1966) was born in Mallorca, but lived in Barcelona from 1907 onwards, studying there with Granados and Pedrell. He studied the folk-music of the Ballearic Islands and contributed to the *Canconer popular de Catalunya*. The symphonic suite reviewed by Gerhard was often just known as *Mallorca*. His output was small but skilled.
61. First published as "Els compositors madrilenys" in *Mirador*, 107 (19 February 1931), 5.
62. Gustavo Pittaluga (1906–75) studied law and music (with Oscar Espla) at Madrid University. He became a member of the Triton group of musicians in Paris in 1935; then from 1936 to 1939 worked at the Spanish Embassy in Washington D.C. (for the Loyalist Government). He remained in the USA and was in charge of the film library of the Museum of Modern Art in New York (1941–49). His musical output declined after the war. His early compositions had rejected both romantic and folk-music influences. His most lasting success was the ballet *La romeria de los cornados* (1927; a concert version preceded it in 1922), which was based on a text by Lorca and Rivas Cheriff.
63. Juan José Mantecón (1897–1964) composed songs and chamber music, but was better known eventually as a music critic, writing under the pseudonym of Juan del Brezo.
64. Julián Bautista (1901–61). He studied with Conrad del Campo and later became Professor of harmony at the Madrid Conservatory. Much of his early music was lost during the Spanish Civil War. He subsequently settled permanently in Buenos Aires, where he spent most of his time composing film scores.
65. Rodolfo Hallfter (1900–88) was mostly self-taught, though he did receive advice from Falla. He emigrated in 1939 to Mexico, where he became an important figure on the musical scene, as professor at the Conservatorio Nacional and as director of the publishers, Edicions Mexicanas de Musica. As his music evolved, it embraced serialism and incorporated elements from Spanish Renaissance music. (See also pp.72–3 above.)
66. Fernando Remacha (1898–1984), was born in Tudela (Navarra) and also died there. He studied first in Pamplona, then with Conrado del Campo in Madrid. He won the Italian Prize in 1923 and continued his studies with Malipiero. On his return to Spain in 1928, he became a violinist in the Orquesta Sinfonica de Madrid, was an active member of the Grupo de los Ocho and amongst the first in Spain to compose film music. With the onset of the Civil War, he stopped composing and worked in the family business at his birthplace, Tudela. He resumed composition in 1957 and became director of the Pamplona Conservatory.
67. Rosita García-Ascot (b. 1906), studied with Pedrell and (in particular) Falla. She was an energetic member of the group known as the "Generation of 27" during its formative years. At the same time she produced a Suite for Orchestra and numerous piano pieces. During the Civil War, all her work was destroyed and she went into exile. Her output thereafter was small: and although she is remembered as an important figure, her music is seldom performed. Her late husband was the musicologist Jesus Bal y Gay (1905–93).

68. Salvador Bacarisse (1898–1963) studied in Madrid with Conrad del Campo and was the winner of three national music prizes (1923, 1931 and 1934). His *Heraldos* (1923) for piano solo caused a scandal on account of its polytonality. Stylistically, he veered thereafter between impressionism and neo-classicism, echoing also the styles of Les Six. Active in organizing concerts and music programmes on radio, he eventually settled permanently in Paris, where he continued to compose prolifically until his death.
69. Ernesto Hallfter (1905–89) was the younger brother of Roldolfo (see n. 65 above) studied with Falla and later became director of the Orquesta Baetica of Seville. But his compositional career was properly launched with his prize-winning *Sinfonietta* (1925). After several years as director of the Seville Conservatory, he settled in Lisbon in 1936 with his Portuguese wife, Alicia Camera, but returned to Spain after the Civil War.
70. First published in *Mirador*, 119 (14 May 1931), 5.
71. First published in *Mirador*, 129 (23 July 1931), 5.
72. Xavier Gols i Soler (1903–38) was born in Tarragon and became the most important member of a family of Catalan musicians. His father, Josep Gols i Veciana (1870–1938), wrote religious music and popular songs. His brother, Joan Gols i Soler (1894–1947), became musical director at the church of Santa Maria del Mar in Barcelona; exiled to Venezuela, he founded the Coral Catalana de Caracas. Xavier Gols became director of the Societat Filharnonica Tarragonina and wrote, amongst other compositions, *Poema de divendres sant,* for mixed chorus and *Tres preludis rurals* for piano and orchestra.
73. First published in *Mirador*, 133 (20 August 1931), 5.
74. First published in *Mirador*, 61 (27 March 1931), 5.
75. Quite the contrary, in fact: the German versions of Verdi's operas by Franz Werfel (1890–1945) were a distinct success and contributed greatly to the renewal of interest in the composer. Werfel's translation of *La forza del destino* (1925) was widely performed on the European continent: it led to his translation of *Simon Boccanegra* (1929), which very soon became equally ubiquitous, likewise *Don Carlos* (1932), undertaken in collaboration with Alfred Wallenstein. Political events made further such projects impossible and Werfel emigrated to the USA with his wife, Alma Mahler-Werfel, where his edition of Verdi's letters (produced in collaboration with Paul Stefan) appeared in an English translation (New York, 1942).
76. First published as "Film Sonor" in *Mirador*, 96 (4 December 1931), 5.
77. First shown in 1932 at a film gala in Paris.
78. Both parts of this essay formed the text of talks broadcast on the BBC Third Programme in 1949 and 1951, respectively.
79. Sir Steuart Wilson (1889–1996) began his career as a tenor before the First World War and went rapidly into the forefront of British singers during the 1920s and 30s, achieving special success in the title-role of Elgar's *The Dream of Gerontius* and as the Evangelist in Bach's *St Matthew Passion.* On his retirement, he began a new career as an administrator, taught at the Curtis Institute, Philadelphia (1939–42), returning to become Music Director of the BBC Overseas Services (until 1945) and subsequently of the newly formed Arts Council of Great Britain. At the time of *The Duenna*, he was Director of Music at the BBC.
80. T. S. Eliot, *The Use of Poetry and the Use of Criticism* (London 1933), 30.
81. Ibid., 30.
82. Dr Samuel Johnson, *Lives of the English Poets* (1779–80), *Gray*: "In the character of his Elegy, I rejoice to concur with the common reader; for by the

common sense of readers uncorrupted with literary prejudices ... must be finally decided all claim to poetic honours."

83. This is the text of two lectures given in 1950 at a London University vacation course and published the following year in *Ballet*, 3 and 4 (April and May 1954), 19–24 and 29–35.
84. E. M. Forster, *The Raison d'être of Criticism in the Arts* (Harvard 1947), reprinted in *Two Cheers for Democracy* (London 1953), 117–31.
85. *Op. cit.*, 124–5.
86. *Don Quixote* was first produced at Sadler's Wells Theatre, London, on 20 February 1950, with choreography by Ninette de Valois, scenery and costumes by Edward Burra and Robert Irving conducting.
87. Stravinsky, *Chronicle of My Life* (London 1936), 50; the ballet under discussion was *The Firebird.*
88. Arnold Haskell, *Ballet* (London: Penguin 1938, rev. edn, 1951, ch. 4), 85.
89. First published in David Drew (ed.), *The Decca Book of Ballet* (London 1958), 153–6.
90. First published in *Mirador*, 165 (31 March 1932), 5. Schoenberg and his wife stayed in Barcelona as guests of the Gerhards between October 1931 and June 1932. It was there that Schoenberg composed Act II of *Moses und Aron* and his Piano Piece, Op. 33b. He also conducted a concert that included his *Pelleas und Melisande.* (See also note 119 below.)
91. First published in *Mirador*, 145 (12 November 1931), 5.
92. First published in *Perspectives of New Music* (Princeton, New Jersey: Spring–Summer 1975), 57–65.
93. H. H. Stuckenschmidt, *Arnold Schoenberg* (Zurich 1951; English transl., Edith Temple Roberts and Humphrey Searle, London 1959), 50.
94. First published in *The Sunday Telegraph* (3 December 1961), 11.
95. First published as one of several contributions by different composers to the English edition of Josef Rufer, *Die Komposition mit zwölf Tonen* (Berlin 1952), English transl. by Humphrey Searle, *Composition with Twelve Notes* (London 1954; revised edition 1969), Appendix I, 183–5.
96. H. H. Stuckenschmidt, *op. cit.*, 85: Stuckenschmidt attributes the remark to Josef Mathias Hauer.
97. T. S. Eliot, "Conclusion", in *The Use of Poetry and The Use of Criticism* (London 1933), 151.
98. First published in *The Score*, No. 6 (May 1952), 28–35.
99. Arnold Schoenberg, *Harmonielehre*, 3rd edn. (Vienna 1922), 487.
100.* 1908 is the year in which Schoenberg's piano pieces Op.11, Berg's Piano Sonata and Webern's *Passacaglia* for orchestra were written.
101. Alois Hába, *Neue Harmonielehre des Diatonschen-, Chromatischen-, Vertel-, Drittel-, Sechstel-, und Zwolftel-Tonsystems* (Leipzig 1927).
102.* Schoenberg, *op. cit.*, 504.
103.* *Op. cit.*, 466.
104. Nicholas Slonimsky, *Music Since 1900* (New York 1937; revised edn 1961), 1315–16 (letter from Schoenberg dated 3 June 1937, Hollywood, California).
105. See *Harmony* in Donald F. Tovey, *The Forms of Music* (Oxford 1943), 4.
106. Gerhard's musical examples from now on refer to those used by Schoenberg in his *Style and Idea* (New York 1950, Engl. transl. London 1951), 151(first given as a lecture at the University of California, 26 March 1941).
107.* In his catalogue of possible chords of 3, 4, etc, up to different notes, Hába has got this and also the other figures wrong [see Hába, *op. cit.*]. The correct numbers are as follows: chords of three notes 19; of four notes 42; of five notes

55; of six notes 80; of seven notes 80; of eight notes 66; of nine notes 42; of ten notes 19; 11 transpositions of the one 11-note chord are possble and there is, of course only one 12-note chord. Such are my powers of argument, however, that I was unable to convince Haba of the correctness of my numbers in the course of a discussion lasting from Victoria [Railway] Station [London] to Glyndebourne [Opera House]. And yet nothing, it seemed to me could be easier than to show the sources of Hába's miscalculations. Let me try it on my reader: Hába lists, for instance, these as different chords: *c–d–g* and *c–f–g*. They are not; the second – take in its first inversion, *f–g–c* – is nothing but a transposition of the frst one, a fourth up. Haba goes on repeating this same mistake over and over again without ever detecting the identity of a chord when it appears in transpositions or inversions which look different to the eye.

108. See *Style and Idea*, 122–23.
109. First published in *The Score*, no. 17 (London September 1956), 61–72.
110.* Should we say twelve-note or twelve-tone? – '*l'un et l'autre se dit*', but on different sides of the Atlantic. Personally, I choose the latter on the authority of the following passage in Sir James Jeans's *Science and Music* (London 1937), 80: '... When we decompose the curve of a vibrating string into simple harmonic curves ... we are in effect decomposing the motion of the string into its separate free vibrations, and these represent the *constituent tones* in the *note* sounded by the vibration' (Gerhard's italics).
111. Schoenberg, *op. cit.*, 117.
112.* The word "arbitrary" easily causes a frown. But it is a mistake to let oneself be disturbed by the overtones which nearly always happen to be uppermost in the colloquial use of the term, as connoting something like abuse of authority. In its non-colloquial meaning, as used here, it is intended to denote "willed", in the sense of deliberately chosen in the light of reason, or as "self-imposed", in contrast to "imposed by nature" or by "natural laws".
113. See *Memoirs of a Poem* (1937), reprinted in *The Collected Works of Paul Valéry,* ed. J. Matthews (transl.), vol. 7, 107.
114. A. N. Whitehead, *Adventures of Ideas* (Cambridge 1947; Penguin edition, 1948), 62. The original read: "But wisdom is persistent pursuit of the deeper understanding of ever confronting intellectual systems with the importance of its omissions."
115. First published in *Mirador*, 361 (16 January 1936), 8.
116. Berg's Violin Concerto received its world premiere in Barcelona on 19 April 1936, with Louis Krasner as soloist and Hermann Scherchen conducting. The programme also included the *Wozzeck* fragments.
117. First published in *Mirador*, 166 (7 April 1932), 5. At Gerhard's invitation, Webern came to Barcelona in April 1932 to conduct two concerts with the Orquesta Pau Casals. His programmes included his orchestration of Schubert's Six German Dances, his own Six Pieces Op.6 and Passacaglia Op.1, Schoenberg's *Bergleitungsmusik* and Mahler's Fourth Symphony. He described the orchestra as "outstanding" and " the best I have ever conducted".
118. First published as "Some Lectures by Webern" in *The Score*, 28 (January 1961), 25–8.
119. Anton Webern (ed. Willi Reich), *Der Weg zur neuen Musik* (Vienna 1960; English translation London 1963).
120. This and succeeding quotations are Gerhard's own English translations from the original German text.
121. First published in *The Score*, No. 20 (London 1957), 38–43.
122. Robert Craft, "A concert for St Mark" in *The Score*, No.18 (London 1956), 35.

123. "I breathe the air of another planet" is the first line of the poem *Entruckung* by Stefan George, set to music in the final movement of Schoenberg's Quartet No.2 for soprano and string quartet (1907–8).
124. This is the text of two talks given at the University of Michigan at Ann Arbor in the spring of 1960.
125.* For a long time I've been puzzled with Occam's razor; you meet him so often in print, and without footnotes, that I at first thought he must have been some celebrated ancient Cambridge worthy (the immensely witty barber, a philosophical Figaro, or something of the sort), until a scholarly friend put me right. Well, I needn't quote Latin at you, but I'm sure you'll agree that it makes a fundamental methodological point.
126. "Mode types" (as between major and minor): see J. M. Hauer, *Von Melos zur Pauke: eine Eifugrug in die Zwölftonmusik* (Vienna 1925; 2nd edn, 1967).
127. See Karlheinz Stockhausen, ... *How time passes* ... in *Die Reihe* (1959), 3, 10–41.
128. E. M. Forster, *Aspects of the Novel* (London 1927; Penguin Books 1990), 149. Forster wrote "trio-scherzo-trio-finale-trio-finale"; Gerhard corrects this inaccuracy.
129. First published in *Tempo*, 11 (old series ed. Ernest Chapman, Spring 1945), 2–3; reprinted in *Tempo*, 100 (new series ed. David Drew, July 1972), 4–8.
130. Jonathan Swift, Letter to Alexander Pope, 29 September 1725.
131. An illustrated talk given at the "Music, Libraries and Instruments" Conference in August (?) 1959. It was later published under its present title in the *Hinrichsen Music Yearbook* no. 11 (London 1961), 30–38. The lecture ended with excerpts from Gerhard's own *Audiomobiles*.
132. *Mutazioni*, for one-track tape, was first broadcast on RAI (Italian Radio) in 1956.
133. *Gesang der Junglinge*, for five-track tape, was first heard in Cologne, Germany, on 30 May, 1956.
134. Originally entitled *Symphonie de bruits*, it was further developed and became *Symphonie pour un homme seul* was completed in 1950; see Pierre Schaeffer, *Traité des Objets Musicaux* (Editions du Seuil, Paris 1966).
135. Originally, a talk given on BBC Radio, on 22 January 1960.
136. Lorca's *Llanto por Ignacio Sachez Mejias* was written in September 1934, a month after Ignacio's death in the arena at Manzanares. It was first read in public in April 1935 by the poet himself. Lorca had first met Ignacio during the centenary celebrations for the poet Gongora. They saw much of each other thereafter, both in Spain and during Lorca's stay in New York, by which time Ignacio had become the lover of a friend of Lorca's, the dancer La Argentinita. When Ignacio received his fatal wound, Lorca made hourly enquiries as to his condition: and at his death – so the poet told his friend and biographer Marcelle Auclair – it was if he had heard of his own death.
137. Two talks – here combined – originally given on the BBC Third Programme on 28 January and 3 February 1965.
138. cf. James Jeans, *Science and Music* (London 1937), V, 186–90.
139. *Collages* was the subtitle of Gerhard's Symphony No.3 for orchestra and electronic tape (1960).
140. A. N. Whitehead, *Modes of Thought* (Cambridge, 3rd edn, 1956), 36: The original contains a word omitted by Gerhard: "The *conceptual* entertainment of unrealized possibility is a major factor in human mentality."
141. This is a conflation of two articles. The first was published in *The Listener* no.

1826 (26 March 1964), 533; the second, originally in German, appeared in *Musical Events* no. 4 (April 1964), 6.

142. From "Robinson Crusoe's Preface" to the third volume of *Robinson Crusoe*.
143. Albert Camus, *The Plague*, transl. from the French by Stuart Gilbert (London, 1960), 251.
144. Camus, *op. cit.*, 251–2.
145. Ibid., 252.
146. Ibid., 252.
147. An illustrated talk given on BBC Radio, 25 October 1958.
148. In Gerhard's revised version of the work as *Metamorphoses* (1967–8), the twelve percussionists were reduced to seven.
149. A lecture given at the University of Michigan, Ann Arbor on 17 May 1960 and published in the University of Michigan Official Publication vol. 62, no. 18 (August 10 1960, School of music series, 2), 3–14.
150. Edward J. Dent, *Terpander* (London 1926; reprinted in 1965 as *Music of the Future*).
151. Charles Burney, *A General History of Music from the Earliest Times to the Present* (London, 4 vols, 1776–1789), I, 427–8.
152. Theodor W. Adorno, *Philosophy der Neuen Musik* (Tubingen, 1949, 3rd edn 1967), transl. Anne G. Mitchell & Wesley W. Blomster (London 1973).
153. Theodor W. Adorno, *Dissonanzen: Musizk in der Verwalten Welt* (Gottingen 1956).
154. Ibid., *Das Altern der Neuen Musik*, 102–5; the quotations are all in Gerhard's own English translation; some are taken from the translation by Rollo H. Myers in "Modern Music is Growing Old", in *Score*, No. 18, December 1956, 18–29.
155. Virgil Thomson, "Music – Ending the great tradition; a modest proposal", in *Encounter*, I, 12.64, 7 January 1959.
156. Adorno, *op. cit.*, 104.
157. Adorno, *op. cit.*,14.
158. Herbert Read, *Philosophy of Modern Art* (London 1951), 171n.
159. Wallace Stevens, "The Noble Rider and the Sound of Words" in *The Necessary Angel* (New York 1942), 29.
160. First broadcast on the BBC Third Programme, then published under the title "Thoughts on 'Art and Anarchy'" in *The Listener*, no. 1669 (23 March 1961), 519–20. It was one of a series of responses to Edgar Wind's Reith Lectures, *Art and Anarchy* (broadcast on the BBC Third Programme and published in *The Listener*, 64, November 17, 24, December 1, 8, 15 and 22 1960, before appearing in book form (London, 1963; 3rd edn, rev. 1985).
161. Wind. op. cit., 10–16.
162. Ibid., 21: Wind wrote: "... what we ourselves, *in the enjoyment of art*, might do ...".
163. Ibid., 20–21.
164. Ibid., 17.
165. Ibid., 23.
166. A. N. Whitehead, *Modes of Thought* (Cambridge, 3rd edn, 1956), 87.
167. Wind, *op. cit.*, 7.
168. Ibid., 7.
169. Ibid., 24.
170. Wallace Stevens, "The Noble Rider and the Sound of Words" in *The Necessary Angel* (New York 1942), 36.
171. Wind, *op. cit.*, 7: Wind refers, in fact, to "... vast aggregates of available images [that] are absorbed with an eagerness and, I may add, with a degree of

intelligence that would have left less adaptable generations dazed."

172. "Imagination as Value" in Stevens, *op. cit.*, 138–9.
173. A. N. Whitehead, *Modes of Thought* (Cambridge, 3rd edn, 1956), 119. Gerhard misquotes one word: the original reads, "The essence of life is to be found in the *frustrations* of the established order."
174. Whitehead, *op. cit.*: Gerhard here conflates two passages. The originals read as follows: (1) "Life degenerates when enclosed within the shackles of mere conformation. A power of incorporating vague and disorderly elements of experience is essential for the advance into novelty." (p.109). (2) "For the essence of great experience is penetration into the unknown, the unexperienced." (p.87).
175. Ibid., 119: the original is slightly different: "... to explain the aim and forms of order"....
176. First published in *Revista Shell* (Venezuela, December 1962), 64–9.
177. A. N. Whitehead, *Adventures of Ideas* (Cambridge 1947), 113–6.
178. José Ortega y Gasset, *Mediationes del Quijote* (Madrid 1921); the translation is Gerhard's own.
179. Luciano Berio, "Aspetto di artigianato formale" in *Incontri musicali: Quaderni internazionali di musica contemporanea*, I (Milan 1959), 99; the translation is Gerhard's own.
180. Heinrich von Kleist, *Uber das Marionettentheater* (1810); Engl. transl. by Idris Parry in *Hand to Mouth and other essays* (London 1981).
181. Ibid., 18.
182. Lecture given at the Berkshire Music Centre, Tanglewood, August 1961.
183. Paul Valéry, *Remerciement à L'Academie Française* : Lecture given on 23 June 1927, published in *Variété,* IV (Paris, Gallimard, 1938), 13. The sentence in which the phrase appears reads: "Le naturalisme et le Parnasse etant au plus haut periode, ils devenient la proie passive de l'inertie; il se trouvaient sans le savoir dans toute la faiblesse des apogées."

Appendix I: Chronological list of Gerhard's writings

This section is based upon the list of Gerhard's writings compiled by Margarida Estanyol in the booklet *Centenari Robert Gerhard* (Generalitat de Catalunya: Departament de Cultura, September 1996), 35–7. In certain respects, I have modified or corrected Sa. Estanyol's text and presented it (in English) in a slightly different format.

1918 *La canco popular catalana*: Catalunyan Archives of Ethnography and Folklore (Barcelona 1918), 5.

1922 "L'obra de Felipe Pedrell" in *Revista Musical Catalana*, vol. XIX (September–October 1922), 231–2.

1930–1936: Articles in *Mirador*
Prelude: 50 (30 January 1930), 7.
Coral: 54 (6 February 1930), 5.
Orquesta Pau Casals: 55 (13 February 1930), 5.
Fuga: al Mestre Millet: 56 (20 February 1930), 5.
Fuga (acabament): al Mestre Millet: 57 (27 February 1930), 5.
Elogi del Saxofon: 58 (6 March 1930), 5.
Concert al Liceu: 59 (13 March 1930), 5.
La Banda Municipal: 60 (20 March 1930), 5.
Opera: 61 (27 March 1930), 5.
Conzertstück: 62 (3 April 1930), 5.
Coda: 63 (10 April 1930), 5.
Variacions: 64 (17 April 1930), 5.
Com escolteu música?: 65 (7 April 1930), 5.
Com escolteu música? II: 66 (24 April 1930), 5.
(Untitled): 95 (27 November 1930), 5.
Film sonor: 96 (4 December 1930), 6.
La Música i el film sonor: 97 (11 December 1930), 5.
Un princep fa opera moderna: 99 (25 December 1930), 5.
Hanns Eisler: 101 (8 January, 1931), 5.
L'opera russa de Paris: 104 (29 January 1931), 5.
Bela Bartók: 105 (5 February 1931), 5.
Bela Bartók a "Audicions intimes": 106 (12 February 1931), 5.
Els compositors madrilenys: 107 (19 February 1931), 5.
Segon concert Conxita Supervia: 109 (5 March 1931), 5.
Artur Rubinstein: 111 (19 March 1931), 5.
C. Badia d'Agustí: 112 (26 March 1931), 5.
Francesc Costa: 114 (9 April 1931), 5.
Pau Casals: 115 (16 April 1931), 5.
Ildebrando Pizzetti: 118 (7 May 1931), 5.
Ernesto Halffter: 119 (14 May 1931), 5.

Baltasa Samper: 120 (21 May 1931), 5.
Música aplicada: 124 (18 June 1931), 5.
Edicions: 129 (23 July), 5.
Edicions de música: Xavier Gols, Suite pour piano: 131 (6 August 1931), 5.
Rodolfo Halffter "Sonatas de El Escorial": 133 (20 August 1931), 5.
La questió de la radio: 140 (8 October 1931), 5.
Un hoste illustre: Arnold Schoenberg: 140 (8 October 1931), 5.
Conversant amb Schoenberg: 145 (12 November 1931), 5.
Arnold Schoenberg: 165 (31 March 1932), 5.
Anton Webern (Música da Camera): 166 (7 April 1932), 5.
La SIMC a Viena: 182 (28 July 1932), 5.
La SIMC a Viena (continued): 185 (18 August 1932), 5.
La SIMC a Viena (concluded): 187 (1 September 1932), 5.
El Mestre Amadeu Vives: 202 (15 December 1932), 5.
La música contemporània (Report from Prague I): 348 (3 October 1935), 8.
"Suite" de música contemporània (Report from Prague II): 348 (17 October 1935), 8.
"Suite" de música contemporània (Report from Prague III): 348 (17 October 1935).
Primer concert de l"Orquesta Pau Casals: 350 (31 October 1935), 8.
La vida musical (Recent concerts I): 351 (7 November 1935), 8.
Francesc Martorell: 351 (7 November 1935), 8.
La vida musical (Recent concerts II): 353 (21 November 1935), 8.
"Maria del Carmen" de Granados: 351 (7 November 1935), 8.
Una nova orquesta de "camera": 356 (12 December 1935), 8.
Alban Berg: 361 (16 January 1936), 8.
Al Conferència Club: "La musica a la cort d'Alfons el Magnanim": 364 (6 February 1936), 8.

1935 *Música i poesia, Quaderns de poesia*: Year I (July 1935), 2, 18–22.

1945 *England. Spring, 1945: Tempo*, 11 (old series, ed. Ernest Chapman, Spring 1945), 2-3; reprinted in *Tempo*, 100 (new series, ed. David Drew, July 1972), 4–8.

1951 *On Music in Ballet* I: *Ballet*, 3 (April 1951), 19–24; II, 4 (May 1951), 28–35.

1952 *Tonality in twelve-tone music: The Score & MA magazine*, 6 (May 1952), 23–35.

1954 "On composition with twelve notes" in J. Rufer, *Composition with Twelve Notes* (London/New York: Rockcliff/Macmillan, 1954), First published as one of several contributions by different composers to the Appendix of Josef Rufer, *Composition with Twelve Notes*, English transl. Humphrey Searle (London 1969), Appendix I, 183–5.

"Reply to George Perle": *The Score & MA magazine*, 9 (September 1954), 59–60.

1955 *Twelve-note composition explained*, BBC Radio talk: 2 April 1965.

1956 *Pau Casals, simbolo de la nacionalidad catalana*: (1) *Libro blanco de Cataluña*

(Buenos Aires); (2) Published in *Revista de Catalunya*, 1956, 16 (in Spanish, Catalan and English).

"The Contemporary Music Situation": *The Score & MA magazine*, 16 (June 1956), 7–18 (Originally a talk given at Bedford College for Women, London).
"Developments in twelve-note technique": *The Score & MA magazine*, 17 (September 1956), 61–72.
Schoenberg reminiscences: Lecture given at Dartington Summer School of Music, published posthumously in *Perspectives of New Music* (Princeton, New Jersey, Spring–Summer 1975), 57–65.
"Twelve-note technique in Stravinsky": *The Score & MA magazine*, 18 (December 1956), 38–43.

1957 "Sound and Symbol": BBC radio talk, 13 August 1957.

1958 "A propos Mr Stadlen": *The Score & MA magazine*, 24 (July 1958), 50–57.
"The composer and his audience": BBC radio talk, 3 October 1958, first published in Rollo Myers (ed.), *Twentieth-Century Music* (London, Calder & Boyars 1960), 52–61.
"Introduction to Symphony 2": BBC radio talk, 25 October 1958.

1959 *Concrete and electronic music composition*: An illustrated talk given at the "Music, Libraries and Instruments" Conference in August (?) 1959. Later published under its present title in the *Hinrichsen Music Yearbook*, 11 (London 1961), 30–38.
Symphony 2: programme note for first performance by BBC Symphony Orchestra at the Royal Festival Hall, London, 27 November 1959.
"Roberto Gerhard's Symphony": *Radio Times* (October 1959), 9.

1960 *Functions of the series in twelve-note composition*: two lectures given at the University of Michigan, Ann Arbor, spring 1960.
Is New Music Growing Old?: Lecture given at the University of Michigan, Ann Arbor on 17 May, 1960 and published in the University of Michigan Official Publication vol. 62, 18 (August 10 1960, School of Music series, 2), 3–14.
"Introduction to 'Lament on the death of a bullfighter'": BBC radio talk, (26 January 1960?).

1961 "Some lectures by Webern": *The Score & MA magazine*, 28 (January 1961), 25–28.
"Thoughts on 'Art and Anarchy'": *The Listener*, 1669 (23 March 1961), 519–20.
"Irrelevant art": talk on BBC Radio (11 March 1961).
"Reluctant Revolutionary": article on Schoenberg in *The Sunday Telegraph* (December 3 1961), 11.

1962 *Musa y música hoy*: *Revista Shell* (Venezuela, December 1962), 64–69.

1963 "Primitive folk music from Spain": BBC radio talk, 6 January 1963.

1964 "The Plague": *The Listener*, 1826 (March 26 1964), 553.
Composer's Forum: *The Plague*, in *Musical Events*, no. 4 (April 1964), 6.

1965 "Sound Observed": two BBC radio talks (28 January and 3 February 1965).

1992 *Apunts: Cultura* (Barcelona, January 1992), 29–42.

Translations

Between 1929 and 1934 Gerhard was active as the translator into Catalan of various important books on music. These are as follows:

Hugo Riemann: *Dictado musical* (Barcelona: Labor 1928) and *Composicion musical* (Barcelona: Labor 1929).
Hermann Scherchen: *El arte de dirigir la orquesta* (Barcelona: Labor 1933).
Hans Scholz: *Compendio de armonia* (Barcelona, Labor 1928?).
Ernst Toch: *La melodia* (Barcelona, Buenos Aires, Labor 1931; reprinted in 1985).
Fritz Volbach: *La orquesta moderna* (Barcelona, Labor 1928).
Egon Wellesz: *Música bizantia* (Barcelona, Labor 1930).
Johannes Wolf: *Historia de la música* (Barcelona, Labor 1934).

Appendix II: List of musical compositions by Gerhard and selected discography

Publishers

BH	Boosey & Hawkes Ltd
BM	Belwyn Mills Music Ltd
CN	Chester Music
EMS	Editions Maurice Sénart
KP	Keith Prowse Music Publishing Co. Ltd
MOR	A. Morelda
OUP	Oxford University Press
TTO	Tritó Edicions, Barcelona
UE	Universal Edition Vienna/London
UME	Union Musical Espanola Barcelona

BBC	Manuscript in BBC Music Library
BIRS	Recordings on tape in British Institute of Recorded Sound
BL	Manuscript in the British Library
CBA	Manuscript in the Concepcion Badia D'Agusti Archive (Biblioteca di Catalunya)
CUL	Manuscript on the Cambridge University Library
IEV	Manuscript at the Institut d'Estudis Vallencs, Valls, Catalonia
SCL/SML	Manuscript in Shakespeare Centre Library/Stratford Memorial Theatre

The Akond of Swat (1954), for voice and percussion, 10 mins
"Scena for Monica and Percussion"
Words by Edward Lear
Ms: CUL
Commissioned by the Music Section, Institute of Contemporary Arts, London
(OUP: facsimile of composer's autograph)
First perf: Heather Harper (soprano), Institute of Contemporary Arts, London, 7 February 1956

Albada, Interludi i Dansa (1936), for orchestra
Ms: IEV
Publ: BH
First perf: BBC radio broadcast, London, BBC Symphony Orchestra/Gerhard, 14 May 1937
Rec: Tenerife Symphony Orchestra/Victor Pablo Perez, Audivis Montaigne MO 782104

Alegrias (1942), for two pianos
Ballet in one act, with Scenario by Gerhard
Choreography by Elsa Brunelleschi
Ms: CUL
Publ: BH
First perf: Ballet Rambert, Birmingham, 16 July 1943
Version for two pianos, arr. Richard Rodney Bennett (1973)

Rec: Andrew Ball & Julian Jacobson
Largo 5119

Suite from the Ballet-Divertissement Flamenco, Alegrias (1942)
Publ: BM; now BH
First perf: BBC Theatre Orchestra/Stanford Robinson (BBC studio recording), 4 April, 1942
1994
Rec: (1) Louisville Orchestra/Whitney, Louisville Orchestra
CRI 646
(2) Tenerife Symphony Orchestra/Victor Pablo Perez,
Etcetera KTC 1095
(3) Orquesta de Cambra Teatre Lliure/Josep Pons
Harmonia Mundi HMC90 1500
also BIRS

All Aboard (1958), 5 mins
Score for cartoon film for Bowater Company
Ms: CUL

Andantino (?1928), for clarinet, violin and piano
Ms: IEV

L'alta naixença del Rei En Jaume (1932), 17 mins
(The Noble Birth of King James)
Cantata for soprano, baritone, chorus and orchestra (1932)
Poems by Josep Carner
Ms: IEV
Publ: BH
First perf. (movements 4 and 5 only): ISCM Festival Amsterdam, cond. Gerhard, 10 June 1933
First perf. (complete): Palau de la Musica, Barcelona, Carmen Bustamente/Enric Serra/Coral Antics Escolans de Montserrat & Cor Sant Esteve del Conservatori de Vilaseca 1 Salon/Orquestra de la Cuitat de Barcelona/Antoni Ros Marba
Auvidis MO 782106
Rec: Anna Cors/ Francesc Gattigosa/Coral Carmina/Orquesta Sinfonica de Barcelona I Nacional de Catalunya/Edmond Colona
Auvidis MO 782106

The Anger of Achilles (1964), 110 mins (duration of whole programme)
Incidental music, for orchestra and tape, for BBC radio production of Robert Graves' play, 15, 24 and 31 May 1964
Ms: CUL
Also rec: BIRS

(Dos) Apunts for solo piano
Ms: CUL
Publ: UME; also in Score & IMA Magazine no. 17 (Sept 6 1956)
Rec: (1) Jordi Camell
A. Morelda 12941
(2) Jordi Maso
Marco Polo 822 3867
(3) Andrew Ball
Largo 5119

Ariel (1934), 20 mins
Ballet with scenario by Gerhard and J.V. Foix, decor by Joan Miró
Ms (2): IEV
Publ: BH
First perf: ISCM Festival, Barcelona, cond. Hermann Scherchen, 19 April 1936
Rec: Catalonian National Orchestra/Edmon Coloner
Auvidis Montaigne 782105

Asylum Diary (1959), 75 mins (duration of complete programme)
Incidental music for BBC Radio play by Christine Lavant
Ms: ?

Audiomobiles I–IV (c. 1958–9)
Electronic composition
No.2 subtitled *DNA*
Also: *DNA in reflection* (1963) – see below, *Ten Pieces for Tape*

Bailete [c. 1930–38?]
Song for high voice and piano
Ms: CUL

El Barberillo de Lavapiés (1954)
For seven singers and orchestra
An arrangement and orchestration by Gerhard of Francisco Barbieri's zarzuela (1874)
First perf: BBC Theatre Orchestra/Stanford Robinson, BBC Radio recording, March 1954
Ms: ?
Publ: BH

Cadiz (1943), 9 mins
A free orchestral fantasia by Gerhard (under the pseudonym Juan Serrallonga) on the zarzuela by Federico Chueca and Joaquin Valverde (1886)
Publ: BH
First perf: BBC Theatre Orchestra/Stanford Robinson, BBC Radio (studio recording), 1943

Caligula (1961), 15 mins
Incidental music for chamber ensemble and tape, for BBC radio production of Camus' play, 1961
Also: concert version for chamber ensemble and tape (1961), 6 mins
Ms: CUL

14 Cançons populars Catalanes (1917), for high voice & piano, 20 mins
Ms: CUL
Publ: UE, with German text by R.S. Hoffmann; English transl. by J.B. Trend; now BH
First perf: Conchita Badia d'Agusti (soprano), Barcelona
Arr. from this cycle: **6 Cançons populars de Catalunya** (1931), for high voice & piano, 10 mins
First perf: Conchita Badia d'Agusti, soprano, Anton von Webern, conductor, ISCM Festival, Vienna, 16 June 1932
Rec: Anna Cors/Francesc Garrigosa/Catalonian National Orchestra/Edmond Colomer
Auvidis Montaigne 782106

Cancionero de Pedrell for high voice and piano, 18 mins
An arrangement by Gerhard of Spanish folksongs collected by Pedrell
Ms: CUL

Publ: KP, now BH
First perf: Sophie Wyss (soprano), Norman Franklyn (piano), Wigmore Hall, London 1942
Rec: Benita Valenta (soprano) Tan Crone (piano)
Etcetera KTC 1060
Version for voice and chamber ensemble (1941)
Publ: KP, now BH
First perf: Sophie Wyss/Ensemble/Leslie Bridgewater, BBC Radio, 1942
Rec: (1) Josep Benet/Orquestra de Cambra Teatre Lliure/Josep Pons
Auvidis MO 782105/Harmonia Mundi HMC90 1500
(2) Anna Cors/Catalonian National Orchestra/Edmond Colomer
Auvidis Montaigne 782106

Three Canciones Toreras (c. 1943), for medium voice and piano, 9 mins
(arranged by Gerhard under the pseudonym Juan Serrallonga)
Ms: CBA
orchestrated version
First perf: BBC Theatre Orchestra/Stanford Robinson, c. 1943

Cantares (1956): Seven Spanish songs for voice and guitar, arr. Gerhard, 18 mins
Ms: CUL
Publ: BM, now BH
First perf: Sophie Wyss (soprano), Julian Bream (guitar), BBC Radio Concert, 1957
Rec: BIRS
(see also Fantasia for Guitar, below)

Capriccio (1949) for solo flute, 5 mins
Publ: BM, now BH
First perf: Edward Walker, ISCM Concert, London 1949
Rec: (1) Ingrid Culliford
Lore LNT 107
(2) Xavier Relats
PICAP CD-90
Also rec: BIRS

Chaconne (1959) for solo violin, 18 mins
Ms: CUL
Publ: BM, now BH
First perf: Yfrah Neaman, Macnaughten Concert, London 1959
Rec: (1) Caroline Balding
Metier Sound and Vision MSV CD 92012
(2) Santiago de la Riva
Several Records (no number)
(3) Barcelona 216
Stradivarius 33404
Also rec: BIRS

The Cherry Orchard (1961),. 40 mins
Incidental music, for chamber ensemble and tape, for production of Chekhov's play at Memorial Theatre, Stratford-on-Avon
Ms: ?

Cristobal Colón (1943)
Incidental music for BBC radio production of the play by Madariaga
Ms: BBC

Concert for Eight (1962) for flute, clarinet, accordion, mandolin, guitar, percussion, piano and double-bass, 10½ mins
Publ: OUP
First perf: Melos Ensemble/Jacques-Louis Monod, BBC Invitation Concert, 17 May 1962
rec: (1) Nieuw Ensemble
Largo 5134
(2) Barcelona 216/Ernst Martinez Izquierdo
Stradivarius 33404
Also rec: BIRS

Concertino for string orchestra (1929)
Arrangement of String Quartet (?1928)
Ms: String Quartet, IEV; Concertino (parts only), IEV
First perf: Orchestra cond. Roberto Gerhard, Palau de la Musica, Barcelona, December 1929
Publ: TTO (ed. M. Bowen)

Concerto for Harpsichord, String Orchestra and Percussion (1955–6)
Ms: CUL
Publ: BM, now BH
First perf: (1st movement only): Thurston Dart/Boyd Neel String Orchestra/Antony Hopkins
First perf. (complete): Thurston Dart/Boyd Neel String Orchestra/Brian Priestman
Geoffrey Tozer/BBC Symphony Orchestra/Matthias Bamert
CHANDOS CHAN 9693
Also rec: BIRS

Concerto for Orchestra (1965)
Commissioned by the Cheltenham Festival
Ms: CUL
Publ: OUP
First perf: BBC Symphony Orchestra/Antal Dorati, Boston, USA
First European perf: BBC Symphony Orchestra/Norman Del Mar, Cheltenham Festival, 1965
Rec: (1) BBC Symphony Orchestra/Norman Del Mar
Argo ZRG 553
(2) BBC Symphony Orchestra/Mathias Bamert
Chandos 9694
Also rec: BIRS

Concerto for Piano and String Orchestra (1951)
Ms: CUL
Publ: BM, now BH
Noel Newton-Wood/Strings of the Aldeburgh Festival Orchestra/Norman Del Mar, Aldeburgh Festival, 16 June 1951
Rec: (1) Geoffrey Tozer/BBC Symphony Orchestra/Matthias Bamert
Chandos CHAN 9693
(2) Albert Attenelle/Orquestra Simfonica de Barcelona/Nacional de Catalunya/Franz-Paul Decker
Auvidis Montaigne MO 782107
Also rec: BIRS

Concerto for Violin and Orchestra (1942–3)
Ms: CUL
Publ: BM, now BH
First perf: Antonio Brosa/Orch cond. Hermann Scherchen, Maggio Musicale, Florence, May 1950
Rec: (1) Yfrah Neaman/ BBC Symphony Orchestra/Colin Davis
Argo ZRG 701
(2) Olivier Charlier/BBC Symphony Orchestra/Matthias Bamert
Chandos CHAN 9599
Also rec: BIRS

Conquistador (1953)
Incidental music for BBC radio production (Archibald McLeish)
Ms: CUL

Coriolanus (1959)
Incidental music for production of Shakespeare's play at Memorial Theatre, Stratford-on-Avon
Ms: SCL/SMT

The Count of Monte Cristo
Incidental music for BBC TV adaptation of Dumas' novel
Ms: CUL

Cymbeline (1949)
Incidental music for production of Shakespeare's play at Memorial Theatre, Stratford-on-Avon
Ms: ?

Don Carlos (1959)
Incidental music for production of Schiller's play
Ms: CUL

The Adventures of Don Quixote (1944): Incidental music for radio
Cervantes/Linklater
Ms: BBC
First perf: BBC Radio, 1944

Ballet: *Don Quixote*, in one act (1940–41; 1947–49)
Scenario by Gerhard after Cervantes (unperformed)
Ms: CUL
2nd (final) version 1947–49)
Publ: BH
First perf: Sadler's Wells Ballet at Covent Garden, 20 February 1950 with Robert Helpmann and Margot Fonteyn
Choreography by Ninette de Valois
Decor by Edward Burra
Conductor Robert Irving
Rec: Orquestra Sinfonica de Tenerife/Victor Pablo Perez
Audivis Montaigne MO 782104

Suite No. 1: Don Quixote (1941), 32 mins
BBC Symphony Orchestra/Constant Lambert, Cambridge 1941
Suite No. 1: Don Quixote (arr. David Atherton) (1973) for 15 players
First perf: London Sonfonietta/David Atherton, Hull, 1973
Suite No. 2: Don Quixote (1947), 24 mins

ISCM Festival, Copenhagen, cond. Andre Souris

Dances from Don Quixote (1958)
Publ: KP, now BH
First perf: BBC Proms, BBC Symphony Orchestra/Basil Cameron in the Royal Albert Hall, London, 1958
Rec: BBC Symphony Orchestra/Antal Dorati
Also rec: BIRS
HMV ALP 2063/ASD 613/Argo ZRG/Seraphim S 60071
Transcription by Gerhard for piano solo (1947) 16 mins
Publ: MOR, now KP, 1957
First perf: Albert Ferber, BBC radio recording, 1947
Rec: Jordi Camell
A. Morelda 12941

The Duenna (1945–47)
Opera in three acts
Libretto by Gerhard based on Sheridan's *The Duenna*
Additional lyrics by Christopher Hassall
Ms: BH
Publ: BH (Performing edition by David Drew, 1991)
First perf: Camden Theatre, London BBC Theatre Orchestra/Stanford Robinson, 1949
Further perfs: ISCM Festival, Wiesbaden, con. Franz-Paul Decker, 1951
BBC radio recording, with Soloists/BBC Symphony Orchestra/Chorus/David Atherton
First stage production: Teatro Lirico Nacional La Zarzuela, Madrid, Opera/Antonio Ros Marba, 19 January 1992
Rec: Soloists/Chorus of Opera North/English Northern Philharmonia/Antoni Rosa Marba
Chandos CHAN 9520(2)
Also rec: BIRS

Interludes and Arias from 'The Duenna' (1961) for mezzo-soprano and orchestra, 14 mins
Text by the composer (based on Sheridan)
Publ: BH
First perf: Marie Collier/BBC Symphony Orchestra/Basil Cameron, BBC Proms, Royal Albert Hall, London, 18 September 1961

Duo concertante (see **Gemini** below)

El Conde Sol (?1927), for trumpet, horn, bassoon,violin, viola, cello and piano
Ms: IEV

Engheno novo for high/medium voice and orchestra (c. 1943), 1½ mins
Song with Portuguese text
Ms: CUL
(Written under the pseudonym Juan Serrallonga)
First perf: c. 1943, BBC

Epithalamium for orchestra (1966), 20 mins
Ms: CUL
Publ: OUP
First perf: Valdgano, Italy, cond. Ettore Gracis
Rec: (1) Spanish National Youth Orchestra/Edmon Coloner
Auvidis Montaigne MO 782101

(2) BBC Symphony Orchestra/Matthias Bamert
Chandos CHAN 9556
Also rec: BIRS

L'Etranger (1954)
Ms: CUL
Incidental music for BBC radio adaptation of Albert Camus' novel
(Ms) *

Fantasia for Guitar, 4 mins
Ms: CUL
Publ: BM, now BH
A postscript to **Cantares** (see above), intended for insertion at mid-point of that work
First perf: Julian Bream, 1957
Rec: (1) Julian Bream
RCA 28-09026 61583-2
(2) Franz Halasz
Grammofon 736
(3) Roberto Casares
Koch International 312802
(4) Barcelona 216
Stradivarius
Also rec: BIRS

For Whom the Bell Tolls (1965)
Incidental music for BBC radio adaptation of Ernest Hemingway's novel
Ms: CUL

Six French Folksongs (1956), 8 mins
Arrangement by Gerhard of traditional folk-songs
Ms: CUL
First perf: Sophie Wyss (soprano), Ernest Lush (piano), French Institute, London
Also version of one song, "La Fille Tombée a l'eau" for soprano and harp
Also rec: BIRS

Funnyhouse of a Negro (1964)
Incidental music for BBC radio adaptation of a play by Adrienne Kennedy, BBC Third Programme, 10 December 1964
Ms: CUL
Also rec: BIRS

Gemini (1966), for violin and piano, 12 mins
Ms: Private collection
Publ: OUP, 1970
Commissioned by and dedicated to Dr and Mrs Morris Hochberg
First perf. (under the title *Duo concertante*): Yfrah Neaman/Susan Bradshaw, Commonwealth Institute, London 24 September 1966
Rec: (1) Nona Liddell/John Constable
Decca Head 11
(2) Caroline Balding/Tim Lissimore
Metier Sound and Vision MSV CD92012
(3) Angel Gimeno/John Snijders
Largo 5134
(4) Gerhard Trio (members)
La Ma de Guido 2021

(5) Barcelona 216
Stradivarius 33404
Also rec: BIRS

Gigantes y Cabeduzos (c. 1943), 9 mins
(Giants and Dwarves)
A fantasia for orchestra by Gerhard (under the pseudonym Juan Serrallonga) on a zarzeuela by Manuel Fernandez Caballero
Ms: CUL
Publ: BH
First perf: BBC Theatre Orchestra/Stanford Robinson, c. 1943

Good Morning Midnight (1956)
Incidental music for BBC radio production (Jean Rhys)
Ms: CUL

7 Haiku (1922, rev. 1958), for male or female voice (mezzo-soprano or high baritone), flute, oboe, clarinet, bassoon and piano, 11 mins
Poems by Josep Junoy
Ms: IEV
Publ: BM, 1979, now BH
First perf: Concepcio Badia d'Agusti (soprano), Esteve Gratacos, (flute), Cassia Carles (oboe), Joan Vives (clarinet), Anton Goxens (bassoon), cond. Gerhard, Palau de la Musica Catalana, Barcelona, 22 December 1929
Rec: Josep Benet/Orquestra de Cambra Teatre Lliure/Josep Pons
Auvidis MO 782105/Harmonia Mundi HMC90 1500
Also: BIRS

Hymnody (1963), for seven wind instruments, percussion and two pianos, 17 mins
Ms: CUL
Publ: OUP
First perf: Virtuoso Ensemble/Jacques-Louis Monod, BBC Invitation Concert, 23 May 1963
Rec: BIRS

Three Impromptus (1950), for piano
Dedicated to the Earl and Countess of Harewood
Ms: CUL
Publ: BM, 1959; now BH; also, facsimile of composer's autograph publ. in *The Score*, no.11, 1955, 23–32
First perf: Albert Ferber, London 1955
Rec: (1) Antoni Besses
(Antologia Historica de la Musica Catalana, orig. EDIGSA)
PDI 801069
(2) Andrew Ball
Largo 5119
(3) Jordi Maso
Marco Polo 8 223867
(4) John Snijders
Largo 5134
(5) Jordi Camell
A. Morelda 12941
(6) Barcelona 216
Stradivarius 33404
Also rec: BIRS

L'infantament meravellós de Shaharazada (Op.1): 12 songs for high voice and piano
Poems by J.M. Lopez-Pico
Ms: ?
Publ: UME 1918
Rec: Benita Valente (soprano), Tan Crone (piano)
Etcetera KTC 1060
Six songs from *L'infantament meravellós de Schaharazada* arr. M. Bowen (1993), for high voice and ensemble
First perf: Rosa Mannion/Nash Ensemble/Lionel Friend, Purcell Room, London 1 March 1994
Publ: TTO
(BIRS has tape-recording of Gerhard reading the poems)

King Lear (1955), 40 mins
Incidental music, for chamber ensemble and tape, for production of Shakespeare's play at Memorial Theatre, Stratford-on-Avon
Ms: CUL

Lamparilla Overture (1956), 5 mins
Overture for orchestra after the zarzuela *El Barberillo di Lavapies* by Francisco Anejo Barbieri (1874)
Ms: CUL
Publ: BH

La fulla el mivol (1940s?)
song for high voice and piano
Ms: CUL

Lament for Death of a Bullfighter (1959) for speaker and tape, 12 mins 58 secs
Text by Federico Garcia Lorca, trans. A.L. Lloyd
realized in part at BBC radiophonic Workshop
First perf: Stephen Murray/tape, BBC Radio 1960
Rec: BIRS

A Leak in the Universe (1955), c. 10 mins
Incidental music, for chamber ensemble and tape, for BBC radio production of play by I.A. Richards
Ms: CUL

Leo (1969), for flute, clarinet, horn, trumpet, trombone, percussion, piano, celesta, violin and cello, 20 mins
Ms: CUL
Publ: OUP, 1970
Commissioned by the Hopkins Centre, Dartmouth USA
First perf: Dartmouth Festival Orchestra/Mario di Bonaventura, Dartmouth, 23 August 1969
First European perf: London Sinfonietta/David Atherton at the Queen Elizabeth Hall, London, 24 November 1969
Rec: (1) London Sinfonietta/Atherton
Decca Head 11
(2) Nieuw Ensemble/Ed Spanjaard
Largo 5134
Also rec: BIRS

Libra, for flute (piccolo), clarinet, violin, guitar, percussion and piano
Commissioned by the BBC

Ms: CUL
Publ: OUP, 1970
First perf: London Sinfonietta/David Atherton, BBC Concert at Cambridge, 26 October 1968
Rec: (1) London Sinfonietta/Atherton
Decca Head 11
(2) Australian Contemporary Music Ensemble/Keith Humble
Cherry Pie CPF 1029
(3) Nieuw Ensemble/Ed Spanjaard
Largo 5134
(4) Barcelona 216/Ernst Martinez Izquierdo
Stradivarius 33404
Also rec: BIRS

Lied (c.1917) for voice and piano
German text, unattrib.
Ms: IEV

Macbeth (1962)
Incidental music for production of Shakespeare's play at Memorial Theatre, Stratford-on-Avon
Also: Excerpts for a TV anthology (1964)
Ms: SCL/SMT

Madrigal a Sitges (c. 1930–37), song for high voice and piano
Ms: Two versions: CUL

The Man Born to be King (1966)
Incidental music for BBC radio production of Dorothy L. Sayers' play
Ms: CUL
Also rec: BIRS

A Midsummer Night's Dream (1954)
Incidental music for production of Shakespeare's play at Memorial Theatre, Stratford-on-Avon
Ms: CUL

Nonet, for flute, oboe, clarinet, bassoon, horn, trumpet, trombone, tuba and accordion (1956–57), 19 mins
Ms: CUL
Publ: BM, now BH
First perf: Dennis Brain Wind Ensemble/Norman Del Mar, BBC Radio, September 1957
Also rec: BIRS

The Overcoat (1961), 15 mins
Incidental music, for chamber ensemble and tape, for BBC Radio production of Gogol's play
Ms: CUL

Pandora (1943–44), for two pianos and percussion, 50 mins
Ballet in one act
Scenario and choreography by Kurt Jooss
Decor by Hein Heckroth
Ms: CUL
Publ: BM, now BH

First perf: Ballet Joos, Arts Theatre, Cambridge, 24 January 1944
Orchestrated version (1944–45), London, Ballet Joos
Scenario and choreography by David Morse
First perf: Sadler's Wells Royal Ballet, Royal Shakespeare Theatre, Stratford-on-Avon, 1976
Rec: Catalonia National Orchestra/Edmon Coloner
Auvidis Montaigne MO 782105

Suite: Pandora (1944–45), for orchestra 21 mins
Publ: BM, now BH
First perf: London Symphony Orchestra/Constant Lambert, BBC Radio recording, February 1950
Publ: BH (score rediscovered 1993)
Rec: Orquestra de Cambra Teatre Lliure/Josep Pons
Auvidis MO 782105/Harmonia Mundi HMC90 1500
Also rec: BIRS

Suite: Pandora (ed. David Atherton and arranged for 17 players), 20 mins
Publ: BM, now BH
First perf: London Sinfonietta/David Atherton, Dartington 1973

Suite: Pandora (version for two pianos and percussion)
Rec: Andrew Ball & Julian Jacobson (pianos)
Richard Benjafield (percussion)
Largo 5119

Pedrelliana (1941), for orchestra
Final movement of Symphony Homenatje a Pedrell (see below)
Ms: CUL
Publ: BH
First perf: BBC studio recording, BBC Symphony Orchestra/Juan José Castro, 1954
Rec : Orquestra Sinfonica de Tenerife/Victor Pablo Perez
Audivis Montaigne MO 782104
Also rec: BIRS

Pericles, Prince of Tyre (1958), 40 mins
Incidental music, for chamber ensemble and tape, for production of Shakespeare's play at Memorial Theatre, Stratford-on-Avon
Ms: CUL

The Philosopher's Den (1963)
Incidental music for BBC radio production of play by Zbigniew Herbert
Ms: CUL

Ten Pieces for tape (1961), 5 mins 12 secs
(excerpts from DNA in reflection)

1. Asyndeton	6. Speculum
2. Bubblecade	7. Stridor
3. Campanalog	8. Suspension
4. Dripsonic	9. Telergic
5. Meteoroids	10. Uncle Ned

Disc: Southern Library of Recorded Music MQ 760 (45 rpm), but nos. 8 and 10 are omitted
Also rec: BIRS

Three Pieces for Small Orchestra (c. 1943), 6 mins
orchestral arrangements by Gerhard of three Schubert piano pieces:
1. Rondo from Sonata in D (D.850)
2. Marche Militaire in D (D.733), no. 1
3 Marche Characteristique in C (D.866), no.1
First perf : Westminster Light Orchestra/Leslie Bridgwater
Ms: CUL

The Plague (1963–64), for speaker, mixed chorus and orchestra, 42 mins
Text adapted from Albert Camus' *La Peste* (Eng. transl. by Stuart Gilbert)
Ms: CUL
Publ: OUP, 1967
First perf: Stephen Murray/BBC Symphony Orchestra & Chorus/Antal Dorati, Royal Festival Hall, London 1964
(OUP, London 1967)
Rec: (1) Alex McCowen (narrator)/BBC Symphony Orchestra & Chorus/Antal Dorati
Decca ZAK 13126
(2) Michael Lonsdale (narrator)/Spanish National Youth Orchestra/BBC Symphony Orchestra/Edmon Colonne
Auvidis Montaigne MO782101

Por do pasaré la sierra (1942), for high voice and piano, $2^1/2$ mins
First perf: Sophie Wyss (soprano), 1942
Ms: CUL

The Prisoner (1954), ?40 mins
Incidental music, for chamber ensemble and tape, for production of Bridget Boland's play at Globe Theatre, London
Ms: ?

The Revenge for Love (1957)
Incidental music for BBC radio production of play by Percy Wyndham Lewis
Ms: CUL

Romeo and Juliet (c. 1949)
Incidental music for production of Shakespeare's play at Memorial Theatre, Stratford-on-Avon
Ms: CUL

Two Sardanas (1928), for trad. ensemble of wind (coblas) and percussion, 11 mins
Ms: IEV; also (1) CUL
First perf: Barcelona "Musica da camera" concert, 1930
Rec: (1) Cobla Sant Jordi/Jordi Leon
PICAP 302007
(2) Catalonian National Orchestra/Edmond Colomer
Auvidis Montaigne 782106

Sardana No. 1 arr. brass band (1940), $5^1/2$ mins
Dedicated to Kenneth Wright
First perf: London Sinfonietta/Elgar Howarth, Queen Elizabeth Hall, London, 6 October 1970

Sardana No. 1 arr. wind ensemble (1956)
First perf: Dennis Brain Wind Ensemble/Norman Del Mar, BBC Radio, 21 October 1958
Also rec: BIRS

Sculpture I (1963), 4 mins 18 secs
Electronic composition based on sound from a small-scale model of sculpture of brass rods by John Youngman

Secret People (1951?)
Sample piece for film contract for violin, clarinet & piano
Score for feature film dir. Thorold Dickinson, cond. Ernest Irving for piccolo, oboe, cor anglais, two clarinets, bassoon, horn, trumpet, tuba and percussion (1951)
Ms: CUL

Sevillana (?1936), for trumpet, horn, bassoon, violin, viola and cello
Ms: score & parts: IEV
(TTO, 1999)

Sevillanas (1943), for high voice and piano, 2 mins
Ms: CUL
First perf: Sophie Wyss (soprano), 1943

Soirées de Barcelone (1936–39) 22 mins
Ballet in three tableaux
Commissioned by Colonel de Basil for his company
Orchestration completed by Malcolm MacDonald, 1995–96
Publ: BH
First perf: BBC Radio 3, BBC Philharmonic Orchestra/Yan Pascal Tortelier, 29 September 1996
Rec: Catalonian National Orchestra/Edmon Colomer
Auvidis Montaigne 782105

Suite: Soirées de Barcelone
First perf: New Philharmonia Orchestra/David Atherton, BBC radio recording, 1972
Ms: CUL
Version for piano solo (c. 1958)
First perf: Michael Blake, Purcell room, 12 January 1985
Rec: (1) Albert Nieto
RTVE Musica 65039
(2) Andrew Ball
Largo 5119
(3) Jordi Maso
Marco Polo 8 223867
Also rec: BIRS

Sonatine a Carlos (1914), for piano
Ms: IEV

Sonata for cello and piano (1956)
Ms: CUL
Publ: OUP
First perf: Florence Hooton/Wilfred Parry, BBC Radio, 10 October 1964
Rec: (1) Jo Cole & Timothy Lissimore(piano)
Metier MSV CD92012
(2) Barcelona 216 (members)
Stradivarius 33404
(3) Gerhard Trio (members)
La Ma de Guido 2021

(4) Carlos Prieto/ Edison Quintana
Urtext 17
Also rec: BIRS

Sonata for clarinet and piano (1928)
Ms: IEV (also version for bass clarinet and piano)
TTO (ed. M. Bowen)

String Quartet No. 1 (1950–55), 19 mins
Ms: CUL
Publ: KP, now BH
First perf: Parrenin Quartet, Dartington, 1956
Rec: Kreutzer Quartet
Metier MSV CD 92026
Also rec: BIRS

String Quartet No. 2 (1960–62), 12½ mins
Commissioned by the University of Michigan
Ms: CUL
Publ: OUP
First perf: Stanley Quartet, Ann Arbor, Michigan, 1962
First European perf: Parrenin Quartet, Dartington, 1963
Rec: Kreutzer Quartet
Metier MSV CD 92026
Also rec: BIRS

Symphony "Homenatje a Pedrell" (1941), 28 mins
Ms: CUL
Publ: BH: see also *Pedrelliana* above
First perf. (third movement only): BBC Symphony Orchestra/Juan José Castro, BBC Radio recording, 1954
First perf. (complete): New Philharmonia Orchestra/David Atherton, 1972
(1) Tenerife Symphony Orchestra/Victor Pablo Perez
Auvidis Valois
(2) BBC Symphony Orchestra/Matthias Bamert
Chandos CHAN 9593

Symphony No.1 (1952–3), 37 mins
Ms: CUL
Publ: BM, now BH
First perf: Sudwestfunk Orchestra/Hans Rosbaud, ISCM Festival, Baden-Baden, 21 June 1955
Rec: (1) BBC Symphony Orchestra/Antal Dorati
Argo ZRG 752 (originally EMI)
(2) Tenerife Symphony Orchestra/Victor Pablo Perez
Auvidis Montaigne MO 782102
(3) BBC Symphony Orchestra/Matthias Bamert
Chandos CHAN 9599
Also rec: BIRS

Symphony No. 2 (1957–9), 28 mins
Ms: CUL
Commissioned by the BBC
First perf: BBC Symphony Orchestra/Rudolf Schwartz
Rec: BBC Symphony Orchestra/Mathias Bamert
Chandos 9694

Metamorphoses: A re-composition of Symphony No.2 (1967–68; last movement (unfinished) 33 mins
Publ: BM, now BH
Ms: CUL
First perf: London Symphony Orchestra/David Atherton, Royal Festival Hall, London (at which the original last movement of the symphony was performed in an edition by Alan Boustead)
Rec: Orquestra Sinfonica de Tenerife/Victor Pablo Perez
Audivis Valois 4728
Also rec: BIRS

Symphony No. 3 (Collages) (1960), 20 mins
Commissioned by the Koussevitzky Foundation
Dedicated to the memory of Serge and Natalie Koussevitzky
Ms: CUL
Publ: OUP
First perf: BBC Symphony Orchestra/Rudolf Schwartz, Royal Festival Hall, London, 1961
(1) *Rec*: Orquestra Sinfonica de Tenerife/Victor Pablo Perez
Audivis Valois 4728
Also rec: BIRS

Symphony No. 4 ("New York") (1967), 26 mins
Commissioned by the New York Philharmonic Orchestra in celebration of its 125th anniversary
Ms: CUL
Publ: OUP
First perf: New York Philharmonic Orchestra/William Steinberg, New York, 1967
First European perf: Stockholm Philharmonic Orchestra/Antal Dorati, Stockholm 1968
Rec: (1) Orquestra Sinfonica de Tenerife/Victor Pablo Perez
Audivis Valois 4728
(2) BBC Symphony Orchestra/Matthias Bamert
CHANDOS CHAN 9556
Also rec: BIRS

Symphony No. 5 (1969), (incomplete)
Ms: CUL

The Taming of the Shrew (1953?)
Incidental music for a production of Shakespeare's play
Ms: CUL

This Sporting Life (1963)
Score for feature film, dir. Lindsay Anderson, cond. Jacques-Louis Monod
Ms: CUL

The Tower (1962)
Incidental music for BBC radio production (Hoffmansthal)
Ms: CUL

Six Tonadillas (1942) for high voice and piano, 9 mins
Ms: CUL
First perf: Sophie Wyss (soprano), Roberto Gerhard (piano)

Trio (?1917), for violin, cello and piano
Ms: IEV

Trio in B major (1918)
Ms: IEV
First perf: Trio de Barcelona, 25 April 1918, Barcelona

Trio (1918) for violin, cello and piano, 20 mins
Ms: IEV
Publ: EMS (1921)
First perf: Trio de Barcelona, Barcelona, 1919
Rec: (1) Trio Mompou de Madrid
(Antologia de la musica espanola, vol. ii)
RTVE Musica 65012)
(2) Cantamen
Metier MSV CD92012
(3) Barcelona 216
Stradivarius 33404
(4) Gerhard Trio
La Ma de Guido 2021

The Unexpected Country (1957), 28 mins (total duration of programme)
Incidental music (electronic) for BBC radio production of play by Olwen Wymark
Ms: ?

Ventall (1930?)
Song for high voice and piano
Ms: CUL

Verger de la Galanies (1917–8), for voice and piano
Text by Josep Carner
Ms: CBA

La Viejecita (c. 1943), 9 mins
An orchestral fantasia by Gerhard (under the pseudonym Juan Serrallonga) on the zarzuela by Manuel Fernandez Caballero (1897)
Publ: (BH)
First perf: BBC Theatre Orchestra/Stanford Robinson, c. 1943

War in the Air (1952)
Score for five BBC TV documentary films, cond. Muir Matheson
1. Battle for Britain
2. Desert Victory
3. Wings over Italy
4. The Rising Sun
5. The Future
Ms: CUL

Wind Quintet (1928), 15$^1/_2$ mins
Ms: CUL
Publ: BM now BH
First perf: Esteve Gratacos (flute), Cassia Carles (oboe), Joan Vives (clarinet), Anton Goxens (bassoon), Ramon Bonell (horn), cond. Gerhard, Palau de la Musica Catalana, Barcelona, 22 December 1929,
***** *Rec*: (1) London Wind Quintet
Argo RG 326
(2) Harmonia Quintet
Hyades Arts 25
Also rec: BIRS

The World's Great Stage (1962)
Incidental music for BBC radio production of Calderon's play
Ms: CUL

Voyzeck (1961)
Incidental music for BBC radio production of Buchner's play
Ms: CUL

You Know What People Are (1955)
Incidental music for BBC TV production (J.B. Priestley)
Ms: CUL

Your Skin (1958)
score for a documentary film for Unilever
Ms: CUL

Selected bibliography

Albet, Monserrat (1996), "Gerhard escriu a Casals", in *Revista Musical Catalana*, **140**, June, 38–41.

——— (1996), "Vinculacio de Gerhard amb Catalunya", in *faig Arts*, **36**, October, 4–11.

——— (1996), "Schoenberg in Barcelona", in *faig Arts*, **36**, October, 33–41.

Anderson, Lindsay (1981), "This Sporting Life", in *Tempo*, **139**, December, 334.

Artis, Pere (1986), "La polèmica Robert Gerhard-Lluis Millet", in *Revista Musical Catalana*, **23**, 28–9.

Ballantine, Christopher (1971), "The Symphony in the Twentieth Century: some aspects of its tradition and innovation" (Symphony No.1), in *Music Review*, **32**, 3.

Blyth, Alan (1969), "Verses for Ensembles" (*Hymnody*), in *Music & Musicians*, **17**, April, 62.

Bradshaw, Susan (1980), "Roberto Gerhard", in Stanley Sadie (ed.), *The New Grove Dictionary of Music and Musicians* (London), 7, 251–55.

——— (1991), "Symphony No. 2/*Metamorphosis* – The Compositional Background", in *Tempo*, **139**, December, 28–32.

——— (1990), "Fickle Fashion. Catalan Composer: the ups and downs of his reputation", in *Listener*, 25 October, 44.

Brown, P. (1965), "Influence of David" (*Hymnody*), in *Music & Musicians*, **14**, October, 43.

Buller, John (1969–70), "Roberto Gerhard's *Leo*", in *Tempo*, **91**, 27–9.

Bye, Antony (1992), "The Duenna", in *Tempo*, **180**, 19–20.

Calderer, Lluis (1996), "En el Centenari de Robert Gerhard: alguns fets i algunes preguntes", in *faig Arts*, **36**, October, 23–8.

Casanovas, Josep (1996), "Pedrell, Falla I Schoenberg en la vida I l'obra de Gerhard", in *Revista Musical Catalana*, **140**, June, 36–7.

Chissell, Joan (1965), "The Proms" (*Hymnody*), in *Musical Times*, **106**, October, 781.

Coleman, Edwin H. (1961), "Roberto Gerhard's *Collages*", in *Musical Events*, **16**, 2, February, 19.

Crichton, Ronald (1972), "Orchestral: Gerhard, Routh", in *Musical Times*, **113**, May 1972, 476; *see also* letter from Lionel Salter (re. Harpsichord Concerto) in *Musical Times*, **113**, July, 668.

Davies, Hugh (1981), "The Electronic Music", in *Tempo*, **139**, December, 35–8.

Del Mar, Norman (1956), "Gerhard as an orchestral composer" (Suite: *Don Quixote*; Symphony *Homenatje a Pedrell*; Violin Concerto), *Score*, September, 13–19.

Dennis, Brian (1970), "Films, electronics. (Reflections on a DNA Molecule)", in *Musical Times*, **111**, January, 66.

Donat, Misha (1983), "The last works of Robert Gerhard", in *Listener*, **89**, March, 349.

Drew, David (1956), "Gerhard: the musical character", in *Score*, September, 39–49.

——— (1970), "Roberto Gerhard", in *Listener*, 15 January, 19.

——— (1970), Gerhard obituary in *Musical Times*, March, 24–5.

——— (1973), "Roberto Gerhard – A Chronology" (and introductory essay), in David

Atherton (ed.), *Programme book for the London Sinfonietta's Schoenberg-Gerhard series*, London, 74–5.
——— (1991–2), "Gerhard's Duenna and Sheridan's", in *Opera*, **42** and **43**, December, 39–38 and January, 40–47.
——— (1993), "Notes on Gerhard's *Pandora*", *Tempo*, **184**, March, 14–16.
East, Leslie (1974), "Schoenberg and Gerhard", in *Music & Musicians*, **22**, February, 39–40.
Ericson, R. (1961), "Relocated Spaniard", in *New York Times*, **100**, 13 August, section 2, 9.
Estanyol, Margarida (1996), "El llegat no musical de Gerhard a la Cambridge University Library", in *Revista Musical Catalana*, **140**, June, 42–4.
Gardner, John (1956), "The Duenna 1945–47", *Score*, September, 20–26.
——— (1972), "The Duenna", *Listener*, **87**, 27 April, 565.
Glock, William (1956), "Comment" (Editorial), in *Score*, September, 5–7.
——— (1991), *Notes in Advance* (Oxford), see esp. 176–8.
Goodwin, Noel (1992), "The music for *Don Quixote*", in *Dance and Dancers*, June, 16–19.
Griffiths, Paul (1973), "Gerhard" (Symphony No.2), in *Musical Times*, **114**, August, 811.
Henderson, Robert (1965), "The Cheltenham Festival" (Concerto for Orchestra), in *Musical Times*, **106**, September, 686.
Homs, Joaquim (1987), *Robert Gerhard y su obra* (Universidad de Oviedo, 1987); [Catalan edition, with extra writings by Gerhard] *Robert Gerhard* I la seva obra (Biblioteca de Catalunya, Barcelona, 1991); [abridged edition, with extra photographic material, *Robert Gerhard* (Editorial Labor, Barcelona, 1992).
——— (1992), "La personalit human de Robert Gerhard", in *Cultura*, **30**, January, 23–4.
Jacobson, Bernard (1964), "Camus' City of Pestilence", in *Music & Musicians*, **12**, 32, May.
Jack, Adrian (1974), "Schoenberg and Gerhard", in *Music & Musicians*, **22**, January, 60–61.
Kay, Norman (1970), "Late harvest", in *Music & Musicians*, March, 44ff, 71.
Keller, Hans (1969), "Roberto Gerhard's Two Ears", in *Listener*, **82**, 121.
Kolodin, Irving (1963), "Music to My Ears", in *Saturday Review*, **46**, 53, 26 January.
——— (1963), "Roberto Gerhard's First Symphony", in *Musical Times*, **103**, 19 February.
León, Jordi (1996), "Reflexions a l'entorn de les sardanes de Gerhard", in *Revista Musical Catalana*, **140**, June, 45–6.
MacDonald, Calum (1972), "Sense and Sound: Gerhard's Fourth Symphony", in *Tempo*, **100**, 25–9.
——— (1981), "Soirées de Barcelone – a Preliminary Report", in *Tempo*, **139**, December, 19–26.
——— (1985), "Rugged Individual", in *Listener*, 22 August, 34.
——— (1996), "Towards a Performing Version" [of *Soirées de Barcelone*] in *Tempo* 198, October, 22–36.
Marba, Antoní Ros (1992), " 'La duena', una obsessio de Robert Gerhard", in *Cultura*, 30, January, 25.
Martorelli, Oriol (1992), "Robert Gerhard dins del context de la musica catalana", in *Cultura*, 30, January, 21–2.
Mason, Colin (1954), "Roberto Gerhard", in Eric Blom (ed.), *Grove's Dictionary of Music and Musicians* (London, 5th edn), 3, 599–601.
——— (1958), "A Spanish composer in exile", *Listener*, 60, 25 September, 484.

——— (1962), "Roberto Gerhard's First Symphony", in *Musical Times*, **103**, 99.

——— (1963), "Chamber Music in Britain since 1929", in *Cobbett's Cyclopedic Survey of Chamber Music*, ed. C. Mason (London & New York, 2nd edn), **111**, 121–22.

McCabe, John (1972), "Gerhard: Creator in Exile", in *Records and Recording*, 15 February, 44–5.

Mitchell, Donald (1952), "The emancipation of the dissonance: a selected bibliography of the writings of composers, theorists and critics", in *Hinrichsen Musical Yearbook*, 7, 144.

——— (1956), "A Note on the Catalan songs", *Score*, September, 11–12.

Montsalvatge, Xavier (1991), "Evocacio de Robert Gerhard", in *Papers autobografics*, **X**, 186–87 (Barcelona).

Nash, Peter Paul (1981), "The Wind Quintet", in *Tempo*, **139**, December, 5–11.

Noguero, Joaquim (1996), "Entrevista a Josep Pons", in *faig Arts*, **36**, October, 12–22.

Northcott, Bayan (1974), "Since *Grimes*: a concise survey of the British musical stage" (*The Duenna*), in *Musical News*, **4**, 2.

Orga, Ates (1970), "Roberto Gerhard 1896–1970", in *Music & Musicians*, 19 October, 36.

——— (1973), "Schoenberg and Gerhard", in *Musical Events*, September, 7–9, 28.

——— (1973), "The Man and his Music: an essay", in David Atherton (ed.), *Programme book for the London Sinfonietta's Schoenberg-Gerhard series* (London), 87–94.

Ottaway, Hugh (1961), "Radio Notes" *Collages*, in *Musical Opinion*, **84**, April, 429.

Padros, David (1996), "L'aspecte estilistic a l'obra de Robert Gerhard", in *faig Arts*, 36, October, 29–32.

Payne, Anthony (1963), "Gerhard [Piano] Concerto", in *Music & Musicians*, **12**, 9 October.

——— (1964), "Roberto Gerhard's *The Plague*", in *Tempo*, **69**, Summer, 26–8.

——— (1968), "First performances: Tavener's *In Alium* and Gerhard's *Epithalamium*", in *Tempo*, **86**, August, 22.

Perez, Oriol (1996), "Critic Creador, Vine ...!", in *faig Arts*, **36**, October, 45–6.

Picken, Laurence (1956), "Roberto Gerhard Intermittently Observed", *Score*, September, 50–53.

Porter, Andrew (1975), "Robert Gerhard: generous and lovable pioneer" (The Plague), in *Hi Fi/Musical America*, **25**, October, 64–5.

——— (1992), *The Duenna* (review of Opera North production), *Opera*, November, 1346–50.

Potter, Keith (1973), "Gerhard's Second String Quartet", in David Atherton (ed.), *Programme book for the London Sinfonietta's Schoenberg-Gerhard series* (London), 95–7.

Redlich, H.F. (1955), "Gerhard Robert", in *Die Musik in geschichte und Gegenwort* (Kassel), **4**, 1786–87.

Sadie, Stanley (1961), "*Collages*" (Gerhard's Symphony No.3), in *Musical Events*, **11**, 28 April, 28.

——— (1996), "Gerhard" (Concerto for Orchestra), in *Musical Times*, **107**, March, 229.

Sarda, Albert (1992), "Robert Gerhard i la musica catalana contemporanea", in *Cultura*, 30, January, 26.

Schiffer, B. (1969), "Kammermusikalische Klangspiele in London" (Libra), in *Melos*, **36**, January, 42.

——— (1973), "Englische Firmen, englische Orchester und englische Festivals vergebenKompositionauftraege", *Metamorphoses*, in *Melos*, **40**, 6, 375–83.

Smith, Sydney (1973), "The War Years in Cambridge", *Programme book for the London Sinfonietta's Schoenberg-Gerhard series* (London), 99–100.
Sproston, Darren (1993), "Thematicism in Gerhard's Concerto for Orchestra", *Tempo*, **184**, March, 18–21.
Thomas, Sarah (1970), "Roberto Gerhard 1896–1970", in *Musical Events*, March, 24–5.
Trumpff, A. (1967), "Gerhard's Konzert fur Orchester", in *Hessischen Tundfunk Frankfurt A.M.* (Reprinted from *Die Welt*, 2 December 1966), in *Orchester*, **15**, 19 January.
Vilar, Josep M. (1996), "Gerhard en CD", in *faig Arts*, **36**, October, 42–4.
Vlad, Roman (1956), "My First Impressions of Robert Gerhard's Music", *Score*, September, 27–34.
——— (1958), *Storia della dodecafonia* (Milan), 137–44.
Walsh, Stephen (1968–69), "Two New Works by Gerhard" (*Libra*, Symphony No.4), *Tempo*, **87**, Winter, 27–9.
White, Julian (1993), "National Traditions in the Music of Roberto Gerhard", in *Tempo*, March, 2–13.
——— (1998), "Symphony of hope" (Symphony No.1), *Musical Times*, **139**, 1861, March, 19–28.
——— (1996), "Gerhard's *Soirées de Barcelone*: Catalan Folk Sources" in *Tempo* 198, October, 11–21 and 72.
Whittall, Arnold (1977), *Music since the First World War* (London), 184–8.

Index